W9-AAL-783

THE STATES AND THE NATION SERIES, of which this volume is a part, is designed to assist the American people in a serious look at the ideals they have espoused and the experiences they have undergone in the history of the nation. The content of every volume represents the scholarship, experience, and opinions of its author. The costs of writing and editing were met mainly by grants from the National Endowment for the Humanities, a federal agency. The project was administered by the American Association for State and Local History, a nonprofit learned society, working with an Editorial Board of distinguished editors, authors, and historians, whose names are listed below.

Massachusetts

A Bicentennial History

Richard D. Brown

W. W. Norton & Company, Inc.
New York

American Association for State and Local History
Nashville

Author and publishers make grateful acknowledgment to the following for permission to quote from archival material:

The New York Public Library, for permission to quote from the Samuel Adams Papers.

The Harvard Law School Library, for permission to quote from Holmes's letter of April 6, 1911, to Franklin Ford.

Published and distributed by W. W. Norton & Company, Inc.
500 Fifth Avenue
New York, New York 10036

Library of Congress Cataloguing-in-Publication Data
Brown, Richard D.
  Massachusetts.

  (The States and the Nation series)
  Bibliography: p.
  Includes index.
  1. Massachusetts—History. I. Series.
F64.B86   974.4   78–17525
ISBN 0–393–05666–X

Printed in the United States of America
2 3 4 5 6 7 8 9 0

Contents

Illustrations

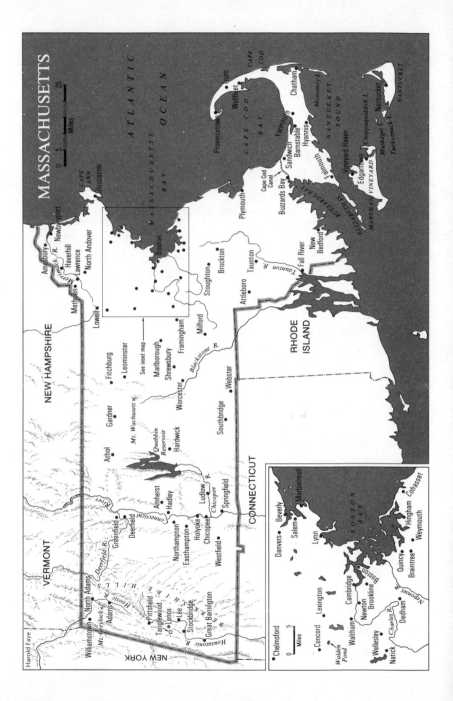

Invitation to the Reader

IN 1807, former President John Adams argued that a complete history of the American Revolution could not be written until the history of change in each state was known, because the principles of the Revolution were as various as the states that went through it. Two hundred years after the Declaration of Independence, the American nation has spread over a continent and beyond. The states have grown in number from thirteen to fifty. And democratic principles have been interpreted differently in every one of them.

We therefore invite you to consider that the history of your state may have more to do with the bicentennial review of the American Revolution than does the story of Bunker Hill or Valley Forge. The Revolution has continued as Americans extended liberty and democracy over a vast territory. John Adams was right: the states are part of that story, and the story is incomplete without an account of their diversity.

The Declaration of Independence stressed life, liberty, and the pursuit of happiness; accordingly, it shattered the notion of holding new territories in the subordinate status of colonies. The Northwest Ordinance of 1787 set forth a procedure for new states to enter the Union on an equal footing with the old. The Federal Constitution shortly confirmed this novel means of building a nation out of equal states. The step-by-step process through which territories have achieved self-government and national representation is among the most important of the Founding Fathers' legacies.

The method of state-making reconciled the ancient conflict between liberty and empire, resulting in what Thomas Jefferson called an empire for liberty. The system has worked and remains unaltered, despite enormous changes that have taken

place in the nation. The country's extent and variety now sur-
pass anything the patriots of '76 could likely have imagined.
The United States has changed from an agrarian republic into a
highly industrial and urban democracy, from a fledgling nation
into a major world power. As Oliver Wendell Holmes remarked
in 1920, the creators of the nation could not have seen com-
pletely how it and its constitution and its states would develop.
Any meaningful review in the bicentennial era must consider
what the country has become, as well as what it was.

The new nation of equal states took as its motto *E Pluribus
Unum*—"out of many, one." But just as many peoples have
become Americans without complete loss of ethnic and cultural
identities, so have the states retained differences of character.
Some have been superficial, expressed in stereotyped images—
big, boastful Texas, "sophisticated" New York, "hillbilly"
Arkansas. Other differences have been more real, sometimes instructively, sometimes amusingly; democracy has embraced
Huey Long's Louisiana, bilingual New Mexico, unicameral Ne-
braska, and a Texas that once taxed fortunetellers and spawned
politicians called "Woodpecker Republicans" and "Skunk
Democrats." Some differences have been profound, as when
South Carolina secessionists led other states out of the Union in
opposition to abolitionists in Massachusetts and Ohio. The result was a bitter Civil War.

The Revolution's first shots may have sounded in Lexington
and Concord; but fights over what democracy should mean and
who should have independence have erupted from Pennsylvania's Gettysburg to the "Bleeding Kansas" of John Brown,
from the Alamo in Texas to the Indian battles at Montana's
Little Bighorn. Utah Mormons have known the strain of isolation; Hawaiians at Pearl Harbor, the terror of attack; Georgians
during Sherman's march, the sadness of defeat and devastation.
Each state's experience differs instructively; each adds understanding to the whole.

The purpose of this series of books is to make that kind of understanding accessible, in a way that will last in value far
beyond the bicentennial fireworks. The series offers a volume
on every state, plus the District of Columbia—fifty-one, in all.

Each book contains, besides the text, a view of the state through eyes other than the author's—a "photographer's essay," in which a skilled photographer presents his own personal perceptions of the state's contemporary flavor.

We have asked authors not for comprehensive chronicles, nor for research monographs or new data for scholars. Bibliographies and footnotes are minimal. We have asked each author for a summing up—interpretive, sensitive, thoughtful, individual, even personal—of what seems significant about his or her state's history. What distinguishes it? What has mattered about it, to its own people and to the rest of the nation? What has it come to now?

To interpret the states in all their variety, we have sought a variety of backgrounds in authors themselves and have encouraged variety in the approaches they take. They have in common only these things: historical knowledge, writing skill, and strong personal feelings about a particular state. Each has wide latitude for the use of the short space. And if each succeeds, it will be by offering you, in your capacity as a *citizen* of a state *and* of a nation, stimulating insights to test against your own.

James Morton Smith
General Editor

Massachusetts

1

The Country the
Englishmen Found

$\mathcal{E}$VERY day the tide rushes in, wave upon wave, rip-
pling and foaming as it reaches land. Softly sloping beaches of
sand and pebble, tumbles of rocks, gray and brown, still meet
the onrushing waters as they have for millions of years. Here, at
the shifting boundary between land and sea, Massachusetts
begins. The lands that lie to the west for 200 miles—coastal
plains and hillocks, uplands furrowed by a thousand streams,
the great river basin, and the high, steep forests beyond—are
what survive after hundreds of millions of years of punishment
by wind, water, and four great glaciers. Ten thousand years
ago, when men first settled what is now Massachusetts, they
came to a country that had already been transformed many
times.

One hundred centuries ago, the first settlers, hunters using
fluted-blade stone weapons, made little impact on the land.
These earliest inhabitants accommodated themselves within an
environment that they could not dominate. Yet during the mil-
lennia that Stone Age peoples occupied the land, they did come
to manipulate the country in significant ways. Over the years
they added farming to their hunting and gathering, tilling the
soil and cultivating crops brought from distant parts of America.
To enhance hunting and gathering as well as tillage, they skill-

3

fully used fire to burn off the young growth on vast tracts of forest. Thus the seemingly new and underpopulated world that Englishmen explored and settled early in the seventeenth century was new only to them and underpopulated only according to the standards of the newcomers. The landscape they discovered had been remade a hundred times by natural forces, and remade again by its Stone Age inhabitants. The newcomers and their progeny would transform Massachusetts once more, and at a speed that was unprecedented.

From the perspective of the land itself, Massachusetts is an artificial creation. Except for the ocean that washes its eastern shore, its boundaries are entirely man-made, straight lines negotiated during the seventeenth, eighteenth, and nineteenth centuries without much concern for topography. Laid out from east to west, across a landscape that includes four distinct regions running from north to south, Massachusetts possesses no natural unity. No great basin or valley unites its eight thousand square miles of territory.

In the east there is a coastal plain thirty to fifty miles wide (much wider if one includes the Cape Cod peninsula); then a central upland region of similar breadth rises to about five hundred feet above sea level. Farther west the broad valley (often a dozen miles wide) of the Connecticut River bisects Massachusetts. This valley is the remnant of a vast glacial lake, which stretched across Massachusetts fifteen thousand years ago. The fourth region, the Berkshire hills that lie to the west, is much like the central upland although the elevation is higher, one thousand to two thousand feet. Here Mount Greylock, the highest point in Massachusetts, rises to a height of thirty-five hundred feet. This upland Berkshire region is itself divided by the narrow valley of the Housatonic River which runs south into Connecticut before emptying into the Long Island Sound.

Just beneath the surface of these four regions, and sometimes cropping up into view lie the bedrocks that have provided the foundation for the land. Heaving up, sliding, and sinking as this particular fragment of the earth's surface cooled and shifted, the rocks were formed as long ago as one billion and as recently as twelve million years. These seemingly indestructible metamorphic rocks, among them gneisses and granite, have crumbled during the centuries and given the land its present character.

More than once Massachusetts was high mountains, comparable to the Rockies today. Such great peaks, some of them volcanoes, were pushed up by the working of the earth's crust hundreds of millions of years ago. Several times they rose, only to vanish as water, wind, and frost wore them down. They became plains, slightly tilted to the south and east so that water ran off in those directions. Their powdered remnants together with the lava from volcanic eruptions provided Massachusetts with a deep, rich soil that supported an abundance of plant life. Two hundred million years ago the Connecticut Valley was a lush, tropical region that teemed with dinosaurs and a hundred other species of prehistoric reptiles. As recently as one million years ago Massachusetts was everywhere a relatively flat if uneven land, its bedrock mostly covered with a thick layer of powdered-rock soil.

Then, for some mysterious reason, the climate of eastern Canada changed. Summers turned cooler by a few degrees so that they no longer melted the winter snowfall entirely. Each year a little more snow accumulated until, after several hundred centuries, great glaciers formed that spread out in every direction. Those that rolled south overspread Massachusetts entirely. The dinosaurs and their cousins were frozen out. The green landscape turned white as an ocean of ice up to ten thousand feet deep covered the land. The weight of the glaciers was so enormous that the earth's crust yielded beneath it, sinking for hundreds of feet.

The ice age spanned about one million years, a relatively brief period compared to the geologic eras that preceded it. Moreover, it was three times interrupted by warmer periods, thousands of years long, when the glaciers melted away, the land turned green again, and animal life lived once more upon it. But though the glaciers were temporary, they gave the surface of Massachusetts its present character. Indeed by the scale of earth history they lasted until yesterday, about fifteen thousand years ago.

When the last glaciers melted, their impact on the land became visible. The soil that had been accumulating for millions of years from the eroding rocks had been scoured off and washed into the Atlantic. In its place rough glacial debris—glacial till—had been deposited, an infertile mixture of clay, gravel, and rocks. In some places bedrock had been scraped off and strewn around in boulders. The rocky surface of Massachusetts and the stony subsoil beneath it are legacies of the glaciers.

The gentle hills (drumlins) one or two hundred feet high that surround Massachusetts Bay were also formed by the glaciers. These hills have no core of bedrock; they are piles of glacial till. Other ridges (moraines), including the high ground on Cape Cod, that rise above the coastal plain were formed by the runoff carrying sand and gravel to the edges of stagnant glaciers. In the same region, and farther west, the retreating glaciers stranded great free-standing chunks of ice, which created numerous ponds and upland swamps as they melted. Some of these filled up with silt, turning ponds into bogs, and swamps into fertile land possessing a deep covering of soil.

The Connecticut Valley at the end of the ice age had a natural dam in central Connecticut, making it one vast lake. For thousands of years this lake trapped the silt that rain and melt water carried off the surrounding hills. Later, when the dam gave way and the lake drained, a deep, rich soil was left covering the valley, making it the most fertile stretch of land in all New England. Farther west, in the Berkshires, the glaciers scraped the narrow valleys making them a little broader, but they also left the characteristic rocky soil, boulders, ponds, and swamps. The ice age had sharply reduced the ability of the land in Massachusetts to sustain life.

Yet the land rebounded rapidly. Even the earth's crust, freed of its burden of ice, sprang upward again, in some places as much as two hundred feet. Within a few thousand years flora and fauna from farther south had migrated to the land and were flourishing. The country that the fluted-blade hunters inhabited provided plenty of game on land, in the air, and under water. The Massachusetts that Englishmen were to "discover" thousands of years later was becoming recognizable.

The renewal of life in Massachusetts depended chiefly on the climate. The global warming trend that destroyed the glaciers gave Massachusetts the moderate climate it still possesses. In January, the coldest month, the mean temperature is 29 degrees Fahrenheit, although in the Berkshires it is about three degrees cooler, and on Cape Cod it is three degrees warmer. The mean temperature during the warmest month, July, is 72 degrees, about two degrees warmer in the western hills and two degrees cooler on the Cape. The difference in growing season at the two extremes is substantial. In the southeast growth occurs for a full six months, whereas in the west it lasts barely four months. Rainfall is everywhere abundant, averaging 39–43 inches each year. These conditions of climate would make Massachusetts a heavily forested land, but because of varying temperatures and soil conditions, the forests would be of several distinct types.

In the southeast where the sandy soil retained few organic nutrients from decaying plants, a forest of pitch pine and scrub oak developed. Along river banks and in coastal marshes grasses and shrubs like bayberries, beach plums, and blueberries came to predominate. In such settings chipmunks and squirrels, rabbits and raccoons, all found food and cover. Shellfish flourished along the shore, feeding themselves on the organic matter in tidal flats and at the mouths of rivers. According to the seasons, alewives, salmon, and shad raced up the rivers and streams to spawn. Offshore, bass, bluefish, cod, and mackerel were common.

Farther north the coastline was much the same, but back of the immediate shore a more substantial forest grew up, with hickory and red and white oak predominating. In these varied woodlands, larger animals roamed. Deer found shrubs and young trees for browsing. Foxes fed on rodents, grouse, partridge, and pheasant. Inland, trout swam in the streams, and bass and pickerel were the masters of the ponds. All along the coastal plains migratory birds were seasonal residents. In and around the streams were beaver, mink, muskrats, and otters.

To the west, in the central upland region, the higher elevations and cooler temperatures produced a somewhat different forest. Here the same varieties of trees were present, but in dif-

ferent proportions. Birch, beech, and maple, the northern hard-
woods, became more numerous, as did hemlock and pine. In
these woods the wildlife, too, was similar to the coastal plain,
but here bobcats, wolves, and black bears prowled. Fewer migratory birds flew inland, but turkeys were more common in the
woods. This same pattern of forest life flourished to the western
edges of the Connecticut Valley.

In the higher, cooler Berkshires, a forest of beech, birch, and
maple prevailed, with a substantial complement of conifers.
Oaks and hickories became scarce, and the acorns, butternuts,
chestnuts, and hickory nuts that fed the chipmunks and squirrels
of central and eastern Massachusetts were seldom found. This
thick-forested region of steeply sloping hills, with few meadows
and brushlands, sheltered large animals, wolves, bear, deer, and
moose. With a shorter growing season and less fertile land, the
western hills fed a smaller population of wildlife.

It is not surprising then that when the fluted-blade hunters
edged their way northward into this land ten thousand years
ago, they came to the coastal plains where fish and game were
readily available and the climate was more like the southern
land of their origin. These paleo-Indian settlers used chipped
stone weapons for hunting, as well as various snares and traps.
In addition to hunting they gathered the food that was accessible—nuts, berries, shellfish. In the spring and fall they constructed dams of wooden stakes to trap the alewives and salmon
that spawned upstream. These fluted-blade hunters were a small
population, and though they may have dwelt there for several
thousand years, ultimately they vanished, leaving scarcely a
mark upon the land.

Their successors, who may have destroyed or engulfed them,
arrived nearly seven thousand years ago. They were more advanced, aggressive, and durable, although they, too, lived by
hunting, fishing, and gathering. The size and character of their
settlements remain uncertain, but their surviving cord-marked
pottery, from about 2500 B.C., links them to Indians of the
south and central portions of North America.

From two thousand to three thousand years ago Algonkin
people arrived, who hunted, gathered, and also farmed. These

were the first people to remake, in a limited way, the patterns of life in and of the Massachusetts forests. These Indians, whose descendants encountered the Norsemen and the English, cultivated the land. They settled on the most fertile locations along the streams and rivers of the eastern and central regions, and they added to the few natural meadows there by clearing flat, low-lying tracts. Their techniques of girdling the trees to kill them and burning the underbrush enabled Algonkin men to clear sufficient farmland for a growing population. The women planted hills of corn and squashes among the stumps, fertilizing the soil with fish. The forest remained dominant, but the crops grown from imported seeds enabled the Algonkins to supplement their diet of meat, nuts, berries, and fish.

Algonkin forest management included setting periodic, sometimes biannual, forest fires to clear away the underbrush, making an open, parklike forest under a canopy of tall hardwood trees. Such a forest provided a maximum of food for the Algonkins' game and for themselves. Oaks and hickories as well as shrubs flourished under these conditions, enabling the small animals and deer to increase. Moreover, the open woods made Indian hunters far more effective in tracking, stalking, and killing game.

Algonkin tribes moved about seasonally in the woods and meadows and along the rivers, but they were attached to the land and possessive of the farming and hunting territory they worked. Over the centuries distinct tribes emerged as masters of a given region—on Cape Cod the Nausets, a fishing tribe; along the south coastal plain the Wampanoags, who farmed, fished, and hunted; to the north the Massachuset tribe. The central uplands were Nipmuc country, and the Connecticut Valley and the Berkshires belonged to the Pocumtucs. All of these tribes possessed common Algonkin origins and characteristics in their languages and social customs, but each was independent and at least latently hostile to the others.

Several families, related through the female line, occupied wood-framed lodges or wigwams covered with bark and hides, which were clustered together in villages. A village was maintained as long as the farming and hunting of its locale within the tribal region would sustain it. Newly cleared land might be good for a decade before it would be allowed to revert to forest.

Boys were reared to be hunters and warriors, possessing nothing but their deerskin garments and the weapons of their trade. When one married he entered the family of his wife, who retained all property rights. Inheritance, whether of goods or political status, was through the women, who cultivated the land and held it in common. These relationships were believed to be divinely ordained and inseparably entwined with the world of natural and supernatural beings. Each person, each family, each clan within a tribe, carried, as did the tribe itself, a mystical relationship with a living creature. The divinities, who expressed themselves in forms such as sun, fire, wind, water, and thunder, were abstract though not entirely impersonal natural forces. They demanded submission, but they might also be placated by appropriate offerings and worship. Each year the clans of a tribe gathered in religious ceremonies where, amid rituals of chanting and dancing, the political leaders of the tribe, the sachems of the clans, met in council.

Although family practices were matrilineal and power came to men through their female kin, political authority was patriarchal. The sachems were middle-aged and elderly men who together made decisions for the tribe, adjudicating disputes, punishing misbehavior, and negotiating with other tribes. The sachems declared war and planned military operations. Warfare itself was an activity of young men, although in the event of a major defeat, old people, women, and children might be captured too and enslaved by the victors. The chief cause of warfare seems to have been territorial incursions.

Over the centuries tribes rose and fell, and with them the extent of their lands. Tribes that survived were of comparable strength. Food supply, disease, and conjugal practices played a much greater role than warfare in maintaining stable populations. When the English arrived at the beginning of the seventeenth century, they found a comparatively old and stable system of rivalries among the tribes and their neighbors. Only the Pequots, to the south in Connecticut, were newcomers to the politics of the New England region.

This region was not a "virgin land," nor a particularly rich or fertile one. Yet the country that revealed itself to English explorers seemed fresh and unspoiled. One exclaimed that "the Land to me seeme[d] paradice: for in mine eie t'was Nature's Masterpeece; Her chiefest Magazine of all where lives her store: if this land be not rich, then is the whole world poore." [1] Even though Algonkin peoples had been living there since 500 B.C., to the English, who had cleared the forest from their own land and who now preserved deer in a few enclaves to give sport to aristocrats, this land seemed pristine. They were so impressed by what they saw that they were inspired to describe it to their countrymen in detail. The land abounded in plant and animal life; it was Nature's storehouse, inviting them to feast upon it.

The climate was more extreme than England's, yet the "sharpe Ayre" of winter did not distress them, since they found "wood in good store, and better cheape to build warm houses and make good fires." Compared to England's, this climate was healthful, for as one early settler reported, "in publicke assemblies it is strange to heare a man sneeze or cough." Fresh water was conveniently found; indeed there could be "no better water in the world" [2] than in the "sweet Cristall fountaines, and cleare running streames" [3] that watered this new land.

As did the Indians, the English also viewed wildlife as game. The coastal marine life, which had regularly brought English fishermen to the shores of New England during the sixteenth century, excited enthusiasm. Even the winter catch was good; and the variety of fishes impressive. Sea bass was the favorite, "a delicate, fine, fat, fast fish." The technique of catching sea bass was copied from the Wampanoags: "the Fisherman taking a great Cod-line, to which he fastneth a peece of Lobster, and throwes it into the Sea, the fish biting at it he pulls her to him, and knockes her on the head with a sticke." Shellfish were so

---

1. Thomas Morton, *New English Canaan* (Amsterdam, 1637). Publications of the Prince Society, 14 (Boston, 1883; reprint ed., New York: Burt Franklin, 1967), p. 180.

2. William Wood, *New England's Prospect* (n.p., 1634). Publications of the Prince Society, 3 (Boston, 1865; printed from the 1764 edition; reprint ed., New York: Burt Franklin, 1967), pp. 4, 5, 16.

3. Morton, *New English Canaan*, p. 180.

common that the Indians and the English seldom ate them. The first English settlers would use clams to feed their swine. Lobsters, weighing up to twenty pounds, were similarly abundant and were collected among the rocks at low tide, but they were "little esteemed and seldom eaten." [4] Indians used them for bait, and only turned to them for food when bass were scarce.

In the woods, deer was the favorite game, supplying both the venison and hides that were staples of Indian life. Rabbits, like other small animals, were hardly worth hunting, and so the English gave them little notice. Birds, however, were a different matter since they could supply the table with choice dinners. The variety of doves, partridges, and pheasants compared favorably with England; but it was the ducks, geese, and turkeys that were most remarkable. Of the geese Thomas Morton avowed "I have had often 1,000 before the mouth of my gunne." They were fatter than English geese and their feathers made "a bedd softer than any down." [5] Turkeys, the equally common year-round residents, came in great flocks, the largest fowls weighing from 40 to 60 pounds. Such riches for the larder dazzled the first English observers.

Nature inspired wonder. The very ground on which one trod offered delectable treats. One found "strawberries in abundance, very large ones, some being two inches about," in addition to blueberries, currants, gooseberries, grapes, huckleberries, and raspberries. Exotic creatures delighted the eye, like the hummingbird, "no bigger than a Hornet, yet hath all the dimensions of a Bird, as bill, and wings, with quills, spider-like legges, small clawes: for colour she is glorious as a Raine-bow; as she flies she makes a little humming noise." [6] Yet though the first English observers marveled at nature, they did not share the sense of mystery and awe toward it, or intimacy, that inspired the Algonkins.

To these Europeans the measure of all things was themselves. They saw lumber in the trees and dinners in the wildlife. When

4. Wood, *New England's Prospect*, pp. 37–38, 39.
5. Morton, *New English Canaan*, pp. 89–90.
6. Wood, *New England's Prospect*, pp. 15, 31.

they studied the habitats of trees or the behavior of animals, it was for practical, utilitarian purposes. Beavers were fascinating because they could do what men did, felling trees "as thicke as a mans thigh, afterwards dividing them into lengths according to the use they are appointed for. If one Bever be to weake to carry the logge, then another helpes him; if they two be too weake, . . . foure more adding their helpe, being placed three to three, which set their teeth in one anothers tough tayles, and laying the load on the two hindermost, they draw the logge to the desired place." Their three-story wooden houses were constructed to cope with flooding and frost, and were "so strong that no creature saving an industrious man with his penetrating tools can prejudice them." Beaver dams aroused "admiration from wise understanding men," [7] while the beavers' social patterns, which included the enslavement of strangers, seemed so human that Englishmen found it tempting to regard them as reasonable creatures.

In time the newcomers would make beavers the forest's first cash crop, harvesting them until they were virtually extinct. Yet Europeans did not themselves have the temperament to hunt the beaver, whose "wisedome secures them from the *English* who seldome, or never kills any of them, being not patient to lay a long siege, or to be so often deceived by their cunning evasions, so that all the Beaver which the *English* have, comes first from the *Indians,* whose time and experience fits them for that imployment." [8] No matter how much the English admired the landscape of the country they explored, they could not fully become part of it, as could the Algonkins, who had hunted over the land for two thousand years. Englishmen were not inclined to adapt themselves to the ways of the beaver or the pace of the forest. When one boasted that "I have fed my doggs with as fatt Geese there as I have ever fed upon my selfe in England," he expressed a profligacy toward nature and its bounties that had hitherto been alien in this land. [9]

7. Wood, *New England's Prospect,* p. 29.
8. Wood, *New England's Prospect,* p. 29.
9. Morton, *New English Canaan,* p. 190.

English settlers would come with the express purpose of transforming what they found. They came as adversaries to a landscape and a way of life that had gradually emerged after the glaciers. Immediately they would make themselves competitors with its Stone-Age inhabitants for possession of the land itself. The coming of the English would open an epoch in the history of the land as important as the ice age. The coastal plain, the inland hills, the rivers, were about to be subdivided and settled in a wholly new way. The creation of a place known as Massachusetts was at hand.

2

The Worlds of Bradford
and Winthrop

*O*N July 29, 1588, Sir Francis Drake, adventurer, seaman, and favorite of Queen Elizabeth, finished his game of bowls in the city of Plymouth and set out to battle the Spanish Armada. Two months later the job was done. Queen Elizabeth's England proudly gloried in this greatest triumph in memory. For almost two centuries England had been a weak and divided nation, torn by dynastic uncertainty and religious conflict. Now, thirty years after Elizabeth's coronation, domestic peace and prosperity had brought England to the front rank of European powers. To Englishmen, this Protestant victory over Spanish Catholics symbolized not only the prowess of the English nation, but Divine favor as well. Some were ready to proclaim: "God is English."

Queen Elizabeth's wise and judicious rule was a major reason why England flourished. Gradually Elizabeth and her advisers had created an English church that combined Calvinism and Catholicism so effectively that it attracted a broad consensus of support. There was no need, nor in Elizabeth's case any desire, to persecute the minorities who remained outside its generous boundaries. Religious tolerance calmed English public life, and opened the way for flexibility and compromise in secular affairs. Working through shrewd and sensible councillors, Elizabeth developed a co-operative relationship with Parliament that

15

enhanced the Commons and the Lords while strengthening the monarchy.

Elizabeth herself was the center of a glittering court life that, in London and in palaces dotting the countryside, brought England into a golden age of Renaissance culture. The arts flourished as never before, and in the poetry of William Shakespeare and the philosophy of Francis Bacon, the creativity of English high culture reached a climax. The ambition to excel bred daring and innovation.

This spirit inspired the earliest English attempts to settle in North America. For at the same time the English were doing battle against the Spanish in Europe they were also competing with them for North America. In 1585 and again in 1587 Sir Walter Raleigh, another of Queen Elizabeth's heroes in the war with Spain, had sent settlers to found a colony at Roanoke Island in Carolina. But they were cut off from supplies from England when the Spanish Armada sailed into the English Channel. Raleigh could not have anticipated this interruption; moreover, he had underestimated the hazards of settlement and the resources necessary to sustain it. So the Roanoke colony collapsed and vanished.

Yet Raleigh's plan itself was reasonable. Where others dreamed of building forts and trafficking in precious goods as the Spanish were doing, Raleigh, who was familiar with English plantations in Ireland, conceived of transplanting English rural society to America. He was the first to send whole families to found a settlement that could be self-sufficient through farming. As it turned out, Raleigh's ideas were ahead of their time. Most of the courtiers and merchants who became interested in America thought of get-rich schemes in narrower terms.

The desire for immediate profits inspired the Jamestown settlement, launched almost twenty years after the Roanoke Island colony disappeared. The first settlers were mostly soldiers and gentlemen-adventurers; among the handful of tradesmen were a goldsmith and a perfumer. The purpose of overseas expansion was trade and the extraction of gold, silver, spices, perfumes. Initially, American ventures were manifestations of the exuberant hopes of Renaissance courtiers and merchants eager to enrich themselves with glory and gold.

Yet there was another England that was the foundation of Elizabeth's realm. This was a land of yeoman farmers and husbandmen, of artisans, laborers, and fishermen who lived in villages. These people, comprising ninety percent of England's 4.5 million population, struggled for survival or, if they were fortunate, savored the amenities of comfortable shelter, plentiful food, and sturdy clothing. For them the thirst for glory and the taste for novelty were alien and viewed with mistrust. Generally speaking, they subscribed to the view that the old ways are the best ways, and in earning their livelihoods they generally shunned innovation. The common adage among farmers was: " 'Tis not the husbandman, but the good weather that makes the corn grow.'' [1] In this world, the self-assertive individualism of Renaissance culture was overmatched by general conformity to age-old community values. The general good was based on people fulfilling the roles prescribed for them by the community. Individual self-fulfillment at the expense of the orderly, everyday routine of social life was intolerable.

The people of this England were roused by the threat of Spanish Catholicism, and celebrated the victory of 1588 with feasting and bonfires. But except for the Devon and Cornwall fishermen who regularly crossed the Atlantic to harvest the waters from Newfoundland south to Cape Cod, none of the common people in England knew or thought much about America. It would be more than a generation before people who lived outside the circle of the Renaissance elite became fully aware that America existed and might even have some bearing on their lives. It was in this country setting that the two principal founders of Massachusetts, William Bradford and John Winthrop, were born and reared.

Winthrop, a native of Edwardston in the East Anglian county of Suffolk, was born a few months after the victory over the Spanish. When John was a child, his father, Adam Winthrop, inherited the family manor house at Groton, and it was here, watching his father, that Winthrop learned the role of a country gentleman. At the age of fifteen he was sent off to Cambridge

---

1. Thomas Fuller, 1662. Quoted in Eric L. Jones, ed., *Agriculture and Economic Growth in England, 1650–1815* (London: Methuen, 1967), p. 5.

for some college education, and when he returned three years later, his father had arranged a marriage for him to Mary Forth of Essex County. Winthrop's bride brought land as a dowry, and within a year gave birth to a son, John, Junior. When Winthrop was twenty-one and the father of two sons, his father allowed him to share in the squire's duty of holding court for the people of Groton Manor. Several years later, Adam Winthrop, himself a lawyer as well as country gentleman, would send John for a stint at the Inns of Court at London so that he, too, might be formally trained in the law. Living under his father's and grandfather's roof, with a wife selected by his parents, and following his father's career, John Winthrop absorbed old family and community ideals continuously. By the time he was an adult, Winthrop was accustomed, by his heritage and upbringing, to a favored place in the communal social order of rural England.

Winthrop's contemporary William Bradford was born just two years later, in 1590, in the Yorkshire parish of Austerfield. Bradford's father, a yeoman farmer, died the following year, and his mother soon remarried, so his upbringing was supervised by his grandfather and uncles, who were resolved that young William should follow his father's calling. Bradford was trained as a farmer, but unlike John Winthrop, he did not follow readily in the path his elders laid out for him. For both Bradford and Winthrop, the Bible was a regular part of their upbringing, but for Bradford the sacred text became supremely important. At the age of twelve or thirteen he began to follow an independent path in religion, joining the Puritan group that met at William Brewster's house in nearby Scrooby. Brewster, twenty-four years older than Bradford, treated him as a son and brother in Christ. Bradford became part of this special community of Puritans who separated themselves from the Church of England in 1606. Forever after, William Bradford was part of this tiny band of separatists, going with Brewster and the others to Amsterdam, Leyden, and ultimately to Plymouth Colony.

While John Winthrop was taking up life as a husband, father, and squire, Bradford was suffering in the wave of religious persecution inaugurated by James I when he vowed that Puritans would "conform themselves" or he would "harry them out of the land." [2] Bradford was briefly imprisoned in 1607, and in the following year he joined his brethren in fleeing across a stormy North Sea to Amsterdam. In 1609 the group moved to Leyden and in that year, the same in which Winthrop first held court at Groton Manor, the nineteen-year-old William Bradford was chosen to be, with Brewster, a ruling elder of the Pilgrim church.

For a decade Bradford and the other Pilgrims lived comfortably at Leyden, "a fair and beautiful city" [3] adorned by a university, and a center of theological discussion. Bradford himself prospered; a family inheritance enabled him to purchase a house, in which he earned his living as a weaver. In 1613 he married Dorothy May and began a family. Bradford learned Dutch and some Latin and Hebrew so that he could read religious texts. While John Winthrop was being trained as an attorney, Bradford profited from the university milieu, schooling himself in Protestant history and classical literature, and collecting a substantial personal library in several languages. Bradford and Winthrop were traveling in different circles. One was already a radical nonconformist in religion, a refugee; the other, a rather conventional Puritan gentleman treading the favored path of his fathers. By 1630 they would both be pioneers, dwelling in the forests at the edge of a vast wilderness. Separate routes, ultimately grounded in religion, would bring them both to Massachusetts.

Bradford's decision to join in leading a group of thirty-five Pilgrims from Leyden to America represented an assertion of a particular identity. The Leyden separatists were, in the eyes of the orthodox, incorrigible individualists who set their own individual views above the wisdom and authority of the entire English political and ecclesiastical establishments. But among themselves the separatists were devoted to an encompassing

---

2. Quoted in George Macaulay Trevelyan, *England Under the Stuarts* (n.p., 1904; Penguin Books, 1960), p. 74.
3. William Bradford, *Of Plymouth Plantation, 1620–1647*, Samuel Eliot Morison, ed., (New York: Knopf, 1963), p. 17.

communal ideal, modeled on the early Christians. Bradford became convinced that to realize this ideal of a select holy community it was necessary to depart Leyden. The danger in Leyden was not persecution, as in England, it was hospitality, a spirit which threatened assimilation within a licentious society that made merry on the sabbath. Already, after a decade, the community had begun to dissolve and scatter. Some saw their children "drawn away by evil examples into extravagant and dangerous courses." Bradford and those who went with him believed "their posterity would be in danger to degenerate and be corrupted," if they remained where they were.[4]

For refuge the elders turned their thoughts to America, which Bradford described as a vast and fruitful land, "unpeopled . . . [excepting] only savage and brutish men which range up and down, little otherwise than wild beasts." [5] They began negotiations for land there in 1617. By 1619 the Virginia Company of London, having given up hopes of gold in America, was vigorously promoting agricultural settlement, eagerly selling land to companies that would send colonists. In that year William Brewster, who had been secretly printing banned religious tracts for sale in England, was seized by Leyden authorities acting on behalf of the English ambassador. Brewster escaped, to London ironically, where he arranged the formation of a company of merchants who obtained land for Pilgrim settlement near the Hudson River. In this backdoor manner the settlement of Massachusetts became linked to the most conspicuous English example of Renaissance imperialism, the Virginia Company.

The actual decision to go to America seriously divided the Leyden community. The Reverend John Robinson and the majority of the church decided to stay put, preferring the known dangers of life where they were to the innumerable unknown hazards of a transatlantic settlement. When the time came to leave in the spring of 1620, only thirty-five of the 240 Leyden church members embarked from Holland. In England about

4. Bradford, *Plymouth Plantation*, p. 25.
5. Bradford, *Plymouth Plantation*, p. 25.

forty more London separatists joined to the group, as well as a handful of ordinary Englishmen. When the *Mayflower* finally slipped away from Plymouth on September 16, its parting aroused no attention. England prospered, and most Englishmen, whatever their persuasion, were not willing to leave it forever.

Yet in the next decade a combination of events would make many people uneasy, and lead a substantial number to consider permanent settlement in America. John Winthrop, an obscure Puritan layman whose chief concern was making a secure and pious life for himself and his family, was one of thousands who saw gloomy portents in the public life of his country. In the past, England had experienced much worse periods than the 1620s, but now, among Puritans particularly, there was a new restlessness. Access to America created new possibilities.

The sense of malaise in England seemed to be general. Some of its roots were economic. Over the long term a population expanding more rapidly than employment was a major source of distress. People who had once been bound to an occupation and a community were now roaming the countryside or gravitating to London, either way exposed to repeated hardships and threatening the order and the property of more fortunate people. The situation was aggravated in the 1620s by a general economic depression, which sharply affected the textile business of East Anglia. Troubles in the economy seemed to be manifestations of less concrete, but equally disturbing changes in common attitudes.

Exactly what these disturbing changes were depended on one's location in the social structure. The vast majority of people who possessed no land believed that the world at least owed them a place, however meager, and that it was the fault of grasping landlords and merchants, not simply God's will, that they were groaning in poverty. The wealthy and privileged, expecting docility and deference from their inferiors, were troubled by the rising expectations and the actual mobility they saw challenging their own positions. "Observe degree, priority, and place," [6] ran the old dictum, but in a competitive, increasingly

6. William Shakespeare, *Troilus and Cressida,* Act I, Scene 3, line 86.

crowded commercial society, people were jostling each other for advantage. Moreover the tolerance of different opinions within the Elizabethan Church had permitted such a degree of religious individualism, that the fundamental common denominators of Christian belief were in doubt. Everything from skepticism to pietism could be found in England. The familiar expectation of uniformity, so conducive to harmony and security, was repeatedly being frustrated by experience.

Uneasiness in English public life bred noisy controversies. The privilege and favoritism of monopolies and royal patronage were sharply criticized in Parliament during the 1620s, and a struggle between the advocates of royal prerogative courts and the supporters of common law courts, attested to a far-reaching division among prominent people over the principles of maintaining order. At the end of the 1620s, when Charles I dissolved Parliament and determined to rule without it, the political conflict reached a climax. When the king succeeded in raising revenue by means of a forced loan, he effectively trampled the principle of taxation by consent in Parliament. Charles's objective was to establish uniformity and order within the realm by means of royal absolutism.

The English Church, which had once been pliant and tolerant, was now headed by William Laud, whose drive for ecclesiastical absolutism was part of Charles's program for his realm. As a result, Puritanism was now treated as a subversive movement to be actively rooted out of the church, the sooner the better. In the past Puritans had been under a cloud. Now the storm burst upon them. Laud believed that he must achieve a total victory over the Puritans, or they would take over the Church. Henceforth Puritans would be ousted from the universities and church appointments, and, where they deviated from Laud's ecclesiastical policies, they would be fined and harassed. Until the end of the 1620s Puritans had clung to the hope that they could redeem an England that was sliding toward Hell. Now, when their own survival was in doubt, gloomy premonitions about the consequences of God's wrath came readily to mind. These were the anxieties that inspired Puritans to create the Massachusetts Bay Company in 1629.

They established the Bay Company from the ruins of the Dorchester Company. During the early 1620s the Dorchester group led by the Reverend John White had attempted to found a farming and fishing colony on the shores of Massachusetts Bay. Although Puritans were conspicuous in this effort, the chief object of the enterprise was commercial. After several preliminary voyages, the Dorchester Company mounted its greatest effort in 1625 when it sent three ships and nearly one hundred men to settle Cape Ann. But as with the earlier voyages, there were no profits. The settlers' chief accomplishment was survival, although they did begin a town at Naumkeag (later named Salem), before most of them returned to England. This was not enough to save the company.

Yet John White, who had come to believe in the necessity of a purified settlement away from England, would not give up. Gaining new sponsors in 1628, White helped found the New England Company, and it was this fragile corporation that became the Massachusetts Bay Company by royal charter in March 1629. When the Massachusetts Bay Company sent its first five ships to Cape Ann in 1629, John Endecott, who had been the head of the Dorchester settlement, was made governor of the colony.

John Winthrop was not among the original one hundred ten investors in the new company. But within the year he was drawn into the enterprise by Matthew Cradock, John Humphry, Isaac Johnson, Sir Richard Saltonstall, and the tireless John White. White's vision of a holy settlement, a fragment of England that could redeem it, appealed strongly to Winthrop. Winthrop's willingness to leave Groton Manor, the estate that had brought his grandfather into the gentry class, grew out of a careful assessment of his family's possibilities at home, and their prospects in New England.

As of 1629, when Winthrop and his third wife, Margaret Tyndal, decided to migrate, they were the parents of eight children. The three eldest, sons of John's first wife, were all grown men, but none had as yet found a secure place in the world. John, Jr., and Henry had each spent some time at university, they had traveled, and Henry had married against his parents' wishes. The third son, Forth Winthrop, was training to be a minister. John Winthrop's landholdings were not sufficient to establish his three eldest sons at his own level, not to mention the younger children. His official position as a magistrate in the London court of wards and liveries, which had initially seemed to be a lucrative rung on the patronage ladder, now appeared no more than a tiresome, break-even post, so Winthrop resigned it. In light of Winthrop's ambition for himself and his offspring, he was ripe for a new proposition.

Moreover, Winthrop was part of a network of Puritan gentry northeast of London. When prominent members of this group, such as John Humphry and Isaac Johnson, brothers-in-law of the greatest Puritan peer, the Earl of Lincoln, discussed their plans for Massachusetts with Winthrop, he listened and was persuaded. For Winthrop nothing could be more satisfying than escaping the corruption and competition of a decadent England in favor of building a colony where Puritans would rule and land was abundant. The Massachusetts Bay Company was led by powerful men whom Winthrop respected, and so it could nourish his visionary hopes while reassuring his practical judgment.

In the summer of 1629 Winthrop became part of a conspiracy within the newly formed company to transfer its government and its charter to the new colony. Initially Matthew Cradock, an important London merchant who was the governor of the company, proposed to the company's stockholders' meeting that the actual government of the settlement be transferred "to those that shall inhabit there." [7] The company in England would thereby allow its colony substantial political independence. But Cradock's idea ran into opposition from those who believed the charter did not allow such a step, and that to take it would lead to the charter's revocation. This discussion led a dozen men, including Thomas Dudley (the Earl of Lincoln's steward), Humphry, Johnson, Saltonstall, and Winthrop, to meet again privately at Cambridge in late August. Here they jointly pledged themselves to be ready, "with such of our severall familyes as

7. Matthew Cradock. Quoted in Charles McLean Andrews, *The Colonial Period of American History,* 4 vols. (New Haven: Yale University Press, 1934), 1:388.

are to go with us and such provision as we are able conveniently to furnish ourselves withall to embark . . . by the first of march next [1630] . . . to inhabite and continue in new England.'' But this agreement was made contingent on a crucial point, that ''the whole government together with the Patent . . . bee first by an order of Court legally transferred and established to re-mayne with us and others which shall inhabite.'' [8] Two days later, on August 28, 1629, this Cambridge agreement was presented at a special meeting of the company's stockholders. On the following day, after a systematic airing of the pros and cons, they voted by a show of hands in favor of the Cambridge plan. Only 27 of the company's 125 members were present. The active minority had succeeded in imposing its will on the company.

The revolution in the company was underscored in October 1629 when John Winthrop was elected governor. During the summer he had emerged as a vigorous, shrewd, and conciliatory leader among a group of pious and prudent merchants and gentlemen. The Cambridge agreement now assured all of them that others of similar resources and personal commitment would share in the trials ahead. They were also assured, unlike members of virtually every other colonial settlement, that they and others who risked their lives and their fortunes would never be placed at the mercy of a company whose interests or objectives differed from their own. The special corporate vision of a purified community of God's chosen people, born in the trying circumstances of England in 1629, would be preserved and developed by those who shared the dream.

That fall and winter of 1629–1630 the members of the company led the way in persuading emigrants to go to their colony. Puritan and family connections were the most effective recruiting mechanisms, as groups of farmers from Suffolk and Norfolk, Essex and Lincolnshire, decided to follow the lead of Puritan gentlemen and clergy who lived nearby. No one of real wealth was tempted to go, but the sons of minor gentry, like Winthrop's own sons, yeomen and their families, and a few ar-

8. Edmund S. Morgan, ed., *The Founding of Massachusetts: Historians and the Sources* (Indianapolis: Bobbs-Merrill, 1964), p. 183.

tisans were ready to gather their resources together and invest in passage to America. Most of England was unaware of the migration that was building, and indeed only a tiny fraction of the population was responsive to the lure of overseas settlement. But when the "Winthrop fleet" of eleven vessels assembled at Southampton and Plymouth in the spring of 1630, there were over one thousand passengers on board, with hundreds of cows, horses, goats, swine, and chickens.

Just before his ship sailed, Winthrop wrote a last letter to Margaret, "mine owne, mine onely, my best beloved." She was expecting the birth of another child, and so with John, Junior, to look after her, she remained behind at Groton. Junior, now twenty-three, was to sell the family land and then, once his father was established in the new country, shepherd his step-mother, brothers, and sisters to Massachusetts. Aboard the *Arbella*, John himself was accompanied by his nine- and ten-year-old sons Adam and Stephen. Winthrop's spirits were high, and his words gave Margaret encouragement: "Our boyes are well and cheerful, and have no mind of home, they lye both with me, and sleepe as soundly in a rugge (for we use no sheets heer) as ever they did at Groton, and so I doe my selfe." In a midnight reverie he joyously mused: "Oh how it refresheth my heart to thinke that I shall yet againe see thy sweet countenance, that I have so much delighted in, and beheld with so great contente!" And he promised faithfully to hold to their agreement that on Mondays and Fridays at five in the evening "we shall meet in spiritt till we meet in person. yet if all these hopes should faile, blessed be our God, that we are assured, we shall meet one day, if not as husband and wife, yet in a better condition." [9] The separation from Margaret, the hardships and uncertainties of what he had begun, could not intimidate Winthrop's faith. He was confident God would protect and prosper their enterprise, and if it was His will that Winthrop and others should die in the attempt, then Winthrop felt certain of his reward. This was the faith that had sustained Bradford and the Pilgrims for twenty years. Now it launched a larger fleet.

9. Morgan, *Founding of Massachusetts*, pp. 184, 186.

Under way, the Winthrop fleet was far more fortunate than the *Mayflower* had been. Although it ran into some stormy weather, it made a seasonable crossing of eight to ten weeks. On board the *Arbella* Governor Winthrop delivered a sermon to his fellow passengers that embodied the corporate vision of what the colony was supposed to be. In England the Puritans had been individualists. Unwilling to submit to the orthodoxy of Laud's church, they had elevated their own individual judgments above church and state authority. Now, in Massachusetts, they sought to establish their own orthodoxy to which individual judgments must yield.

The foundation of the new community, Winthrop avowed, was a special contract with the Lord: "Thus stands the cause betweene God and us, we are entered into Covenant with him for this worke." If "the Lord shall please to . . . bring us in peace to the place wee desire, then hath hee ratified this Covenant and . . . will expect a strickt performance of the Articles contained in it." [10] Strict performance meant that the colony must be an exemplary Christian community. Speaking as the elected governor of the company, Winthrop proclaimed a utopian mission:

> wee must entertaine each other in brotherly Affeccion, wee must be willing to abridge our selves of our superfluities, for the supply of other necessities, wee must uphold a familiar Commerce together in all meekenes, gentlenes, patience and liberallity, wee must delight in eache other, make others Condicions our owne[,] rejoyce together, mourne together, labour, and suffer together, allwayes haveing before our eyes our Commission and Community in the worke, our Community as members of the same body, soe shall wee keepe the unitie of the spirit in the bond of peace, the Lord will be our God and delight to dwell among us, as his owne people and will command a blessing upon us in all our wayes. [11]

Whether or not the people of the Massachusetts Bay colony would keep the covenant and join together in building a community of love, justice, and piety was a supreme test, not only for

10. Morgan, *Founding of Massachusetts*, pp. 202, 203.
11. Morgan, *Founding of Massachusetts*, p. 203.

them, but for reformed Christianity. Certain of the covenant in his own heart, Winthrop presented his fellow settlers with a heroic view of the significance of what they were about. For if they lived up to the covenant:

> . . . wee shall find that the God of Israel is among us, when tenn of us shall be able to resist a thousand of our enemies, when hee shall make us a prayse and glory, that men shall say of succeeding plantacions: the lord make it like that of New England: for wee must Consider that wee shall be as a Citty upon a Hill, the eies of all people are uppon us; so that if wee shall deale falsely with our god in this worke . . . wee shall be made a story and a by-word through the world, wee shall open the mouthes of enemies to speake evill of the wayes of god . . . wee shall shame the faces of many of gods worthy servants, and cause theire prayers to be turned into Cursses upon us till wee be consumed out of the good land.[12]

The cause of the Massachusetts Bay Colony was no temporal venture aimed at profit. It was not just an effort to secure a place to live and worship as the settlers willed. Its founders believed it was a holy adventure in which the future of all mankind was at stake.

The self-consciousness of Winthrop and the Bay Company and the generous scale of its enterprise stood in sharp contrast to the Pilgrim effort that had preceded it. The *Mayflower* had sailed alone, because its companion vessel leaked too badly to risk an Atlantic crossing. Because they were delayed, Bradford and the other *Mayflower* passengers crossed the sea during the stormy autumn months. At one point in mid-ocean one of the ship's main timbers buckled; but using "a great iron screw" the ship's carpenter raised "the beam into his place" and braced it "with a post put under it, set firm in the lower deck." [13] So the *Mayflower* survived its nine-week voyage and came into harbor on November 11, 1620, at the eastern end of Cape Cod, over two hundred miles northeast of its Hudson River destination.

The sailors, the separatists, and the nonseparatist passengers suffered a quarrelsome journey, and now that the ship had

---

12. Morgan, *Founding of Massachusetts,* pp. 203–204.
13. Bradford, *Plymouth Plantation,* p. 59.

landed outside the jurisdiction of the Pilgrims' patent, the question of civil authority was in doubt. To provide order, the separatists drafted a simple agreement to join in creating a regular government, "to enact, constitute and frame such just and equal Laws, Ordinances, Acts, Constitutions and Offices, from time to time, as shall be thought most meet and convenient for the general good." [14] Before going ashore, all the healthy men signed this Mayflower Compact, establishing from necessity a government by the consent of the governed. Its first act was to confirm John Carver, an intimate of Brewster and Bradford, as governor of the colony.

Since the Pilgrims had not arrived at their destination, the most immediate question was where they should spend the winter. For three weeks they explored the cape on foot and in an open boat, discovering fresh water and a hoard of Indian seed corn and beans. Then on the night of December 8 the exploring party sailed into Plymouth Bay in a snowstorm. After passing two days on an island, they went ashore at Plymouth Rock on December 11. Here, Bradford reported, they "marched into the land and found divers cornfields and little running brooks, a place (as they supposed) fit for situation. At least it was the best they could find, and the season and their present necessity made them glad to accept of it." Now the explorers returned with the good news to their ship. But when Bradford arrived, he was greeted by the news that his wife, his "dearest consort, accidentally falling overboard, was drowned." [15] Dorothy Bradford had been traveling for nine months, now she found herself staring at the bleak, sandy wastes of America, separated from her young son who had stayed in Leyden and from her husband who was off exploring. It appears that she was a suicide, succumbing to the depression that struck some Englishwomen when they came face to face with the new land they must now call home.

The winter that lay ahead in new Plymouth presented the most devastating test of their faith. Living in lean-tos and shelters they dug in the ground, not equipped to feed themselves

---

14. Bradford, *Plymouth Plantation*, p. 76.
15. Bradford, *Plymouth Plantation*, pp. 72, xxiv.

with fish, the people fell sick. Bradford, one of the dozen heads of families who survived, related that "in two or three months' time half their company died, especially in January and February, being the depth of winter." During the worst period:

> there died sometimes two or three of a day. . . . there was but six or seven sound persons who to their great commendations, be it spoken, spared no pains night nor day, but with abundance of toil and hazard of their own health, fetched them wood, made them fires, dressed them meat, made their beds, washed their loathsome clothes, clothed and uncloathed them. In a word, did all the homely and necessary offices for them which dainty and queasy stomachs cannot endure to hear named; and all this willingly and cheerfully, without any grudging in the least, showing herein their true love unto their friends and brethren.[16]

It was a cruel sifting, and their bodies yielded to it, but not their humanity or their trust in God.

When the winter broke in March, the Pilgrims' health and their fortunes improved. After several minor brushes between the Pilgrims and Indians, an Algonkin called Samoset, who had learned to speak English among fishermen in Maine, came to Plymouth, and with several gifts Pilgrim diplomacy began. In a few days Samoset returned with the sachem of the Wampanoags, Massasoit. On his arrival Massasoit was greeted by Governor Carver, accompanied by several musketeers with drum and trumpet: "after salutations, our Governor kissing his hand, the King [Massasoit] kissed him." [17] The friendly spirit of the meeting quickly led to a durable treaty of peace and mutual defense based on the principle that neither the Pilgrims nor the Wampanoags would injure the other, and that in the event of any injury or theft the offending person(s) would be returned to their own kind for punishment. Each pledged to support the other in the event of war. The newcomers were fortunate that their Plymouth settlement did not trespass on the Wampanoag territory but was instead on the land of the Patuxets, a small

16. Bradford, *Plymouth Plantation*, p. 77.
17. [Thomas] *Mourt's Relation*, quoted in Bradford, *Of Plymouth Plantation*, 80n.

tribe that had been wiped out by disease (perhaps measles) in 1617. Only one Patuxet, who had been kidnapped by English fishermen and thus absent in the fatal year, survived. His name was Squanto.

For the Pilgrim outcasts struggling to survive, the orphaned Squanto appeared a godsend. For it was Squanto who showed them how to plant corn, "and after how to dress and tend it." He taught them how to catch the alewives coming up the streams, and how to use them to fertilize their corn and beans. The value of his help proved inestimable since the "English seed they sowed, as wheat and pease," [18] failed entirely that first year.

While the Pilgrims were getting their first crop planted, the *Mayflower* departed. Soon after, Governor Carver, hard at work in the fields, suffered a sunstroke and died. Now the small remnant of the men elected Bradford their governor, a post he would retain through repeated elections for over thirty years. Bradford was energetic yet stolid, reliable, and self-effacing; his sound judgment and devotion to the common good made him the lasting choice of the Plymouth colony. Under his leadership they bore their afflictions and in time prospered.

When the first anniversary of their arrival came round, it was apparent they had passed through the fire. "Being all well recovered in health and strength," their harvest gathered, the settlers "had all things in good plenty." [19] Every family was provided with a generous store of codfish and bass, ducks, geese, turkeys, venison, and cornmeal. Then Bradford organized a great feast of thanksgiving. He sent four men hunting who, in a day, returned with enough wild fowl to feed the settlement for a week:

> At which time, amongst other recreations, we exercised our arms, many of the Indians coming amongst us, and amongst the rest their greatest king, Massasoit with some 90 men, whom for three days we entertained and feasted. And they went out and killed five deer

18. Bradford, *Plymouth Plantation,* p. 85.
19. Bradford, *Plymouth Plantation,* p. 90.

which they brought to the plantation and bestowed on our Governor and upon the Captain [Miles Standish] and others.[20]

The colonists still mourned the loss of so many of their brethren, but they rejoiced that God had made them a community. They looked to the future with optimism.

Now, however, there were a number of strictly temporal problems that needed solutions. The colonists possessed no English title to the land they had settled, and the merchant company that had sponsored their crossing wanted a return on its investment. The first issue was resolved soon after the *Mayflower* arrived again in England. Using as a model the patent they had held from the Virginia Company, they obtained a new grant from the Council for New England in June 1621. The colony was required, under the grant, to pay a quitrent of two shillings per hundred acres. In addition, however, the merchants would have to be paid.

At first, under Bradford's leadership, property was held in common with an annual drawing for garden plots. But by 1624 the planters persuaded Bradford to make permanent allotments, so that those who improved the land would enjoy the benefits. Eight years later, when new arrivals swelled the colony to three hundred people, the move to private ownership was extended by permanent divisions of meadow and pasturelands outside the village. Farming sustained the colony during the 1620s, but it could not yield profits for the company; so the stockholders would provide no further assistance. The value of their stock plunged. As a result the Pilgrims concluded in 1626 that they must attempt to buy out the company and liberate themselves from its control. They did so, but at a fearfully high cost considering their resources: they would pay for the shares at the rate of £200 annually for nine years, and in addition pay off the company's £600 debts. By this agreement the colony itself became, *de facto,* a joint-stock corporation. Fifty-three men in the colony owned its assets as well as its debts, and the land and livestock were allotted among them.

20. Edward Winslow, letter of Dec. 11, 1621, printed in *Mourt's Relation,* 60–61, and quoted in Bradford, *Of Plymouth Plantation,* 90n.

In order to accumulate the capital necessary to pay the new obligations, it was clear that the colony would need to develop trade aggressively. Accordingly Bradford and seven others secured permission from the settlers to form a partnership to manage the colony's trading activities until the debts were retired. This partnership and the need to pay the debts rapidly altered the orientation of the colony toward trade. Here the friendly relations with the Wampanoags were a great asset as the Pilgrims exchanged steel hatchets and knives for furs, fish, and corn. Pilgrim trade, however, extended all along the northern coast, from New Amsterdam to Maine, where they established important posts along the Kennebec and Penobscot rivers. In the 1630s agriculture, too, added to the profits, with sales of cattle, corn, and wheat to the newcomers in Massachusetts Bay. Yet it was not until 1639 that the five remaining trading partners succeeded in completing payment to their London creditors, and in order to raise the final £400, they all had to sell portions of their real estate.

The growth of Plymouth during the 1620s, while large in percentage terms, was actually quite modest. The survivors of the *Mayflower* voyage, less than sixty in all, were later joined by two hundred more separatists and others arriving at various times on four different ships. One of these, in 1623, carried the widow Alice Southworth of the Leyden church and her two young sons. Soon after arrival, she and Bradford were married. The three children born of this marriage, like the other children born in Plymouth, marked an important milestone in the settlement, the emergence of a new generation—people who were not refugees and who knew only the landscape of the frontier. As yet they were only youths, subject to family discipline. But the colony would one day be theirs.

Now, however, in 1630 the separatist settlement at Plymouth, so painstakingly built up over a decade, was suddenly dwarfed by the new Puritan colony to the north. When Winthrop and the thousand other settlers landed in June and July 1630, they came to a region that their own agents had carefully reconnoitered, and they were greeted by John Endecott, former governor and leader of the handful of "old planters" of Cape Ann. In contrast to the Pilgrims, the Puritans, well financed, supplied, and numerous, were off to a running start. Indeed from the outset there was a keenly competitive element in this new colony.

Prime land was the first source of rivalry. Since Massachusetts was mostly heavily wooded, years would pass before it could be put to the plow. The Dorchester Company's people had already taken up some of the best cleared meadowland on Cape Ann, so there was an immediate scramble for tillage elsewhere. Within two or three months the new settlers—three or four hundred families—scattered themselves around the bay, principally along the Charles River at Charlestown and Watertown, along the Mystic River, on the Shawmut peninsula, which they named Boston, and farther south at places called Roxbury and Dorchester. Their first tasks were building shelters before winter, preparing defenses against Indian attack, and, wherever possible, getting in a crop.

Governor Winthrop and the other rulers of the colony, the assistants, were anxious about this rapid dispersion. It drastically weakened their possibilities for control, while undermining the colony's ability to defend itself. But in the turmoil of establishing government and settlement simultaneously, they had little recourse but to accept this dispersion. At the same time they made a vigorous effort to govern, holding court at Charlestown in August and September, and at Boston in October 1630. Here they appointed constables, assessed taxes, and began imposing justice on Puritans and everyone else within their jurisdiction. Their laws were the charter, the customs they knew, and their collective judgment as to what was best. Winthrop and the assistants were struggling to establish order and their own authority according to their own lights. Elsewhere local government was beyond their reach, and so reverted to the settlers themselves to establish as best they could according to the various borough, manor, and open-field customs they had known in England.

The Puritans' winter of 1630–1631 was hard, though not as deadly as that of the Pilgrims a decade earlier. Two hundred settlers, including Assistant Isaac Johnson and his wife, died of malnutrition and disease, and within the year one hundred more returned to England. The non-Puritan settlers, a few of whom had been there for years, chafed under the imposition of Winthrop's version of a purified community. What had seemed so fresh and promising in June 1630 was already in doubt by October.

Winthrop's flexibility and shrewd judgment were largely responsible for setting things right. At the October 19 meeting of the company stockholders, General Court, Winthrop and the Assistants disregarded the charter and allowed all men present to vote on the issues before it, not just the stockholders. This bold step broadened the government's base of consent. Soon after, Winthrop and his colleagues invited all who wished the privilege, to become "freemen," thus returning the suffrage within the rules of the charter. By the following spring the Bay Colony government was far more secure, and in the towns Puritan churches had been established. The laxity and disorder of the first months had been surmounted, and now Winthrop turned his efforts toward fulfillment of the corporate dream.

A first step was to assure that the rule of the godly would never again be jeopardized. Accordingly Winthrop, after being elected governor once more on May 18, 1631, urged the adoption of an oath of fidelity to the Massachusetts Bay Company and its officers in New England. The freemen accepted the oath, and the majority then went on to accept Winthrop's proposal that from that day forward "noe man shalbe admitted to the freedom of this body politicke [the General Court and its electors], but such as are members of some of the churches within the limitts" [21] of the colony. Frankly elitist in their views of society and government, the rulers of Massachusetts Bay believed that only those who were actual converted members of the churches, not merely those who attended church, were fit vessels for authority in running the colony. In contrast to Bradford and the leaders of Plymouth who, once survival was assured, had turned their eyes to trade in order to secure independence from outside control, Winthrop, Dudley, and their colleagues now set about building the "City upon a Hill."

21. Quoted in Andrews, *Colonial Period,* 1:435.

In retrospect their self-confidence is awesome. By 1635 it was apparent that Winthrop was prepared to affirm the total independence of Massachusetts Bay Colony from the authority of any English institution whatever, including the monarchy. This self-confidence was founded on religious faith, but it was also underwritten by the fact that after the first year, the colony was growing and prospering at a rate that could only reinforce its leaders' sense of divine support. By the mid-1630s immigrants, chiefly Puritans, were coming to Massachusetts at the rate of two thousand annually. They were bringing the manpower, tools, and livestock required to develop the colony at a rapid pace. By 1640 there were some three hundred university-trained Puritan clergymen among the settlers, who vigorously promoted the religious objectives of the colony. Under these circumstances it is no wonder that Winthrop and the assistants developed a heady sense of power. In a few short years they had gone from being semi-outcasts of modest rank in England, to being the exclusive leaders of a great Christian experiment.

The sense of certainty of the Bay Colony leadership is illustrated in its responses to crucial policy issues it faced during the mid-1630s. In light of the rapidly expanding population, territorial questions were most pressing. Massachusetts's response was unequivocally expansionist. With the blessing of the governor and General Court its people settled all along the seaboard, northward along the Maine coast and southward to open land on both shores of Long Island Sound. They encouraged interior settlement as well. Ignoring Dutch claims on the Connecticut River, colonies of migrants from Massachusetts Bay began farming and trading in the rich valley, where they founded the towns of Hartford, Saybrook, Springfield, Wethersfield, and Windsor. A more compact, readily controlled pattern of settlement would have been preferable to Winthrop, since settlers were in some cases moving beyond the Bay Colony's jurisdiction, but he and his colleagues supported expansion all the same.

They supported expansion even though, as they anticipated, it led to a major war with the Pequot Indians of the Connecticut region in 1637. While the immediate causes of the war were conflicts between English traders and Indians, the war was prosecuted on a scale and with a finality that was intended to eliminate the Pequot tribe and extinguish its territorial claims. Certainly after the surprise attack on the main Pequot fortified village, where the English set the encampment on fire, encircled it, and then shot those who fled from the flames, it is obvious that the war was not aimed at the restoration of amicable trading relations. The English captain who led the battle estimated that in half an hour six or seven hundred Pequots died, men, women, and children. The remnants of the Pequots were sold to neighboring tribes as slaves. The land was immediately occupied by Englishmen under the leadership of John Winthrop, Jr., who in 1635 had become the colonial agent for the English owners of Connecticut lands. English expansion, and the victory over the Pequots, set an example to the other tribes of southern New England that they must accommodate the newcomers.

Within Massachusetts Bay itself, in Boston and the neighboring towns, the influx of people put intense pressure on the concept of orthodoxy. Puritans all rejected the ceremonial ritualism of Anglican worship in favor of concentration on preaching, but they were not an entirely uniform or coherent body. Some tended toward Presbyterianism, others toward separatism, and many still favored controlling and reforming the episcopal hierarchy. Dissenting religion possessed a powerful affinity with individualism. The concept of Puritan orthodoxy was itself new, and putting it into practice generated a major crisis in the Bay Colony.

The conflict that emerged with the Reverend Roger Williams in 1635 was symptomatic. Williams had come over with the Winthrop fleet in 1630, and was highly regarded, being named minister by the Salem church in 1635. But Williams's religious views were in flux, and from the Salem pulpit and in religious meetings at his home he denied the authority of the Bay Colony and its General Court to act in religious matters. Contradicting directly the fundamental position of the leadership, he called for an absolute separation of church and state. In addition Williams became a separatist, denying any legitimacy for the Anglican Church. At a time when Massachusetts Bay governors were

seeking to consolidate their power, Williams's loudly proclaimed views were intolerable. The General Court moved
quickly and decisively to end his subversive challenge by ban-
ishing him from the colony. To have tolerated his insubordi-
nation would have opened the door to a wide variety of civil and
religious views that were simmering in Boston and in the scattered settlements of the colony.

The following year, 1636, similar issues erupted around Anne
Hutchinson. These were far less easy to contain because she had
the backing of a prominent young Puritan, Sir Henry Vane, who
had just arrived in the colony. Vane, the eldest son of one of the
king's privy councillors, was elected governor in 1636 because
of his high rank, excellent English connections, and apparent
zeal for the Puritan cause. Vane was impressed with Anne
Hutchinson's extraordinary gifts for theological discourse and
her intense piety. As a result he was reluctant to take action
against her when she began holding prayer meetings in her
home, where she pronounced sharp criticisms of conventional
piety and of the clergy who encouraged it. She claimed direct,
personal revelation from God on matters of doctrine, which Anglicans and Puritans agreed was heresy. Together with the Reverend John Wheelwright of the Boston church, Anne Hutchinson self-righteously challenged the emerging religious
establishment frontally. Wheelwright threw down the gauntlet at
the beginning of 1637 when he preached to his followers:
"When enymies to the truth oppose the way of God . . . we
must kille them with the worde of the Lorde." If this meant "a
combustean in Church and Commonwealth," so be it.[22] Sir
Henry Vane, who would distinguish himself a decade later as a
champion of religious liberty in the English Revolution, became, in effect, the patron of this insurgent movement in the
Boston church.

The conflict came to a head in 1637 when the General Court
tried Wheelwright and, not withstanding Vane's defense of his
actions, convicted him of the civil crimes of sedition and contempt of authority. Sentencing was delayed, and when the Gen-

---

22. Quoted in Darrett B. Rutman, *Winthrop's Boston* (Chapel Hill, N.C.: University
of North Carolina Press, 1965), p. 120.

eral Court met again, Vane attempted to have the decision reversed. But the deputies, led by Winthrop, stood firm against reopening the case and then went on to elect Winthrop as governor. Three months later the twenty-four-year-old Vane returned to England, depriving Wheelwright, Hutchinson, and their followers of their most effective secular spokesman.

Winthrop and the deputies, backed by the clergy, pressed their advantage. In the fall they banished Wheelwright from the colony, and disfranchised his two supporters (Boston deputies) in the General Court, as well as others who had actively supported Wheelwright's subversive activity. Taking the threat of sedition seriously, the General Court ordered fifty-eight Bostonians to give up their muskets until they were ready to recant their sins. Those who would not—a substantial number—ultimately left, going to New Hampshire with Wheelwright or to Rhode Island.

Hutchinson was now virtually defenseless. She faced the choice of quiet submission or punishment when the authorities whom she had attacked brought her to trial before the General Court in March 1638. Here, after a virtuoso defense in which for hours she recanted nothing while cleverly avoiding any self-incrimination, she finally revealed the views that had brought on the conflict: loftily she exclaimed that her testimony was direct from God, "by an immediate revelation," [23] and that her accusers and their posterity would be accursed, for "the mouth of the Lord hath spoken it." [24] Though the trial was anything but fair—even by seventeenth-century standards—she had finally convicted herself out of her own mouth; so the ministers present voted to excommunicate her, and the magistrates voted her banishment.

These struggles with Williams, Wheelwright, and Hutchinson were crucial for the definition of orthodoxy in the Bay Colony. The disputations among clergymen that had surrounded the judgments against the three dissidents established the outer boundaries of consensus among the orthodox. Moreover the

---

23. Quoted in Edmund S. Morgan, *The Puritan Dilemma: The Story of John Winthrop* (Boston: Little, Brown, 1958), p. 152.

24. Quoted in Rutman, *Winthrop's Boston*, p. 121.

close, mutually supportive though distinct roles of church and state authority were delineated in the conflicts. In the process something that was not Anglican, or Presbyterian, or separatist, was coming into being—the New England Way—through which conventions of clergymen, meeting periodically, established their own discipline and criteria for uniformity. This arrangement allowed for a substantial degree of congregational independence, which, considering the volatile religious spirits the Bay Colony had attracted, was vital to the establishment of a peaceful, relatively harmonious Christianity. Here a durable balance was struck between individualism and corporate orthodoxy. In a few years when Harvard College, the seminary founded in 1636, would begin supplying Massachusetts with clergymen trained in the New England way of orthodoxy, its future would be assured.

The triumph of orthodoxy between 1635 and 1638 encouraged Winthrop to believe that Massachusetts Bay Colony might indeed build a virtuous city on a hill. But the establishment of orthodoxy in religion, while absolutely necessary, was not sufficient. Maintaining the colony's integrity was a continuous battle, both against English interference, repeatedly invited by malcontents within the colony, as well as against indigenous tendencies toward backsliding. In the latter case economic individualism was the chief danger. Acquisitiveness, in real estate and in trade, flourished during the booming conditions of the 1630s as every year more land was settled and more furs brought to market. When the migration to Massachusetts abruptly ended in 1640 because hope for Puritanism was blossoming in England, the land boom stopped. Prices of land, livestock, and crops slackened, but not the desire for individual gain.

Winthrop's response, analogous to the enforcement of communal religious standards, was to seek central control of business activities as well. A major portion of Winthrop's "Model of Christian Charity" sermon had been devoted to an explication of the proper terms of moneylending for Christians. With their governor, the representatives in the General Court believed in the idea of the "just price," rather than a floating, "anything-the-market-will-bear" law of supply and demand. Coming from a land where rents commonly remained fixed for fifty or one hundred years and the prices of basic commodities were often fixed, they were unsettled by the inflation and rapid fluctuations in prices during the 1630s. Setting prices on commodities and on wages, the General Court used the depression as a time to retrench. From the end of the 1630s onward, both secular and religious sanctions were brought to bear on those who violated the general sense of fair dealing.

In order to preserve the stable social hierarchy that was crucial to the corporate ideal, the General Court resorted to sumptuary laws. Hoping to keep people in their proper places, it prescribed codes of dress so that artisans and their wives would dress with the simplicity that suited their stations. Winthrop, the other magistrates, and the clergy made every effort to establish a society in which an inbred sense of mutual obligations between masters and servants, parents and children, rulers and subjects, would provide for a harmonious and stable community. But the pressures they faced, within themselves as well as from below, never faltered. One observer remarked in the 1650s that: "An over-eager desire after the world hath seized on the spirits of many . . . as if the Lord had no farther work for his people to do, but every bird to feather his own nest." [25] Religious dissent could be banished, but not acquisitive self-seeking. At best it could be kept at bay.

Ultimately the question was whether the new generation of colony leaders would share the founders' commitment to the utopian vision of Massachusetts Bay Colony. The experience of Plymouth Colony was not promising. The Pilgrims had never possessed the powerful commitment to central institutions that Massachusetts Bay had, but their colony was so much smaller and more intimate that during its first two decades the personal influence of Bradford and the other elders had sustained its unity far more effectively than all the courts and ministerial consociations of Massachusetts Bay. Yet the same pressures were everywhere.

In Plymouth many settlers had departed from the old village to take up lands across Plymouth Bay at Duxbury and Green's

---

25. Edward Johnson, quoted in *Winthrop's Boston*, p. 245.

Harbor (Marshfield), and even farther away at Barnstable, Sandwich, and Yarmouth along the Cape. Those who remained became dissatisfied with the "barrenness" of their lands, and so Bradford reports:

> . . . the church began seriously to think whether it were not better jointly to remove to some other place than to be thus weakened and as it were insensibly dissolved. . . . Some were still for staying together in this place, alleging men might here live if they would be content with their condition, and that it was not for want or necessity so much that they removed as for the enriching of themselves. Others were resolute upon removal and so signified that here they could not stay; but if the church did not remove, they must. . . . And thus was this poor church left, like an ancient mother grown old and forsaken of her children, though not in their affections yet in regard of their bodily presence and personal helpfulness; her ancient members being most of them worn away by death, and these of later time being like children translated into other families, and she like a widow left only to trust in God.[26]

Already in the 1640s Bradford was lamenting the passing of his world. His community, initially formed at Scrooby in 1606, had survived persecution in England, exile in Holland, and the most severe physical and emotional tests of settlement, only to be undermined by the lure of material success.

Bradford's counterpart in Massachusetts Bay was not yet so gloomy, though Winthrop too regretted how much "self-love" had gained a foothold and "how little of a public spirit appeared in the country." [27] Both men, and hundreds of families who had come to America sharing their visions of Christian communalism within the framework of the English social hierarchy, still held fast to this vision. But now, as settlements became widely dispersed in the region and conditions of farming and settlement no longer required intense co-operation, their vision of New England was in doubt. Though Bradford and Winthrop still ruled as governors, their world was fading, and a dynamic provincial era was beginning.

26. Bradford, *Plymouth Plantation*, pp. 333–334.
27. Quoted in Rutman, *Winthrop's Boston*, p. 245.

3

Piety and Plenty in the American Canaan

N 1649 John Winthrop died at the age of sixty-one. Eight years later the death of William Bradford in his sixty-eighth year marked the end of an era. A few children of Queen Elizabeth's England still lingered on, but both in Plymouth Colony and Massachusetts Bay, leadership had passed to younger men. The founders had met their most basic challenge masterfully, creating settlements that could endure. Large, healthy families were making the settlements grow rapidly. Year in and year out, farmers were converting great oaks, pines, chestnuts, and hickories into lumber and firewood, as they cleared thousands of acres for planting. In Boston, chiefly, merchants were establishing long-distance trade, selling fish, furs, lumber, cattle, and foodstuffs to Virginia, the West Indies, and England. By the 1650s the colonies had recovered from the slump of the early 1640s and were building the foundations for prosperity.

But Pilgrims and Puritans had not come to America for the sake of mere survival or material success—the Pilgrims had prospered in Leyden, and the great majority of Puritans, and their property, survived very well in England. Among the founders of Massachusetts Bay a sense of community had been formed during a period of special adversity when a ''corrupt'' society had treated them as outcasts and when they struggled to survive in the wilderness. Now that their children were the majority, in control of public and ecclesiastical power, what could weld them together? The test that lay ahead was whether the society they and their children were creating would be truly pious, or whether it would become merely a distant colony of provincials living the ways of the English countryside. The tension inherent in this situation proved a dynamic force over the next century as people struggled over their identity. Beneath it lay the question of whether the colony's corporate ideals should override individual goals or promote their fulfillment.

If the survival of the missionary vision of Massachusetts Bay Colony had rested on a handful of leaders such as Winthrop and the Assistants, or even the broader group of leaders, the clergy, then it would have had only a short and contentious life after the restoration of the Stuart monarchy in 1660. Outside pressure from England, combined with the ambitions of farmers, fishermen, and merchants in an expanding economy would have buckled the leadership. But, in fact, the original impulse had been broad as well as intense and never limited to a few lay or clerical leaders. Most Massachusetts Bay households were headed by yeomen farmers, and it was the attachment of these families to the ideal, reinforced by the policies of the General Court and the clergy, that enabled the ideal to persist.

The community of Dedham, founded in 1636, demonstrates the widespread commitment to Puritan corporatism and the way that local institutions and central authority were used to sustain it. The thirty men who founded Dedham were all part of the great Puritan migration, arriving in Massachusetts between 1630 and 1635. They were strangers from several different counties in England, but their common bond was a desire to live and own land in a Christian community. The General Court yoked these objectives in its requirements for granting townships, because it would allot them only to groups of settlers, not to individuals or absentee owners. This approach to the distribution of land was a powerful incentive for community formation.

From the beginning, the Dedham settlers planned on creating their own "Citty on a Hill"; indeed, they proposed to the General Court that, if their petition should be granted, the town be named Contentment.[1] The court granted the group an extensive tract (some 200 square miles) southwest of Boston, but rather than innovate, the court named it after a village in the shire of Essex. The founders cleared their title with the Wampanoags of the region and rapidly began their settlement in 1636.

Their first action together in Dedham was to draw and sign a community covenant. Its first article was a mutual pledge to "practice one truth according to that most perfect rule, the foundation whereof is everlasting love." [2] In addition they agreed to obey the common rules made by the group. The covenant included a procedure whereby any disputes between Dedham people would be submitted to an arbitration committee selected from among their neighbors. The Dedham settlers wished theirs to be a harmonious community of like-minded people, but they were not totally exclusive. The covenant provided that others might settle if it appeared that the newcomers would be "of one heart with us" and were prepared to sign the covenant.

The willingness to practice what they preached is evident in the way the settlers treated their land. Instead of dividing it all up among themselves to satisfy individual speculative ambitions, they parceled it out to create a compact village within their extensive township. Since they believed in a social hierarchy, the land was not divided equally, but the range between largest and smallest grants was narrow and depended largely on the family's ability to work the land and the number of people in a household. The grants were so sparing, so oriented to present ability to improve the land, that twenty years after Dedham was settled, when the number of admitted families had grown from thirty to seventy-five, the town still retained 97 percent of its original grant.

After the selectmen had laid out the village, the townspeople

1. Petition quoted in Kenneth A. Lockridge, *A New England Town, The First Hundred Years: Dedham, Massachusetts, 1636–1736* (New York: Norton, 1970), p. 4. In this book, *township* refers to a tract of land with political boundaries. *Town* and *township* are used synonymously; *town* does not mean an urban center, and the term *townspeople* refers to farmers and village dwellers within the town.

2. Lockridge, *A New England Town,* pp. 4, 5.

began work on forming a church. Their first task was to know each other's minds so they could work out their common fundamentals for inclusion in a church covenant. Since they had not come from any one parish and were not the followers of a particular clergyman, it was a lengthy task. Meeting weekly from late 1637 into the following year, the people spoke their minds and gradually came to agree on principles. Though only God could know who was truly saved, theirs would be a church of "visible saints," of people whose outward and inward piety were so well known that it seemed probable that they were God's elect. Several of the most pious men, including the Reverend John Allin, were chosen to act as an admissions committee to interview every prospective member. One year after the townspeople had begun discussing a covenant, they were ready to form a church, so, in the presence of clergymen from other churches and magistrates from the General Court, they signed their covenant and inaugurated their church. It had no meetinghouse; it was a body of visible saints. Within a decade four-fifths of the men and women in Dedham became admitted members of the church.

Dedham's first twenty years fulfilled the villagers' ideal of a Christian community. Working and praying together, they accommodated their wishes to one another. The arbitration system was so effective that Dedham people had no need for courts. The town meeting, where heads of households elected local officials and voted on town policy, operated through consensus, and the decisions of the annually elected executives, the selectmen, were never challenged. Common interests—material and spiritual—furnished a setting in which a harmony based on orthodoxy flourished.

Then, in the year of Bradford's death, the people of Dedham laid down a policy that, while aimed at preserving their community just as it was, signaled the legitimation of self-seeking at the community's expense. The immediate decision was to stop admitting new settlers into Dedham so the town's growth would be limited to their own descendants. Otherwise, they feared, the town would become too large and diverse to remain a unified community. However, the way in which the policy was spelled out suggests that selfishness was also at work. The public land of Dedham, which had been thought of as belonging to the community, was now made the common property of the specific individuals who were presently members of the town. They made themselves the proprietors of the town land, and only they, their heirs, and people to whom they *sold* proprietary shares would partake in future divisions of the town's remaining 125,000 acres. Until now Dedham had been a corporation open to like-minded Christians. Now it became a hereditary corporation, although membership could also be purchased. While the immediate consequences of the new policy were minimal, its implications were profoundly significant for the Puritan ideal of community. In time the people of Dedham would be divided into two classes: one, the descendants of proprietors, with hereditary access to land within the township; the other, newcomers and their progeny, much less securely rooted, having to purchase land whenever and wherever they could.

In the church, too, were omens of decline. By the early 1660s the percentage of young people experiencing conversion had fallen so sharply that the day was approaching when only a minority of Dedham people would be church members. For a time the church rejected the "halfway covenant," a widely used innovation whereby the children of admitted members could be allowed into the church (except for communion) provided they committed themselves to living by the Bible. Dedham had made access to communal land a hereditary privilege, but it was not until the 1670s that people were prepared to accept a similar principle in the church, and even then there were misgivings. If incoming clergymen had not demanded the adoption of this provision in order to expand membership and their own base of support, it seems unlikely that the Dedham church would have accepted the halfway covenant. The circle of people devoted to the original faith was contracting, but it did not disappear.

When Dedham and communities like it were challenged by the dispersion of a growing population away from the old villages in the late seventeenth century, their responses were ambivalent. Usually the process began, as it had in Bradford's Plymouth, with the requests of people living distant from the center to be permitted to form a separate church society in their own locality. Often this proposal met heated opposition, since the original church would be left with fewer people and smaller revenues. After separate religious societies were formed, it was often only a matter of time until the same people sought full political separation from the parent town. That, too, meant a loss in revenues. But, generally, the old towns and their deputies in the General Court accepted this process of division because it preserved and renewed the communal ideal which was tied to settlements of no more than several hundred families. The easiest way to recapture a sense of community in a town where rancorous, geographically based divisions had erupted, was to create new towns through legislative surgery. As the population of Massachusetts Bay grew to over 100,000 by 1700, the average size of towns was stabilizing in the range of 200 to 300 families.

By this time, however, a community covenant such as that of Dedham was becoming rare. Even in the 1630s all towns had not begun with Christian covenants. The fishermen of Gloucester and Marblehead, many of whom were not Puritans, scorned to give up the least iota of their individual rights. Even Puritan farmers such as those who settled the town of Sudbury, ten miles northwest of Dedham, did not enter a town covenant. For them, as for others, town-founding had been a secular matter, and material questions had made their town meeting a forum of conflict even though the townspeople organized a church and worshiped as a group.

The fact that all towns were not harmonious Dedhams, and that from time to time bickering and even serious divisions occurred, does not mean that the corporate impulse and the sense that individual judgments and actions should be subordinate to the common good had died. Everywhere it remained a powerful force shaping people's expectations and behavior.

Its initial strength of course, as at Dedham, had been drawn from religious commitment. But from the beginning it also depended on secular attitudes and institutions that were common to agricultural settlements in much of Britain and the Continent in the seventeenth century. Here the crucial decision had been made by the General Court when, both for religious and practical reasons, it had determined that settlement would be by groups of people clustered in towns, in contrast to the scattered, isolated grant system that was used in colonies to the south. Granting land to groups of people and requiring them to establish communal institutions—town government, churches— meant the creation of a highly localized pattern of face-to-face relationships, frequently renewed. Since the land grants were large enough to provide for several generations of inhabitants, the basis for continuity was established at the outset. Loyalties to familiar people and places were bound to grow, reinforcing the vitality of the community.

Pulling together for the common good in frontier settlements was also highly functional in the most mundane, practical terms. Road construction was literally a public-work project, demanding the collective efforts of townsmen; and erecting the frame for every house and barn in a settlement required the labor of several families, at least. In the absence of specialized workers and a cash economy, subsistence required co-operation and common labor from settlers. The physical creation of a village and its amenities, such as roads and bridges, contributed substantially to the formation of a psychological community even in towns where a covenant like Dedham's was never considered.

Over time, the political and ecclesiastical structure of the colony reinforced the corporate identity. Towns and congregations were not mere administrative subdivisions of Massachusetts Bay. Collectively, they *were* the colony. Within wide and generally flexible boundaries fixed by all the towns and churches, each town and each congregation displayed autonomy. Towns conducted their elections, tax collection and disbursement, and other internal business, even relations with neighboring towns, without supervision from outside. Their conformity with colony laws was voluntary for the most part, and coercion from the General Court, which came in the form of fines, was infrequent and subject to negotiation. The colony's military force was composed of town militia units that were largely self-trained and self-governing. Formal secular institutions provided a structure to sustain the vitality of community.

The New England Way of church polity allowed an even greater degree of liberty. Churches hired their own clergy and managed their own affairs. Outsiders were called in only rarely, and then to confirm local decisions or to adjudicate disputes. After a church was founded, total autonomy was common for a generation or two. Under these circumstances, where local institutions were controlled by local people, the town belonged to its people in the fullest sense and group possessiveness toward the community flourished. Informally as well as officially, townspeople effectively squelched selfishness when it interfered with common goals.

Consequently the survival of a vigorous corporate ideal was never in doubt. But was it Winthrop's ideal community? Did people "uphold a familiar Commerce together in all meekenes, gentlenes, patience and liberallity;" did they "delight in eache other, . . . rejoyce together, mourne together, labour, and suffer together . . . in the bond of peace?" [3] To some degree they did. But the communal ideal now showed evidence of a good deal of earthy secularism. Group economic interests often came before Christian generosity. Poor people who were not born in a township were quickly sent away to become charges of their native locality. Even Dedham, with its abundant supply of land, was insistent about maintaining control of every acre within its boundaries when, in the 1670s, the Indian missionary John Eliot needed some land for Christian Indian farmers. Piety flourished, but it was a *social* piety more than a *soul* piety. People still favored the common good over the individual, but in defining the good, the balance had shifted from salvation toward material security and well-being.

It was this trend that made the halfway covenant so generally desirable in the late seventeenth century. In the second and third generations of settlement new church memberships were no

3. Quoted in Edmund S. Morgan, ed., *The Founding of Massachusetts* (Indianapolis: Bobbs-Merrill, 1964), p. 203.

longer common, especially among young men. Whereas church members had once included the majority of heads of families in each town and nonmembers had been in the minority, now the situation was reversed. The political consequences were serious. Enthusiasm for supporting churches waned, and pulpits sometimes remained empty for several years. Moreover, the circle of voters eligible to choose representatives to the General Court contracted. Since the pillars of the social order—the church and the state—were both founded on regenerate Christians, the colony faced the choice of letting these institutions become separate from the body of the people, governing them substantially without their consent, or else letting every man participate, church member or not. In light of their ruling principles, neither of these courses was acceptable. To clergymen especially, the idea that the population would become generally outsiders to the church was a dismal reproach. Their influence would decline, and infidelity would flourish.

Taking the lead in solving this problem, a synod of ministers agreed in 1662 to allow the children of members into church membership without requiring conversion. The church would become theirs, and, it was hoped, they would later come into full membership. The halfway covenant was a recruiting device for the churches and a means of promoting a broader colonial political franchise. Yet because of the congregational church structure, the synod's decision was in no way binding. Each church had to become convinced that it should open its membership in this way. Gradually in the forty years following the synod the new arrangement gained acceptance. When members saw their children and grandchildren straying from their own path, they came to adopt this practical, if doctrinally doubtful measure. Together with hereditary access to town lands, the halfway covenant promoted an almost tribal sense of family identity that became intertwined with communal bonds.

In the late seventeenth century there were two major external threats to the colony that tested community vigor and unity, one from Indians and the other from the king. The first began in June 1675 when Wampanoag braves attacked the village of Swansea in Plymouth Colony, burning part of it. Several days later, as Plymouth prepared its defenses and called on God's assistance through fasting and prayer, eleven Swansea men were killed and King Philip's war began in earnest. Now the Bay Colony joined with Plymouth in seeking to isolate Massasoit's son and successor Metacom, whom the English called Philip, and the Wampanoags. Their first measures were diplomatic, sending messages to their Indian allies the Narragansetts in Rhode Island and the Pocumtucs in the Connecticut River valley. Then, together with Plymouth forces, they moved to capture Metacom. But during the summer of 1675 the Wampanoag chief eluded them and gained Indian allies of his own in what was becoming a drive to curtail English settlement and reassert Indian supremacy. By autumn both the Narragansetts and the Pocumtucs joined the Wampanoags.

When the Nipmucs in the central upland region joined, too, the settlers faced the worst military threat in their entire history. Communications between east and west were disrupted, and the valley towns, including Springfield, Hadley, and Northampton were burned. By the beginning of the winter of 1675–1676 most of the frontier had to be abandoned. In this first phase of King Philip's War the Indians clearly won.

But the tide turned. In late December Governor Josiah Winslow of Plymouth led militiamen from both colonies in an attack on Chief Canonchet and the Narragansetts, the most powerful of King Philip's allies. The Indians were encamped (as the Pequots had been forty years earlier) on a rise in the middle of a great swamp located along the Chippuxet River, ten miles west of Narragansett Bay. Ordinarily this would have been a secure defensive position. But cold weather froze the swamp, and the militia mounted a fierce attack. By the day's end the colonists had suffered 240 casualties; their enemies lost over 900 killed and wounded. The Narragansetts were not destroyed, but they were neutralized, allowing Plymouth and Massachusetts Bay to concentrate their efforts on defense.

Yet the crisis was not over. Through the months of February, March, April, and May, increasingly desperate Indian attacks continued. For now the Indians vitally needed to capture food supplies, so they raided settlements. Dozens of towns were attacked; one, Medfield, originally part of Dedham, was only eighteen miles west of Boston. As people fled to the safety of garrison houses and to relatives in towns surrounding Boston, their hard-won homes, their tools, their scanty furnishings, were destroyed. Scores of settlers were killed, and others taken prisoner.

As terror mounted, atrocity stories bred vengeance on friendly Christian Indians as well as allied tribes. The authorities at Boston, unable to protect the praying Indians in their villages from irate frontiersmen, put many of them in protective custody on an island in Boston harbor. Later, in the summer of 1676 Christian Indians were in the vanguard of the settlers' counterattack, making a major contribution to the ultimate victory of the white settlers. For Philip and his followers lacked the resources for sustained warfare. Their aggressive tactics brought them through the winter, but when spring came, they needed to return to fishing and farming if their tribes were to survive another year. So King Philip's warriors gradually slipped away, and Metacom himself returned to his home camp. There on August 12, 1676, an English musket shot ended his life and the war.

For Plymouth and Massachusetts Bay the war had been a severe test. Nearly five hundred of their militiamen died of battle wounds, exposure, and disease; many civilians died as well. The loss of capital goods—buildings, tools, and livestock—set the economy back substantially, impoverishing the colonies for years. But the colonial governments functioned adequately, and loyalties were strengthened. In contrast to the hard times of the Pequot War and the early 1640s, when there had been a significant re-migration of settlers back to England, almost no one abandoned Massachusetts in 1676. Most of the settlers who had fought Metacom and his braves were American natives too.

The threat posed by England ten years later was more complicated and less immediate than Indian warfare. The colonies in New England, since their founding, had been free of English control. Indeed, during the period of Cromwell's commonwealth, in the 1650s Massachusetts Bay had begun minting currency and operating very much as an independent state. With the Restoration of the Stuarts in 1660, however, the dissenters in Massachusetts began to be subjected to English control. King Charles II and King James II did not forget that New England had given sanctuary to the men who had killed their father. There were others eager to garner the profits of empire now that the region was flourishing; they wanted to exploit New England trade and real estate. Consequently, in 1685 the crown founded the Dominion of New England to rule over colonies in what are now New York, Massachusetts, and New Hampshire, as well as Rhode Island and Connecticut. The plan was to create a central administration, operating out of Boston, that would control trade, land, and defense against the French and their Indian allies. The first president of the council of the dominion, appointed by the crown, was Joseph Dudley, a native of Roxbury, Massachusetts, and the son of Winthrop's colleague Thomas Dudley.

The extent to which some of Massachusetts Bay Colony's sons had departed from the ideals of their fathers is illustrated by their complicity in overturning the colony's charter. Joseph Dudley, who possessed "as many virtues as can consist with so great a thirst for honor and power," [4] had been sent by the General Court to London in 1682 to head off the threatened revocation of the charter. Betraying this trust, Dudley secretly encouraged the king to dispense with the charter, and to give him a major post in the new regime. Dudley and other Boston entrepreneurs recognized tremendous possibilities for insiders to profit from the new dominion. The scope of Boston trade as well as administrative fees would expand, and the insiders would dispense the favors of the government, its patronage, supply contracts, and land patents. Massachusetts Bay leaders had long sought to expand the jurisdiction of the colony and had recently purchased the patent to a vast part of Maine. In the minds of those supporting the dominion, and they included one of John Winthrop's grandsons, opportunity lay at hand.

4. Thomas Hutchinson, *The History of the Colony and Province of Massachusetts-Bay*, edited by Lawrence Shaw Mayo, 3 vols. (Cambridge, Mass.: Harvard University Press, 1936), 2:160.

But after Sir Edmund Andros assumed the governorship of the Dominion of New England in December 1686, the distressing consequences of losing the autonomy of the charter became apparent. Andros, setting aside the General Court, imposed taxes as an executive act. Townspeople bristled, and at Ipswich the Reverend John Wise led a determined effort to nullify Andros's taxes as being contrary to Magna Carta and the rights of Englishmen. Andros jailed Wise and then fined him, and so succeeded temporarily in gaining the upper hand. Settlers complained, but they submitted.

This opposition, however, led Andros to take another crucial step. He forbade town meetings except for the sole purpose of the annual selection of town officials. Now the dominion struck at the heart of civil communities everywhere in Massachusetts Bay. Andros went on to deny towns the right to collect church tithes used to support the clergy. At the same time he commandeered a Congregational meetinghouse and used it ostentatiously to promote Anglican worship in Boston. Puritan church members and the clergy were enraged, even Joseph Dudley, the young Winthrop, and the merchants who had supported the dominion began to be uneasy.

Andros completed the alienation of the people by threatening them with quitrents. In the past land had been granted in fee simple—full ownership. Now future grants would be subjected to a quitrent of one pound per eight hundred acres. For Dedham this would have come to over two hundred pounds. Existing land titles, on which there was no such rent, would be reviewed by Governor Andros, who would personally establish what sum should be paid retroactively to re-establish titles. Within one short year the dominion was undermining the foundations of political, religious, and economic security.

Had the dominion become entrenched and its policies enforced, Massachusetts Bay Colony would have been extinguished as an entity. A pattern of exploitation of New England paralleling English rule in Ireland would have emerged. But the dominion's potential success rested on English support, so when news arrived in Boston in April 1689 that Andros's sponsor, King James II, was being overthrown by Protestants behind

William of Orange, the people of Boston, led by their old magistrates, staged a coup, capturing Andros and his associates.

The insurgents, acting as a "Council for the Safety of the
People," put forward the eighty-six-year-old Simon Bradstreet
to resume his term as governor, which had been interrupted by
the dominion. Bradstreet, one of the few survivors of the original migration of 1630, the husband of the poet Anne Dudley
Bradstreet (Joseph's older sister), and father of eighteen children, was the epitome of the Puritan patriarch. Immediately he
called for a meeting of town representatives, and when they
learned that William III had indeed succeeded in the Glorious
Revolution, the old charter government was restored. Acting on
their own, the people vindicated the political principles of the
Puritan commonwealth.

But the leaders of Massachusetts Bay, both lay and clerical,
could not turn the clock to the 1630s or 1640s. Imperialism was
gaining strength in England, and the autonomy that Plymouth
and the Bay Company had enjoyed was no longer acceptable to
royal administration, Protestant or Catholic. A mercantilist trading system was being developed, and political control over the
colonies was necessary to promote a coherent system that would
serve the needs of British trading and real estate interests. A
new charter, consolidating Plymouth and the Bay Colony and
setting a royal governor over the new province of the Massachusetts Bay, was written.

Yet the Boston leaders did have some voice in shaping the
new charter. The Reverend Increase Mather, son of the great
preacher Richard Mather, and a Boston native, had been sent to
England even before the Glorious Revolution to see if Governor
Andros could be replaced. In 1690 and 1691, he helped negoti-
ate a charter which restored the General Court as the legislative
assembly, the legal system, and allowed the deputies in the
lower house of the General Court to nominate the members of
the Governor's Council, the upper house. The new charter also
permitted the Congregational establishment and its seminary,
Harvard College, to remain intact, although a policy of religious
tolerance for other sectarians—chiefly Baptists, Anglicans, and
Catholics—was now required.

Increase Mather was particularly successful in lobbying for a compatible governor. The appointee was Sir William Phips, a newly knighted sea captain from Kennebec in the Maine district and a Puritan follower of Mather in the Boston congregation. In contrast to Andros, the new governor was friendly to the religious as well as the secular objectives of the tradition-oriented Massachusetts Bay elite.

It was partly for this reason that he fell prey to the witchcraft anxiety that captured Massachusetts Bay in 1692. For when Governor Phips arrived in 1692 bringing the new charter, he was greeted by news of a satanic epidemic at Salem, twenty miles northeast of Boston. Here, in the sharply divided second parish the daughter of the Reverend Samuel Parris and several of her friends were claiming to be attacked by witches. Their tormentors, they said, were middle-aged women outcasts and the Reverend Mr. Parris's opponents in the congregation. Phips took all of this very seriously, and not being one to appear soft on Satan, he quickly created a special court to deal with the suspects.

The court, which met during the spring and summer of 1692, condemned to death by hanging nineteen villagers, both men and women, including the congregation's former minister the Reverend George Burroughs, who had taken a pulpit in Maine. One more victim of the proceedings was Giles Corey, an elderly farmer who wished to assure his heirs possession of his property, and therefore refused to plead. In the circumstances Corey figured that if he pled not guilty, he would be convicted, executed, and his property confiscated. But if he refused to plead, he could not be convicted. His death came when, in accordance with English custom, he was pressed (by placing stones upon his chest) until he was willing to plead. But Corey was determined not to plead. His final words were "more weight"; [5] then his chest caved in.

The prosecutions were postponed at the end of 1692, and later stopped as the General Court, seeing that hundreds now

5. Quoted in Marion L. Starkey, *The Devil in Massachusetts* (Garden City, N.Y.: Doubleday, 1961), p. 205.

stood accused in Salem and neighboring towns, reasoned that something was amiss, and that innocent people were being victimized outrageously. Salem itself had become the epitome of the perversion of Christian community, where half-forgotten grievances were resurrected to settle old scores. The Reverend Mr. Parris, a stranger to charity and love, secured his tenure in the congregation by venting his hostility; but the well of community spirit remained poisoned for years thereafter.

Massachusetts Bay recovered slowly. The majority of towns had not been touched by witchcraft accusations, but concern for the preservation of the old Puritan values and anxiety about the devil and sinful conduct were general. The turmoil connected to the Dominion of New England had been profoundly unsettling, especially because it had revealed a major divergence in the aims of the Bay Colony's leaders. Some, it seemed, were ready to jettison the heritage of pious, frugal independence in favor of imperial political and commercial integration. England, after all, was no longer the realm of James I or William Laud. Parliament controlled the monarchy, and dissenters were now officially tolerated. Massachusetts Bay natives, who had never known religious persecution but who had suffered the economic hardships of King Philip's War firsthand, were eager for the prosperity that British commercial development promised.

The feelings of many were ambivalent. In Boston a competitive, ostentatious "codfish aristocracy" was emerging which delighted in the latest English fashions. Perhaps the most visible symbol of the mixture of attitudes was the new pretentiousness of meetinghouse architecture. The ambition to match London was evident in soaring spires, richly carved interiors, and the brilliance of cut-glass and brass chandeliers. Pulpits rose to new heights, complete with paneled sounding boards. The men who stood in the pulpits and preached to the prospering merchants, tradesmen, and their families were themselves equivocal in their aspirations. They yearned to recapture the holiness of the early settlers and preached nostalgically of the golden age of the great migration. Scolding their congregations for backsliding, they coaxed them to return to the simplicity and humility of their grandparents. Yet at the same time the clergy longed to cut figures of distinction in this world.

Cotton Mather, son of Increase Mather, was born in Boston in 1662, the year that the halfway covenant was approved and he illustrates the conflicting impulses that were generally at work. As the son and grandson of notable divines, and as his father's assistant, he was eager to restore and revitalize the religiosity of the founders. Indeed, filial piety was an ever-present theme in Mather's sermons. Of the hundreds of titles he published in a forty-year career, Mather's history of the Puritan churches in America, *Magnalia Christi Americana,* was his greatest work. It stood as a monument to the founders of Massachusetts and as both an exemplar and a reproach to their heirs.

Yet Cotton Mather did not himself live the life of his grandfathers, Richard Mather and John Cotton. He was terribly aware of his provincial situation within the British empire, and labored tirelessly to distinguish himself on the larger stage. His mania for writing was not introspective; he wished to exhibit his brilliance and erudition to the world. He did not confine himself to theology because as a dissenter he could never gain the plaudits of the English establishment; he turned also to natural science. Ultimately his efforts in astronomy, botany, and physics were rewarded with an international correspondence among natural philosophers and with election to the Royal Society in 1713. Considering the resources of turn-of-the-century Boston, a town of 12,000 people, Mather's achievements were truly extraordinary. But what is most significant is the way Mather combined the desire to maintain the old Puritanism with the thirst for cosmopolitan experience and fame. Other clergymen, Harvard professors, merchants, and magistrates shared these same ambitions, if not always with the same intensity.

In time, however, as the eighteenth century progressed, the intense devotion to the Puritan past waned among ordinary farmers as well as wealthier, more cosmopolitan people. In the port towns, Boston, Salem, Newbury, and a handful of others, commercial prosperity encouraged more and more involvement with the Atlantic trading world. Sailors speaking foreign tongues and worshipping alien gods became part of the land-scape, and in Boston prostitution became a fact of life. In the country towns no such exotic influences were visible, but secu-larism was rife among farmers, whether they were frontiersmen clearing their land or yeomen who marketed their surplus crops, gradually improving their living standard with imported luxu-ries.

In Boston, religious tolerance, forced upon Massachusetts Bay by the new charter of 1692, gained general acceptance. By the 1720s Cotton Mather was proud to announce that he personally had admitted Baptists and Lutherans to communion in addition to Anglicans and Presbyterians. This broad-minded cordiality would have been unheard of when Mather was first ordained in the 1680s. In most Massachusetts congregations such tolerance remained alien. Cosmopolitanism, secular and religious, did not penetrate far into the province socially or geographically. Insu-larity and communal intolerance were widespread in towns that, by the 1720s and 1730s, were genealogically extended cousin-ages. Old ways, in social and religious life, were the best ways, and the forms of old Puritanism, if not always the substance, survived notwithstanding cupidity and profane ambitions.

But in the 1730s a reaction set in against empty piety and covetous secularism. By this time church membership had so diminished that in most congregations only a minority of towns-people, including just a handful of men, were members. The halfway covenant had slowed the decline in the late seventeenth century, but now even it was too stringent to attract most peo-ple. Sexual morality, one indicator of piety in practice, had become so relaxed that the parents of children born within seven months of marriage were frequently treated as if they had not engaged in fornication, even though its fruits were publicly ac-knowledged. Since one-third to one-half of all first children being born in the 1730s were conceived out of wedlock, it is ap-parent that among betrothed couples chastity was a dying virtue. Communal values were following individual behavior, not pre-scribing it.

A reaction in favor of total submission to the will of God began in the town of Northampton, a major farming and trading community in the northern part of the Connecticut River valley. For over sixty years the Northampton congregation had been the home of the Reverend Solomon Stoddard, a vigorous evangelist who had been instrumental in promoting the halfway covenant. In 1729 his successor in the Northampton pulpit was his grandson Jonathan Edwards, a native of Connecticut who had been graduated from Yale in 1720. Edwards was a brilliant scholar who would become the most original intellectual in eighteenth-century New England. At the beginning of the 1730s Edwards, like many other clergymen, was preaching against depending on merely pious behavior for salvation. Instead, as of old, he called on people to rely on God's power to bring forth a redeeming experience, for conversion and salvation. Then, at the end of 1734 and in the early months of the new year, Northampton was mysteriously transformed by a remarkable spiritual awakening. Suddenly scores of people were converted. By springtime the church boasted over three hundred new members, and the whole community became thoroughly absorbed in religion. Never before, Edwards reported, was the town "so full of Love, nor of Joy, and yet so full of distress." [6]

Originally the revival was a purely local affair. But while Edwards's gifts were unique, his message was not, and the spiritual needs of his congregation were very much like those of people elsewhere in Massachusetts. In a few years, partly as a result of Edwards's writing about the Northampton revival, it began to sweep over the entire province. By 1740, when the English evangelist George Whitefield visited Massachusetts, a general revival was at hand. Whitefield preached for a month at Boston, converting hundreds of people, sailors, slaves, and apprentices as well as merchants and manufacturers. He went on, to cross the colony, preaching at Concord, Sudbury, Marlborough, Leicester, and Edwards's own Northampton before heading south to Connecticut and New York.

Whitefield's tour more than Edwards's effort set off a wave of revivalism in Massachusetts and Connecticut. Loose women,

6. Merrill Jensen, ed., *English Historical Documents,* 12 vols. (American Colonial Documents to 1776; New York: Oxford University Press, 1962), 9:538.

impudent boys, and hardened sinners suddenly felt themselves filled by the workings of the Lord's spirit. The message of God's unique power to redeem sinners spoke directly to people who were guilty about the ways in which they had abandoned the soul piety of the early Puritans. The preaching techniques that emerged in the revival, flamboyantly exploited by George Whitefield, moved people emotionally as conventional preaching had never done before. Revival sermons were dominated by bold metaphors and similes drawn from common experience instead of logic and appeals to reason, and they awakened heartfelt identification among audiences. Whitefield himself pulled out all the stops in a lush, sentimental approach—pointing the finger of accusation, throwing his hands up to heaven, shouting, weeping, crying aloud. Often his listeners responded in kind, writhing in torment, crying in exaltation. At their most extreme, revival preachers were chiefly concerned with immediate effects, and they tried to capture souls with emotion in place of reason.

This assault on the time-honored plain style of Puritan preaching aroused defensive reactions from clergymen who neither knew nor wanted any other way, as well as laymen who had long been pious without such "artificial" stimulation. When Whitefield began to draw distinctions among clergymen, pointing out those associated with him as being especially close to God, he encouraged a divisive censoriousness. One minister was more Christian than another, one church more regenerate, one congregation saved and another damned. This Great Awakening, inaugurated in Massachusetts by Edwards and dramatically extended by Whitefield, would not unite townspeople in the Christian harmony of early Dedham. In the end it divided the people into two camps, those who saw the new light, and those who, unmoved, continued to worship under the guidance of the old light.

The Great Awakening recalled seventeenth-century Puritan experience in the intensity of religious involvement and in the way it turned people away from material concerns. Yet in its focus on individual emotional spirituality, it approached the Puritanism of Anne Hutchinson more nearly than John Winthrop and orthodox Puritans. For it set great store on individual judgment, rather than on the reasoned wisdom of expert, ordained clergy. Consequently, it provided the impulse—and the rationale—for numerous church divisions as "new lights" struggled with "old lights" for control of parishes. By the mid-1740s the Great Awakening left Massachusetts society more divided than ever before. Corporatism lost much of its meaning for towns where congregations had divided, and two different strains of the Puritan faith were now competing with each other. Originally town and congregation had been overlapping communities—now as a result of dispersed settlement and religious differences, they were distinct. Both lost a crucial dimension.

Though people were reluctant to accept it, Massachusetts had become pluralistic. The ideal of uniformity remained alive, but actually economic development had laid the foundation for a complex social order, and religious controversy had shattered the illusion of one orthodoxy. Piety remained a powerful force, and the zeal for harmony through uniformity lived on in country towns; however, they had to compete with other values in a province that was economically integrated into the world of imperial commerce.

By the middle decades of the eighteenth century that imperial world of affairs impinged more and more on Massachusetts. Indeed, in the 1740s its people participated actively in an imperial war that did not directly affect their borders or their safety. England and France, enmeshed in a series of dynastic rivalries, went to war in 1740 for reasons that had nothing to do with Massachusetts. In America the conflict generated frontier hostilities and was called King George's War. Still, Massachusetts could have followed the war at a distance, in dispatches from London. It could have limited its participation to trading with the active parties to the dispute, as indeed it did for several years. Yet in 1745, supporting the leadership of the Royal Governor William Shirley, Massachusetts enthusiastically mounted a 4,000-man attack on the French stronghold of Louisburg on Cape Breton Island guarding the Gulf of St. Lawrence. An armada of nearly 100 ships, mostly merchant and fishing vessels, carried the militiamen to their destination. Here, after a 50-day cannonade that dropped 9,000 cannonballs on the fort, the French surrendered the gateway to Canada. Although its soldiers were not rewarded with much booty, Massachusetts Bay had won a great victory for the British empire.

The victory at Louisburg was the fruit of a new spirit in the province, British patriotism. Fifty years before, even twenty-five, the General Court would not have committed its constituents to overseas warfare, and if the idea had been presented by the royal government, it would have encountered vigorous opposition from Massachusetts farmers as well as their leaders. But during the years when the province was declining as an insular Puritan stronghold, identification with Britain had grown. There had been new immigrants from the old country, there had been the official encouragement of the royal governor and his entourage and, together with the rising standard of living, there had been a broad importation of British culture. English secular books and newspapers had become the common fare among influential people. Most important, the Hanoverian monarchy ruling in conjunction with Parliament had become the fortress of Protestant power and the emblem of constitutional liberty in the world. From a Puritan standpoint the Glorious Revolution had substantially redeemed the mother country; it had not become the home of papist tyranny. So the descendants of Bradford and Winthrop chose to view its recent history as compatible with their own forefathers' hope for England.

The peace treaty that temporarily ended the war in 1748 dealt a significant, disillusioning blow to Massachusetts's nascent British patriotism. The crown decided that Louisburg could be returned to the French, effectively repudiating the great Massachusetts victory. Parliament passed an act reimbursing the province for most (not all) of its expenses, but pounds sterling were small recompense for patriotism scorned. The colonists could not return to the mentality of the founders, where the secular pride of nationality had no place. Massachusetts needed patriotism to create the sense of unity that people craved in a diverse and competitive society. The willingness to sacrifice for the common good was still esteemed as a civic virtue—among

old lights and new lights, Anglicans and Baptists, among frontiersmen and Atlantic merchants.

In the century that had passed, Massachusetts had changed so
dramatically that Bradford and Winthrop would have been
aliens in the prosperous British province that their struggling
settlements had become. They would have mourned the distance
that had widened between church and state, the diversity, the
self-interested competition, the enthusiasm for things of this
world that gripped their progeny. That the first magistrate, the
governor, was now an Anglican chosen in the king's court
would have grieved them deeply. Massachusetts was no longer
theirs. But in the concern for the common good, in the
seriousness with which laymen viewed questions of religion and
morality, and in the sense of separateness that still ruled Massachusetts, the world of Bradford and Winthrop endured.

4

Revolutionary Vanguard

N 1750 the future direction of Massachusetts and its people was uncertain. The dissenting spirit of spartan moralism and earnest self-improvement flourished together with a righteous Yankee independence. Town meetings, a distinctive New England institution, symbolized the emergence of indigenous culture. At the same time the influences of eighteenth-century British society proliferated. Royal government brought contemporary English ways to the capital at Boston and into the county seats, the "shire towns" from Falmouth in Maine to Barnstable on the Cape and Springfield in the Connecticut Valley. Commerce, a far more pervasive force day-to-day, brought London tastes in fabric and pottery and, more important, in polite letters and social customs to every village in the Bay colony. At mid-century, Yankee culture and British culture—the one ascetic and oriented toward fulfilling the aspirations of common farmers and tradesmen, the other, frankly elitist and cosmopolitan, aimed at refinement, excellence, and order—were rivals for the future dominion of Massachusetts.

In the 1760s British policy brought these two hitherto indistinct, parallel, and overlapping streams of social development into direct conflict. Enforcement of the new commercial legislation following the French and Indian War, culminating in the Stamp and Tea acts, polarized not only Massachusetts politics but social visions as well. Promoting obedience to British government came to signify an attachment to the orderly, hierarchical world of patronage and privilege. To counsel resistance became emblematic of the Yankee heritage of Puritan ancestry, political autonomy, and the lean, thrifty ways of life practiced by independent freeholders, Consequently the Revolution, which was fundamentally a political conflict, carried broad social implications that would become explicit in the republicanism it spawned. By the 1780s the people of Massachusetts had become self-conscious republicans who, building on their new state constitution, were eager to establish a republic of virtue as a successor to the Puritans' city on a hill.

The very earliest stirrings of the revolutionary impulse can be traced far back into the eighteenth century and even back to the overthrow of Governor Andros. Certainly the idea of provincial autonomy based on a constitutionlike charter was a Puritan legacy. Yet in the sense of a continuously connected set of events, the first sparks of revolutionary opposition to British government began in the early 1760s. In the following decade the royal governor Thomas Hutchinson and the future president of the United States John Adams, two very different but *very Massachusetts* people, both traced their "genealogies" of the Revolution back to the events of the first year or so of Governor Francis Bernard's administration. Hutchinson and Adams, sharing an inflated, provincial sense of the importance of what happened in Massachusetts, began their stories of the American Revolution with the same individual, James Otis. But the differences in the way they viewed people and events, even each other, reveals the conflicting visions of what Massachusetts was and what it should be, that gave the Revolution there its unique character.

Thomas Hutchinson, born in Boston in 1711, was distantly related to Anne Hutchinson, but his own heritage was one of mercantile materialism rather than religious intensity. His father, also named Thomas and also a native Boston Congregationalist, was the scion of a line of merchants and tradesmen stretching back to sixteenth-century London. His mother, Sarah Foster, came from a similar Boston background. Thomas himself aspired to succeed in the manner of his ancestors, as a merchant. At Harvard in the 1720s, while other students kept spiritual accounts in nervously written diaries, Hutchinson "kept a little paper journal and ledger, and entered in it every dinner, supper, breakfast, and every article of expense, even of a shilling, which practice," he later recalled, "soon became pleasant." [1] Where his classmates spent their undergraduate leisure dreaming of excellence in poetry and rhetoric, Hutchinson concentrated on investments. While at Harvard, by "adventuring at sea," he multiplied many times the small capital (several hundred pounds of fish) his father had given him for the purpose.[2] When he married, advantageously, several years after graduation, he had already become a successful Boston merchant.

Shrewd, prudent, rational, and wellborn, Hutchinson built a public career on the same advantages and talents that established his commercial prosperity. At the age of twenty-six, the young merchant was elected, by the Boston town meeting, to its two highest offices, selectman and representative to the General Court. To begin a political career at such an elevated level was extraordinary. It marked Hutchinson's outstanding reputation among Bostonians and his distinguished lineage as grandson of a Governor's Councillor and son of a current Councillor who had been holding office for nearly twenty years. For most provincial officeholders election as selectman or representative represented the pinnacle of their careers, attained only after a generation's service in lesser offices. But Thomas Hutchinson was someone special.

In the General Court he quickly became an active member of the inner circle of legislative committeemen who led the delegates. A decade later, after almost continuous re-election to the court, he became its speaker. By then Hutchinson had become a leading spokesman for the hard-money Boston merchants, but at the same time his base of support was narrowing, and in 1749

1. Thomas Hutchinson, *Diary and Letters,* 1:46. Quoted in Bernard Bailyn, *The Ordeal of Thomas Hutchinson* (Cambridge, Mass.: Harvard University Press, 1974), p. 21.
2. Hutchinson to Francis Bernard, March 25, 1770, Massachusetts Archives, 26:471. Quoted in Bailyn, *Ordeal,* p. 12.

the Boston town meeting turned him out of the General Court. Following the family tradition, however, he was chosen to serve in the Council, where he remained for the next seventeen years. In 1752 Governor Shirley appointed Hutchinson a judge of probate and of common pleas in Suffolk County (which included Boston and 18 other towns). Within the Massachusetts elite, he had become a key figure who could always be relied upon for carefully calculated, reasonable advice on delicate provincial or imperial questions, whether details of patronage or large issues of transatlantic significance. As Massachusetts's delegate to the Albany Congress in 1754, convened to promote intercolonial military co-operation, Hutchinson, with the Pennsylvania delegate Benjamin Franklin (a Boston native five years his senior), became a major proponent of intercolonial union. Provincial in his background, Hutchinson had been led by his political and mercantile experience to embrace a British imperial vision of the colonies. No one was better qualified by training, prior service, or political acumen than Hutchinson when he was appointed lieutenant-governor in 1760.

Hutchinson was an ambitious, self-serving man. He cultivated opportunities for political preferment and financial gain. Yet he was not consumed by ambition or avarice; he was content with his achievements. His personal pleasures were refined and retiring. In Boston he dwelled in a mansion inherited from his maternal grandfather and redecorated in the "modern" taste. At Milton, several miles southeast of Boston, in 1743 he constructed an unpretentious country residence for weekends and summers with his family. He had no desire to overawe his neighbors in Milton or in Massachusetts at large. Indeed his highest ambition was to become the foremost, the exemplary Massachusetts subject. With a zeal surpassing even Cotton Mather's, an awesome figure during his Boston youth, Hutchinson made himself the archivist and historian of his native colony. For decades he collected documents and privately labored over them, drafting a systematic political narrative of Massachusetts that was a model of factually correct, balanced, eighteenth-century scholarship. In it he made Massachusetts's rough edges smooth, vindicating it, and himself, for posterity.

He pictured his own role as that of steward, the champion and conservator of the Massachusetts traditions with which he identified.

Coming to the politics of the 1760s from this position of moral certainty, it is hardly surprising that he viewed his opponents' motives as wrong-headed at best and vicious at worst. Personally acquainted with all of the major figures in provincial politics and fully cognizant of their families' reputations, Hutchinson, naturally, and characteristically for his age, understood events in highly personal terms. The opposition of Samuel Adams, he believed, was rooted in Adams's father's reversals in the land-bank conflicts of 1739–1742 when Hutchinson had emerged on the winning, anti-land-bank side. John Adams's attachment to the antiadministration cause he attributed to Adams's frustrated ambition to become a great man instantly. Indeed, looking back on the origins of the Revolution from his vantage point as an exile in England, Hutchinson was inclined to focus on the implacable enmity of the Otis family. James Otis, angry over Hutchinson's appointment to the judgeship that Otis's father coveted, had declared war on Hutchinson, and so the Revolution had begun. "From so small a spark," Hutchinson concluded, "a great fire seems to have been kindled." [3]

When Hutchinson interpreted John Adams's conduct in terms of towering ambition, he grasped an essential truth about Adams's personality. Born to a family of yeoman farmers who had worked the stony fields of Braintree for a century, John Adams developed the most intense, romantic ambitions for greatness. His father, a respectable farmer, shoemaker, and deacon of the First Church, was himself ambitious and compelled John to prepare for Harvard. Thereafter his son's aspirations needed no further encouragement. All his life Adams thirsted for fame based on the intellectual and moral excellence he ceaselessly sought to cultivate. Adams, an outsider to Boston in the 1760s, relatively poor, yet eager to establish a reputation among Massachusetts lawyers and men of affairs, envied Hutchinson keenly. This was one reason why, in his first year in

3. Hutchinson, *History of the Colony,* 3:64.

Boston, Adams fixed on Hutchinson as villain and identified with James Otis as hero in the drama he saw unfolding.

Over fifty years later John Adams would vividly sketch the scene in the Council chamber of the Town House (Old State House, today) where the Writs of Assistance case, testing officials' powers of entry and search, was tried in February 1761. Here "round a great fire, were seated five Judges, with Lieutenant-Governor Hutchinson at their head, as Chief Justice, all arrayed in their new, fresh, rich robes of scarlet English broadcloth; in their large cambric bands, and immense judicial wigs." All the barristers of Boston and of neighboring Middlesex County were seated as spectators at a long table in their "gowns, bands, and tie wigs." On the walls hung "two portraits, at more than full length, of King Charles the Second and of King James the Second, in splendid gold frames . . . these were as fine pictures as I ever saw; the colors of the royalermines and long flowing robes were the most glowing, the figures the most noble and graceful, the features the most distinct and characteristic." As the case proceeded, "Otis was a flame of fire!" With "a profusion of legal authorities" and "a torrent of impetuous eloquence, . . . [he] hurried away every thing before him. . . . Then and there the child Independence was born." [4] Both Adams, seated at the long table with the other barristers, and Hutchinson, sitting impassively in a great chair by the fire, later saw the emergence of the Revolution in this modest room, removed from the people of Massachusetts and distant from the seat of empire.

That participants personalized these events and possessed such a heightened sense of their importance illustrates the character of provincial politics in the 1760s. For at the time Massachusetts possessed a compact political community, including crown officials, the judiciary, the members of the General Court, and a handful of others dwelling in and around Boston. The chief actors in the Revolutionary crisis were already prominent—the Adamses, Bowdoin, Hancóck, Hutchinson, the Ol-

---

4. John Adams to William Tudor, Quincy, March 29, 1817, *Works of John Adams,* edited by Charles Francis Adams, 10 vols. (Boston: Little, Brown, 1856), 10:245, 247.

ivers, the Otises, the Quincys, the Sewalls, the Warrens. In the next decade scarcely a stranger would intrude as Boston and the General Court became arenas for repeated imperial confrontations. Here events large with significance for Massachusetts and all the colonies possessed a local, personal character for eyewitnesses. But forces much greater than one person's pride or another's thirst for power were operating. Gradually the protagonists came to take on symbolic importance as representatives of constituencies in England and in Massachusetts that diverged more and more. They became heroes to their friends—King George III would hold a reception in Hutchinson's honor, and John Hancock would commission a portrait of Samuel Adams to adorn his drawing-room—and villains in the eyes of their enemies—Hutchinson the traitorous serpent, and Adams so vicious that if one "wished to draw a picture of the Devil, . . . he would get *Sam Adams* to sit for him." [5] Between 1765 and 1775 the people of Massachusetts mobilized around these leading figures and the outlooks and ideologies they personified.

From the time popular revolutionary activity began in opposition to the Stamp Act in 1765 until the battles at Lexington and Concord a decade later, the conflict in Massachusetts, as elsewhere, centered explicitly on the question of taxation and representation. The Stamp Act, designed to raise a revenue to help support imperial administration, set taxes on legal and commercial documents, newspapers, and playing cards. It was a form of excise long used in England and later employed by the United States government. The taxes were a nuisance from the colonial standpoint, but though they did threaten to drain off some hard money, they did not possess major economic importance. Their actual economic impact would probably have been exceeded by the commercial regulations successfully imposed the previous year by the Revenue Act (also called the Sugar Act). But the Revenue Act only affected merchants immediately, and though the Boston town meeting protested it on constitutional grounds, Massachusetts, like the other colonies, accepted it within the es-

5. Peter Oliver, *Origin and Progress of the American Rebellion,* edited by Douglas Adair and John A. Schutz (Stanford, Calif.: Stanford University Press, 1961), p. 39.

tablished framework of imperial regulation of commerce. People outside of Boston and the port towns paid little attention to it. In contrast, the Stamp Act, which touched the general population directly and concerned not only merchants, but also newspaper readers, printers, and attorneys on a daily basis, crystallized opinion broadly. The issue of taxation became the focus for a powerful assertion of political autonomy founded on eighteenth-century Yankee culture.

In Boston, as in other colonial ports where the stamps would be landed and the act first implemented, there were peaceful as well as violent demonstrations in July and August that forced officials who were commissioned to administer the law to resign. Here self-proclaimed "Bodies of the People" declared opposition to taxes and, indeed, to any law made without the consent of the people or their delegates. Outside Boston for the first time there were widespread assertions of political rights. The specter of direct taxation by outsiders was so fearsome that selectmen and other local leaders brought the issue directly to the attention of their neighbors in town meetings.

Here, in gatherings where for over a century nearly all men had been eligible to vote on town policy as well as election of officials, the culture represented by the Adamses spoke its mind. In Braintree, it was John Adams, still an obscure young provincial lawyer, who drafted the town's sentiments in the form of instructions to their representative. The substance of the statement as well as its form bespoke the intensity of the popular commitment to individual liberty within the context of corporate self-government.

The Braintree Instructions concentrated on the three major evils of the Stamp Act which together made it so alarming. In the first place, the townspeople asserted, it "would dreign the Country of Cash, strip multitudes of the poorer people of all their property and Reduce them to absolute beggary." Even if the law had been constitutional, which Braintree denied, it would destroy the economic subsistence which Yankees believed was crucial for personal independence and political liberty. The act was unconstitutional because it contradicted the principles of Magna Carta, "that no Freeman should be subjected to any Tax to which he has not given his own consent in person or by proxy.'' Even worse, the enforcement of the law was under the jurisdiction of vice-admiralty courts where ''no Juries have any concern,'' and ''one Judge presides alone.'' Stripped of their property without their consent, denied the right of trial by jury, the Braintree town meeting warned that people would soon become ''the most sordid and forlorn of Slaves.'' [6]

To John Adams's surprise, the declaration of principles he prepared for his neighbors in Braintree spoke also for Massachusetts townspeople generally. Within a few months forty towns adopted these instructions as their own manifestoes. Adams himself discovered that ''the People, even to the lowest Ranks, have become more attentive to their Liberties, more inquisitive about them, and more determined to defend them, than they were ever before.'' [7] This spirit, manifested in varying degrees among the colonies, was ultimately influential in bringing Parliament to repeal the Stamp Act in 1766.

When word of the repeal arrived in Boston, there were bonfires and celebrations. In the West Church the pastor, Jonathan Mayhew, took as his text ''the snare is broken, and we are escaped,'' a sermon thanking God for delivering Massachusetts ''from a slavish, inglorious bondage.'' [8] The Sons of Liberty, a loose association of defenders of the province, mounted a major parade and procession, culminating in a vast open-air feast to commemorate their demonstration that had led to the Stamp Master's ouster the previous year. Many believed that the imperial threat to their way of life had been ended.

Yet what had actually occurred was not so simple or clearcut. Parliament had accompanied repeal with a Declaratory Act asserting its total competence to legislate, ''in all cases whatsoever,'' so the threat of imperial control remained alive.[9] More-

6. Samuel A. Bates, ed., *Records of the Town of Braintree, 1640 to 1793* (Randolph, Mass., 1886), pp. 404–406.

7. John Adams, *Diary and Autobiography of John Adams,* L. H. Butterfield, Leonard C. Faber, Wendell D. Garrett, eds., 4 vols. (Cambridge, Mass.: Harvard University Press, 1962), 1:263.

8. J. Mayhew, *The Snare Broken* (Boston, 1766), pp. 1–2.

9. Jensen, American Colonial Documents, p. 696.

over the resistance of 1765 had begun to shake the foundations of Massachusetts society.

No one was more aware of this than Lieutenant-Governor Hutchinson who, in spite of his record and reputation for public service, had become the local target of enmity. In August his ancestral mansion in Boston had been all but destroyed by a nighttime mob from which he himself had only barely escaped. The furnishings, the silver, the contents of the wine-cellar, were destroyed or stolen, and the building was left open to the sky, in ruin. Hutchinson, the native son who advocated submission to Parliament while himself enjoying the privileges and emoluments of imperial favor, had become the symbol of the political and cultural forces that Massachusetts Yankees found most alarming. His gorgeous mansion, his luxurious furnishings, his multiple office-holding (three judgeships, a Council seat, and his lieutenant-governor's position) and Oliver family connections, his intimacy with Anglicans and English functionaries, combined to make Hutchinson appear a turncoat who would make Massachusetts over in the corrupt English style. Viewing his behavior, suspicious outsiders to Hutchinson's exclusive circle could not take his professions of concern for Massachusetts seriously; they were a subterfuge for self-aggrandizement.

The attack on Hutchinson's house expressed these hostilities, but it was also unsettling to Bostonians in general. Hutchinson himself feared that Boston had become prey to a leveling mobocracy, and local property holders, whether friendly to the lieutenant-governor or not were worried by the implications of the attack for the security of property. Except for crown officials, no one was eager to publicly identify and prosecute the men and boys who had participated in the affair, but Bostonians did not want the scene repeated. Even Jonathan Mayhew, who had preached on the right of revolution as long ago as 1750 and who was the most outspoken clerical opponent of British policy, drew back from the vision of chaos he had glimpsed in Boston. In the same sermon in which he celebrated Repeal, Mayhew reminded his listeners of how close they had come "to anarchy" when "some profligate people . . . took an opportunity to gratify their private resentments [by] . . . committing abominable outrages and excesses on the persons or property of others.'' Resistance to Britain had exposed the long-standing tension in Massachusetts between liberty and license, a tension that John Winthrop had elaborated in a speech in the 1640s, and which Mayhew now recalled in a quotation from the Apostle Paul: ''Brethren, ye have been called unto LIBERTY; only use not LIBERTY for an occasion to the flesh, but by love serve one another.'' [10] Liberty meant the right to do that which was just, good, and lawful in the eyes of the community, not the untrammeled expression of personal will. The perennial problem for revolutionary Massachusetts was to assert and maintain liberty without degenerating into licentiousness. It was the old question of reconciling individual and corporate rights in a new form.

From this time onward, resistance to British measures was more self-controlled than it had been in 1765. No more houses were destroyed, in Boston or in any other towns. But a year later, when news arrived of the passage of Prime Minister Charles Townshend's Revenue Act of 1767, laying duties on a variety of imports, Bostonians again took the lead in organizing opposition. Drawing a lesson from the Stamp Act resistance, merchants began by joining in a nonimportation movement that embraced all the major colonial ports from Portsmouth, New Hampshire, to Savannah, Georgia. Peaceful economic pressure, they hoped, would lead English shippers to join the colonists in pressing for repeal as they had two years earlier. The newspapers of Massachusetts blazed with the rhetoric of approaching slavery, corruption, and tyranny, but people in Boston and in country towns remained quiet. In the Connecticut River valley, where even the Stamp Act had not aroused much notice, the established leaders who were tied to Lieutenant-Governor Hutchinson by bonds of friendship and patronage remained serene. Conversing with them at court sessions, and reading their letters, Hutchinson was reassured that Massachusetts was returning to normal and that the frightening events of 1765 had been an aberration fomented by Samuel Adams and the handful of malcontents surrounding him.

10. Mayhew, *Snare Broken*, p. 20, title page.

To one who had gradually become distant from the day-to-day existence of ordinary farmers and tradesmen, to one who had not attended town meetings around the province, such a view was as persuasive as it was wishful. Certainly the idea that Massachusetts people were on the verge of denouncing British government and society and of asserting their own independence was unthinkable. In reality, however, it was people like Samuel Adams and his cousin John who had an accurate understanding of public opinion. Yankees had no taste for a closer relationship with England and were apprehensive about imperial innovations. When word arrived in 1768 that royal troops would be stationed in Boston, ostensibly to defend the city against French invasion but actually to strengthen British administration, especially customs enforcement, Massachusetts recoiled. Still, there was no violent opposition to the landing of the troops.

The governor, Francis Bernard, blocked efforts to bring the General Court back into session since he was reluctant to give his opponents a forum for recriminations. To his surprise, the Boston town meeting issued a call for a convention of towns as a surrogate for a legislative session, and about one hundred towns sent delegates. This Convention of Towns, whose members came chiefly from eastern and central Massachusetts and southern Maine, was ridiculed as ineffectual by Bernard and Hutchinson. Certainly it did not head off the peaceful landing of the troops. But had crown officials been more perceptive, they would have been alarmed by the fact that so many towns, where the majority of the population lived, chose to join Boston in an extra-legal body to protest administration measures. Selectmen and other townspeople believed that they had the right to meet, speak their minds, and join with other towns, freely—whether the governor liked it or not. The belief in political autonomy was widespread in Massachusetts, and deference to the prestige, pomp, and dignity of royal government was waning.

Still, for nearly a year and a half after the landing of troops, Massachusetts was peaceful. By 1770, when all of the Townshend duties were repealed (except for the duty on tea), the nonimportation movement in Massachusetts and other colonies was flagging. Ironically, it was at this moment that the British blunder of stationing troops in Boston brought on the bloody fray known as the Boston Massacre. After months of abrasion between Bostonians and the troops, where name-calling and fist fights had been common, there was finally an explosion. On the night of March 5, 1770, groups of soldiers seeking to settle a score over a previous fight, broke the curfew that required them to be in their barracks after eight P.M., and instead went out in the streets with clubs looking for victims. Townspeople quickly turned out, and a vast crowd collected, which ultimately concentrated on the lone redcoat guarding the Custom House. When a handful of soldiers was sent to assist him, they were pelted. In self-defense they leveled their muskets to threaten the crowd. Then they fired pointblank, killing five civilians. Now Boston was on the threshold of warfare. Troops and more civilians poured out. Fearing the worst, Lieutenant-Governor Hutchinson hurried from his home to address the crowd. Stepping out onto the balcony of the Town House, from the chamber where, nearly a decade earlier, he had listened with John Adams to James Otis's flamboyant rhetoric, Hutchinson appealed for order under the law. Murder would not go unpunished; he would order an inquiry immediately and, he promised, "The law shall have its course!" [11]

Although some Bostonians jeered Hutchinson's words, many more decided to heed his entreaty and return to their homes. The Boston selectmen were circulating in the crowd giving the same message—go home. For the moment at least, most people seemed chastened by the gunfire and carnage. But the following morning, after people had reflected on what they now called a "massacre," Bostonians resolved that the troops must leave the town. A hastily arranged town meeting sent the selectmen to Hutchinson and the Governor's Council to urge their removal, and a committee led by Samuel Adams reported to Hutchinson that only the departure of the soldiers would pacify Boston. The lieutenant-governor, who believed that yielding to public pressure would be disastrous, refused to give such an order, arguing that he lacked authority over the troops. By the afternoon, however, after the councillors unanimously advised him to comply

---

11. Quoted in Bailyn, *Ordeal of Thomas Hutchinson*, p. 158.

with the popular demand, Hutchinson yielded and requested (not ordered) the commanding officer to move the troops to Castle William in the harbor. Within the week they were gone, and if Boston was not quiet, at least the danger of a general battle had been forestalled.

Now the clamor was to prosecute the eight soldiers who had committed the "murders." Few attorneys wished to defend them, and for their own safety the soldiers wanted lawyers who were popular in Boston as defenders of colonial rights, so they appealed to John Adams and Josiah Quincy, Jr., to take their cases. The two agreed, after consulting with Samuel Adams, who was eager for the trials to demonstrate that mobbish anarchy did not prevail in Boston as Tories claimed. Boston, he hoped the trials would prove, was a town where the people were committed to constitutional principles of justice.

In the end perhaps the trials lent support to that view. After weeks of investigation and deposition taking, and following several months of delay at the hands of the newly appointed Governor Hutchinson, the soldiers were tried. The jury, packed in favor of the defendants as far as Hutchinson was able, and presided over by Peter Oliver, a close friend of the governor's and related by marriage, was lenient. Six were acquitted of all charges, and two were convicted of manslaughter for firing prematurely. By using the legal loophole "benefit of clergy," they escaped serious punishment and were sentenced to branding upon the hand. From Hutchinson's perspective the outcome was satisfactory. Boston and Massachusetts seemed pacified, and though the troops had not been entirely exonerated, they had not become scapegoats to popular rage either.

But the massacre was not forgotten. Bostonians opposed to the royal government, Whigs, used it as the occasion for an annual memorial oration, in which they repeatedly warned against the tyrannical tendencies of standing armies in a free state. From the perspective of royal officials and those attuned to the social outlook of contemporary English gentlemen, the episode was merely a popular tumult that furnished additional evidence of the turbulence in Massachusetts society. But to Yankees the massacre represented the logical outcome of needlessly station-

ing a corrupt military among subjects who were loyal to both
the crown and the constitution. Massachusetts did become
calmer than it had been at any time since the Stamp Act, but
while the occasions for direct conflict between colonial and English expectations had diminished, the divergence between them
continued to increase.

On the surface, however, Massachusetts seemed to have returned to the halcyon days of Governor Shirley's rule in the
1750s. Trade prospered, agricultural prices were favorable to
farmers, and popular involvement in provincial affairs declined
to a level which Governor Hutchinson believed proper. Many
hoped that time would heal the political wounds of the past
decade so that, if the clock could not be turned back to Shirley's
time, at least Massachusetts could remain as it was, a prosperous British colony enjoying a close commercial relationship
with the empire together with substantial political autonomy.

But in little more than a year, in late 1772, Massachusetts
politics became heated once more. Now a spiral of conflict developed, which led to independence. It began in the spring of
1772 with what seemed to many a minor issue—the salaries of
the governor and judges. In the past the General Court had
always paid these salaries out of provincial revenues, but now
the administration announced that they would be paid by the
crown. The object was to integrate these offices into the British
civil list and thus eliminate any dependence they might have on
the colonists. If their pocketbooks and taxation were all the people of Massachusetts cared about, the crown's taking over of
these salaries would have been welcome. Indeed, had it been
done a generation or two earlier, it is unlikely that such a move
would have caused any protest. By 1772, however, Massachusetts Whigs had embraced a view of politics that explained
virtually every action of the cabinet and Parliament as part of a
scheme to subvert English and American liberty. They believed
that power-hungry conspirators close to the king wished to pay
Massachusetts officials so they would always do their bidding
and loyally serve the cause of tyranny. People like the Adamses, who believed that officials should be responsible to the constituents they served rather than to their patrons in the royal ad-

ministration, saw the salaries issue as fundamental to the liberty of Massachusetts. If the governor and judges were perpetually bribed against the subjects, what hope could people have? In the Boston town meeting, in the General Court, in the *Boston Gazette*, Samuel and John Adams raised the hue and cry.

On half of the issue, the payment of the governor's salary, they lost. After all, if it was constitutional for the crown to appoint a governor, as provided in the Massachusetts Charter, then surely it was proper for the crown to pay that appointee. True, it had always been customary for the General Court to appropriate the governor's salary, but it had often been done with ill will, and this custom had no constitutional standing in the eyes of most observers. The General Court protested the innovation, but the protest died there. Most people took little notice, nor were they eager to pay for Hutchinson's luxuries out of their own pockets. By the summer of 1772 the clamor died, and Hutchinson pocketed his stipend without incident.

In the autumn, news arrived of the other part of the scheme, to pay the judges as well. Once again Whigs protested. In Boston Samuel Adams, who had for some time been weighing a plan to create committees of correspondence to keep alive Whig views of constitutional liberty, chose this occasion to act. After fruitlessly trying to persuade the governor to assemble the legislature and consider the issue, Adams persuaded the Boston town meeting to adopt his motion and create a committee of correspondence to state the town's views and to solicit the opinions of all the communities in Massachusetts. At the time the governor and his friends believed this was the desperate tactic of a dying opposition faction. They fully expected that the issue of the judges' salaries would be even less controversial than that of the governor. Such questions were not matters of local concern, they believed, so townspeople would go about their business and ignore the antics of Samuel Adams and the Boston town meeting.

Hutchinson was wrong. Viewing the countryside from atop his hill in Milton, he saw in it an image resembling rural England where, had such a question ever been raised, it would have been quietly snuffed out by the local gentry. Yeoman farmers, busy with their fields, their orchards, their herds, would not have blinked. But, as he learned to his distress, Massachusetts was not an English county. Towns with English place names were radically different from their home-country counterparts. The local response to the Braintree Instructions in 1765 and to the Convention of 1768, it turned out, had been merely preludes to the political excitement that now rippled across eastern and central Massachusetts.

The Boston Committee of Correspondence had asked townspeople to consider current affairs and to communicate their sentiments to Boston so that the views of the inhabitants generally would no longer be liable to misrepresentation by the governor. To ease the way, the committee provided each town with a highly partisan expression of Boston's views in pamphlet form. The "Boston Pamphlet," as it became known, contained a statement of the colonists' rights "as men, as Christians, and as Subjects," [12] in addition to a lengthy list of grievances. In the pamphlet the issue of the judges' salaries was emphasized within a larger pattern of repeated violations of the Massachusetts Charter and the British constitution. People were exhorted to inform themselves of their rights, and to assert them vigorously if they meant to remain free men rather than allowing themselves and their posterity to slide into slavery. While Hutchinson's politics, and that of imperial officials generally, was grounded on a calculating pragmatism, Whigs like Samuel Adams turned the issues into a moral drama and called on the people of Massachusetts to defend the virtuous legacy of their forefathers in terms that Yankees, both Old Lights and New Lights, often found irresistible.

By December 1772 the local response to the judges' salaries and the larger drift of British policy began to emerge. Although their specific language and emphasis varied, a consensus of political views was made explicit. People reasoned that their forefathers had spent their blood and treasure on settling in the "howling wilderness of" Massachusetts because they wanted to

12. *The Votes and Proceedings of the Freeholders and Other Inhabitants of the Town of Boston* . . . (Boston, 1773), p. 1.

enjoy "civil and religious" liberty.[13] Their ancestors had not risked their lives in order to diminish their own rights. It was self-evident then that the inhabitants of Massachusetts should of right possess the same liberty as Englishmen. Central to that liberty was the right to hold property without being subjected to arbitrary taxation, and the right to impartial justice. Without the secure possession of these rights everything they had or would ever have would be insecure, and they would effectively become dependents on the will of officials. This meant slavery. Faced by such a threat, townspeople were eager to put themselves on record as defenders of their heritage and stewards for their posterity.

As Governor Hutchinson learned of the favorable response that the Boston Pamphlet was eliciting, he grew alarmed. His assumptions about the broad support the administration possessed and the merely factional character of opposition were cast in doubt. Now he called the General Court into session so as to lead a swift counterattack that would cut through the demagogy and bring the light of informed reason to the well-meaning but oft-deceived majority. In the first days of the new year Hutchinson put the finishing touches on his clear, carefully argued speech. On January 6, 1773, he appeared before nearly 200 councillors and representatives pressed into the same chamber where he had heard the Writs of Assistance case.

Standing not a hundred yards from the site of the Boston Massacre, Hutchinson approached his listeners in his recognized role as the pre-eminent authority on Massachusetts history, lecturing the assembly on the colony's long-standing recognition of Parliamentary supremacy. Until recently, he reported, no one had doubted that Acts of Parliament were binding in the Bay province. But now people were making novel claims that the General Court, a subordinate legislature, possessed exclusive powers to legislate wholly beyond the competence of the supreme Parliament. They were even asserting that English subjects residing in a colony must enjoy all the liberties of English-

13. Town of Gorham (Me.), Proceedings, January 7, 1773. Massachusetts Historical Society, Boston Committee of Correspondence letters received, photostat 274.

men in England. These claims, he said, had no basis in the Massachusetts Charter; they were wholly fallacious. If someone left England, that person voluntarily relinquished the right to representation in Parliament. No one could claim that because he had left, Parliament no longer possessed supremacy in the empire. Migrants could not dictate the authority of Parliament or compromise its powers by the fact of their migration. Starkly exposing the central constitutional issue, Hutchinson carried his argument to a climax that he hoped would shock his listeners to their senses: "I know of no line that can be drawn between the supreme authority of Parliament and the total independence of the colonies." [14] By raising the bogeyman of independence as the only alternative to submission to Parliament, Hutchinson dared the members of the General Court to oppose him at their peril.

The delegates were stunned. Doubtless, many of them had long been aware of the ultimate implications of the constitutional debate, but to have their seasoned governor and colleague, the Thomas Hutchinson who was famous for prudence and circumspection, speak so boldly was breathtaking. Their immediate response was silence, and Hutchinson believed that he had successfully opened people's eyes to the necessity of submission. It was more than two weeks before the Council and the House of Representatives formally answered his address, and by then he was so convinced of his success that their rejoinders only stimulated him to press his points home in further debate. If they meant treason by pressing for independence, he wanted the issues brought out into the open where he was certain loyalty to Britain would triumph.

But Hutchinson had blundered grievously. The members of the General Court, and the people generally, rallied around Whig arguments rooted in the legacy of the Puritan commonwealth, that the General Court did enjoy the exclusive right to tax. If a line must be drawn between submission to Parlia-

---

14. Quoted in Richard D. Brown, *Revolutionary Politics in Massachusetts: The Boston Committee of Correspondence and the Towns* (Cambridge, Mass.: Harvard University Press, 1970), p. 88.

ment and independence, they were not afraid to choose the latter; although they had no wish to draw any such line, nor would they propose one unilaterally, without the consent of "all the other Colonies . . . in Congress." The House of Representatives reproved Hutchinson by grieving that "the ill policy of a late injudicious Administration" had raised the question, and that the governor had "reduced us to the unhappy Alternative, either of appearing by our Silence to acquiesce in your Excellency's Sentiments, or of thus freely discussing the point." [15] Hutchinson, they made clear, must bear the onus for whatever consequences flowed from the challenge he had thrown down. John Adams's reactions crystallized Massachusetts's response to the debate over "the greatest Question ever yet agitated." Like others, Adams was "amazed at the Governor, for forcing on this Controversy." In contrast to Hutchinson's wishful assessments, Adams's own post-mortem on the affair proved accurate: "He will not be thanked for this. His Ruin and Destruction must spring out of it, either from the Ministry and Parliament on one Hand, or from his Countrymen, on the other." [16] Hutchinson's superiors in England saw his polemicizing as self-defeating, the worst possible tactic to regain the tranquility they sought, and his adversaries in Massachusetts were delighted that he was now on record explicitly as an opponent to constitutional liberty. Several months later, when Benjamin Franklin furnished the legislature with a collection of Hutchinson's private letters from the 1760s, they would be published to underscore Hutchinson's view that a colonist could not possess the full measure of "English liberties." [17]

By that time the governor's isolation from the people of the province was almost complete. Scores of towns, a majority, had now responded to the Boston Pamphlet in kind, and even in western Massachusetts Hutchinson's allies in Hampshire and Berkshire counties reported that the countryside was growing

15. *The Speeches of His Excellency Governor Hutchinson, to the General Assembly . . . with the Answers of His Majesty's Council and the House of Representatives Respectively* (Boston, 1773), 57, 58.

16. Adams, *Diary and Autobiography*, 2:77.

17. Quoted in Bailyn, *Ordeal of Thomas Hutchinson*, p. 227.

restless. In June the House of Representatives, stung by the contempt for colonial assertions of right revealed in the letters, had condemned Hutchinson and his brother-in-law, Lieutenant-Governor Andrew Oliver, by the overwhelming vote of 101 to 5, calling upon the king to remove them from office. Hutchinson, repudiated in his attempts at the art of persuasion, at last realized that he no longer possessed a substantial base of support in Massachusetts. Thereafter, believing that any lenity on the part of the administration was self-defeating, he became inflexible. Personally he was deeply hurt, not only because his speech had failed to block the tide of opposition and his private letters had been published, but also because, as John Adams had predicted, the Ministry in London frowned on his judgment. Governor Hutchinson longed for an opportunity to vindicate himself and to bring the force he believed was necessary to bear on his enemies, the opposition in Massachusetts.

Several months later, in the autumn of 1773, controversy over the recently passed Tea Act provided the occasion he had been seeking. For the Tea Act, which was specially designed to relieve the East India Company of its surplus inventory, promised to interrupt if not destroy the existing system of tea trading by giving the company the opportunity to sell its tea directly in the colonies through its own agents (consignees), with duties payable on arrival of the goods in America. If it succeeded, tea smuggling would end, enforcement of the customs revenue would increase, and tea traders who were not fortunate enough to be consignees would be cut out of most of their business. Up and down the seaboard, colonial merchants and their allies in elective offices protested the political and economic consequences of this new Parliamentary statute. In Massachusetts where trade and politics centered in Boston, that was where protests began.

They started in an extralegal, or in the governor's eyes an illegal, way when Boston's North End Caucus called for a public meeting at the Liberty Tree, where the consignees would be called upon to renounce their commissions and so block the implementation of the new law. If public demonstrations could stop the Stamp Act, they could also nullify the Tea Act. But the consignees, two of whom were Hutchinson's own sons and strongly backed by the governor himself, refused. Several days later, after the Boston town meeting had formally adopted resolves opposing the Tea Act and calling for the consignees' resignation, they continued to stand firm. Now the involvement of the colony as a whole broadened as the Boston Committee of Correspondence invited committees from neighboring towns to join in the resistance effort. Later, after the tea ships arrived, the Committee of Correspondence would call a great Meeting of the People where men from the surrounding towns joined Bostonians in resolutions forbidding the consumption of the tea, and again pressing the consignees to resign. But Governor Hutchinson, confident that he was upholding the law and that the navy would support him, held the consignees loyal to the East India Company and their commissions, while refusing to allow the tea ships to leave unless the duties were first paid according to law.

Finally, on December 16, 1773, time ran out. Either the tea would be shipped back or the duty paid. Here the Meeting of the People, under the guidance of Samuel Adams and the Whig leadership of Boston, made one final effort to have the tea sent back, obtaining the consent of all the interested parties except the governor. Hutchinson, reached by express rider at his home in Milton, again refused to bend or break the law and allow the vessels to leave. He would vindicate himself in the eyes of the ministry by his staunch devotion to the enforcement of law; and if the opposition did anything radical or violent, then the need for repression would be evident in London. Whatever the event, Hutchinson believed, the soundness of his own behavior, past and present, would be demonstrated.

But the Tea Party that evening still shocked him. He had expected the Whigs to back down. He was not aware that the North End Caucus and other Whig groups had anticipated his refusal to let the ships pass and had made their plans accordingly. The governor had not the least inkling of the plan to send dozens of men (perhaps as many as sixty), disguised as Mohawks, aboard the ships to dump the tea, 90,000 pounds of it worth £9,000, into the harbor. So he was distraught when he learned the next morning that in two hours the tea, all of it, had been destroyed. Immediately he had private second thoughts about his own conduct, but officially he set out to defend his policy and argue the necessity of strong measures against Boston and Massachusetts.

His adversaries were jubilant. "The Sublimity of it, charms me!" John Adams exclaimed, gloating over the near-surgical precision of the Mohawks. "The Town of Boston was never more Still and calm," he said; "all Things were conducted with great order, Decency, and *perfect Submission to Government.*" The only private property that had been destroyed, other than the tea, was a single brass padlock, and that was carefully replaced. Considering the entire period "since the Controversy, with Britain, opened" in his first year at the Bar, Adams concluded that now "the Dye is cast: The People have passed the River and cutt away the Bridge: . . . This is the grandest Event, which has ever yet happened." [18]

Once again John Adams's political judgment after the event was more acute than Hutchinson's judgment beforehand. For Hutchinson, who believed fundamentally that, if left to themselves, the people of Massachusetts were sound, docile, and capable of following wise leaders as they had in the 1740s and 1750s, could never accept the idea that his enemies, Whig leaders like the Adamses, truly represented the people. He was convinced that they were merely demagogues who held power through deceitful machinations, and so he repeatedly returned to the hope that ultimately their extremist follies would expose them for what they were, once and for all separating them from the yeomanry of the province. Briefly he clung to this hope in the aftermath of the Tea Party.

Samuel Adams knew otherwise. Letters arrived almost every day assuring Whigs "that our Friends in the Country approve of the Conduct" of the opposition. Adams was confident "we have put our Enemies in the wrong," [19] and in the early months

18. Adams to James Warren, December 17, 1773, *Warren-Adams Letters,* 2 vols. (Boston: Massachusetts Historical Society, 1917, 1925), 2:403–404. The *Warren-Adams Letters,* vols. 1 and 2, were published as vols. 72 (1917) and 73 (1925) of the Massachusetts Historical Society *Collections.*

19. Samuel Adams to James Warren, December 28, 1773, *Warren-Adams Letters,* 1:20.

of 1774 the consolidation of province-wide support behind Whig leadership confirmed his judgement. For the moment the Tea Act had been nullified, not only in Massachusetts, but in all the colonies. The next move was up to the British government.

In England news of the Tea Party had caused a furor. The attention of the political nation now turned to the American colonies as never before. Parliament and the ministry had been insulted, and for those who believed in stern measures the moment had come to rally support. The ministry, led by Lord North, proposed that the port of Boston be closed to all trade as of June 1, 1774, if the town refused to make restitution to the East India Company and to pay the duty on the tea. Members of Parliament who argued that, according to this logic, the port of London should also be closed owing to recent political riots there, were derided by the majority who passed the bill in March. The Port Act, intended to punish Boston and teach the colonies submission, was quickly succeeded by a series of administrative reform bills, which would be known in America as the Coercive Acts. Their chief focus was Massachusetts.

These Coercive Acts were drawn up and passed in the heat of anger over the Tea Party, but their substance reflected long-standing complaints of colonial officials like Governor Hutchinson. He and others had frequently complained that Massachusetts suffered from too much popular participation in government—democracy—and that crown officials were unable to do their duty free of public pressure. The Administration of Justice Act, sealed by King George on May 20, 1774, spoke directly to the latter point by providing for the transfer of royal officials charged with capital crimes to England for trial. Since customs officials had sometimes been intimidated with counter-suits and criminal-trespass charges which were tried in local courts, the act strengthened officials considerably.

The Massachusetts Government Act, passed the same day, spoke to the larger question of the province's political structure. At a stroke it nullified the Charter of 1692 and strengthened royal power. Now it prescribed the royal appointment of the Governor's Council in place of its election by the lower house; it authorized the governor to appoint and remove all judges; it empowered the governor's appointees, the sheriffs, to appoint juries instead of the town selecting them; and it limited town meetings to one annual meeting for the purpose of managing strictly local affairs, as authorized by the governor. In a single statute the ministry, following the lines of criticism it had long been hearing from its appointees in Massachusetts, attempted to terminate the system of responsive government by consent that the inhabitants had developed over generations. Deliberately, although unwittingly, the ministry was fulfilling the prophecies of the Braintree Resolves of 1765 and the more recently expressed fears of scores of towns and thousands of people all over Massachusetts.

Three days later the last of the Coercive Acts, the Quartering Act, became law. Feeding ancient horrors of quartering a standing army among civilians, and recalling the Boston Massacre, the bill paved the way for stationing troops in any American colonial settlement. It empowered governors to open uninhabited buildings for the use of soldiers whenever they saw fit. Violating the sanctity of private property, it seemed to foreshadow military rule by Englishmen over the colonists. In conjunction with the other acts which remade Massachusetts government along authoritarian lines, the Quartering Act gave notice to all the colonies that their own governments and liberties existed at the sufferance of the Parliament. The colonial response to the Coercive Acts would be not to let Massachusetts suffer alone as the ministry hoped, but rather to see the case of the Bay Colony as their own at one remove, and so to call for a Continental Congress to plan concerted opposition.

For Massachusetts the test of public commitment to government by consent, according to ancestral ways, came during the summer of 1774. Boston town meeting would not reimburse the East India Company for the damages of the Mohawks, nor would the people of Boston now yield to duress and pay the tea duty that they continued to oppose on principle. Consequently the blockade of Boston began in June, entirely cutting off its economic lifeblood, water-borne commerce. Within weeks, large-scale unemployment and the specter of impoverishment became Boston's most threatening concerns, and a wartime mentality began to emerge.

The province as a whole was outraged. Frontier communities along the Kennebec River in Maine, towns in the Berkshires one hundred miles west of Boston, now joined in an opposition that was far broader and deeper than ever before. Judging from public reactions, the Coercive Acts were tantamount to a declaration of war on Massachusetts, and in meeting after meeting called in disregard of the new law, townspeople considered what must now be done. For the most part they were led by the same selectmen and representatives who had earned their trust in years past, although in a few places like Worcester and Springfield, where local officials were loyal to their friend and patron Governor Hutchinson, it was necessary to raise up new leaders. In nearly every town the determination to resist approached unanimity.

The hard question was how to resist. The lesson of past conflicts was that economic pressure through nonimportation, nonconsumption, or a total boycott of English goods, was effective. However, the choice among these alternatives was not clearcut. The decision, and its timing, could damage colonial merchants as well as people in particular trades and divide the colonial cause if it was not made carefully. When the Boston Committee of Correspondence pressed for an immediate boycott of all English goods, to be backed up by a secondary boycott against those who declined to join in the primary boycott, people in Massachusetts declined to take up this initiative. Some of their neighbors and commercial associates would suffer, while local and provincial unity would be sacrificed. Surely, they believed, they could find more satisfactory ways of resisting if they took the time to consult each other.

As towns met to determine their course of action a solution emerged—county conventions. If delegates from all towns within a county deliberated together, they could be sure that decisions, whatever they were, would enjoy broad support and that no town would be isolated by its intemperate or idiosyncratic action. Between July and September 1774, the towns in eight of the nine Massachusetts counties, excepting only Barnstable on Cape Cod (where Hutchinson's allies retained control) and one of the three Maine counties (Cumberland), held conventions to determine the next steps. As Hutchinson departed for England in June 1774, and turned over the royal government to his successor General Thomas Gage, an insurgent government was already beginning to appear. That summer it was the county conventions that functioned as a loose interim government until the autumn when a transformed General Court, calling itself a Provincial Congress, became the effective central government of Massachusetts.

During the summer the conventions agreed on the basic pattern of Massachusetts conduct. Asserting their general support for a boycott, they would take no immediate action with respect to trade. To be effective it would have to be a joint, intercolonial effort, so the matter of designing a boycott and establishing its effective date would be left to the Continental Congress, which was scheduled to meet in Philadelphia at the beginning of September. In the meantime it was necessary to assert fundamental political principles, that the people of Massachusetts enjoyed the same natural and constitutional rights as Englishmen, and submission to the Coercive Acts would mean the surrender of those rights. From the outset, the conventions made it clear that they were not going to acquiesce in the destruction of their liberty, and they took immediate steps to nullify the Massachusetts Government Act. Appointees under the act were pressed to resign their positions, and meetings of the people, great crowds (Tories called them "mobs"), were called to prevent any courts from sitting under the new law. Quickly the county conventions made the Massachusetts Government Act a dead letter; and they went on to recommend that town militia companies be activated and that military supplies be laid by, ready for immediate use. Massachusetts assumed a defensive posture.

All the while popular enthusiasm blossomed. The patriotic fervor was expressed in dozens of large public acts, and thousands of private ones. Bostonians found to their great relief that their countrymen really believed the town was "suffering in the common cause," as donations of food, clothing, and cash flooded into Boston. From all over Massachusetts, and from colonies near and far, pork and mutton came in on the hoof, together with bushels of flour and barrels of wheat. Merchants in Salem, setting past rivalries aside, volunteered the use of their facilities to blockaded Boston merchants. Bostonians could only be elated when contributions from persons and places unknown—like £50 from the Fairfax County, Virginia, planter George Washington—came in. For Massachusetts a year of almost ecstatic patriotism, self-sacrificing, self-righteous, and intolerant of contradiction, had begun.

The ardor was so explosive that on September 1, 1774, a rumor, the Powder Alarm, nearly touched off a war. That night British troops, who had occupied Boston as part of the blockade, marched to Mystic and destroyed the gunpowder that had already been collected there. Rapidly, the false rumor spread through the countryside that Boston was being attacked, that cannonballs from British ships were destroying the town, and that the streets ran with the blood of the inhabitants. Immediately militiamen armed themselves and began marching to the relief of Boston. By morning some 3,000 men had collected on Cambridge common, and 10,000 more were within twenty miles, converging on the capital. As far west as the Connecticut Valley the minutemen had been alarmed, and reports came in of 40,000 or 50,000 surrounding Boston by nightfall. A few days later Samuel and John Adams, who had joined the Continental Congress at Philadelphia, learned that "the people from Hampshire County crowded the county of Worcester with armed men; and both counties received the accounts of the quiet dispersion of the people of Middlesex with apparent regret, grudging them the glory of having done something important for their country." [20] Psychologically, Massachusetts was ready to fight, perhaps even ready for independence.

Yet no one wanted Massachusetts to stand and fight alone. Even the most eager and impulsive patriots recognized the need for intercolonial co-operation in order for resistance to succeed. The Continental Congress rather than unilateral action repre-

20. Joseph Warren to Samuel Adams, Boston, Sept. 4, 1774, quoted in Richard Frothingham, *Life and Times of Joseph Warren* (Boston, 1865), p. 356.

sented their best hope. So Massachusetts rejoiced when Congress, barely two weeks after the Powder Alarm, publicly endorsed the resolutions of the Suffolk County Convention, denying the authority of the Coercive Acts, calling for a stoppage of trade with Britain, and directing the people to prepare for war. For John Adams, "this was one of the happiest Days of my Life. . . . This Day convinced me that America will support the Massachusetts or perish with her." [21] For the present, the task of patriots was to remain peaceful while readying their defenses.

Through the autumn and winter of 1774–1775 Massachusetts stood firm. After the Continental Congress voted a trade boycott in October, and resolved to meet again the following May, people could be confident that people in other colonies would join them in defense of "the common cause." In the blockaded town of Boston there was a war of nerves that repeatedly threatened to ignite a conflagration. If Boston could not trade, then neighboring towns decided they would not supply General Gage's troops with provisions, lumber, or skilled workers. Finally, with his men facing a winter in tents on the Boston Common, Gage imported workers and materials from Nova Scotia and New York to construct barracks. Meanwhile many patriots departed the occupied capital, taking their families to reside in outlying towns among family and friends.

On the surface Massachusetts remained quiet during this winter of waiting. But public attitudes that had become polarized during 1774, rather than moderating, became more and more fixed. One tiny incident, related by a Boston merchant, reveals that even schoolboys were politically conscious. For when General Haldimand's servant destroyed their sledding path by strewing ashes on it, "the lads made a muster, and chose a committee to wait upon the General, who admitted them, and heard their complaint . . . that their fathers before 'em had improved it as a coast for time immemorial." Haldimand redressed their grievance by ordering their path repaired. When General Gage learned of it, he reflected that "it was impossible

21. Adams, *Diary and Autobiography*, 2:134–135.

to beat the notion of Liberty out of the people, as it was rooted in 'em *from their Childhood.*'' [22]

Gage's comment revealed his own ambivalence about his mission in Massachusetts. Deep down, he did not really believe that coercion would bring about the loyal submission Britain craved. But his duty to reassert imperial authority, at gunpoint if need be, was clear. Faced with this dilemma, he stalled, hoping that the ministry would send him the thousands of additional troops he believed necessary to make an effective show of force. But British officials were skeptical. Gage was the governor, after all, and he already possessed a force of 4,000 regulars. Surely, they reasoned, he should be able to overawe the troublemakers and restore the supremacy of the multitudes who, they supposed, were loyal to Britain. Thomas Gage, who had a long record of experience in the colonies and whose wife was American, had witnessed the Powder Alarm, and he knew better. So he delayed, if he did not receive reinforcements, there was always the chance that a political solution might be found. War, he recognized, could be had any time.

But time would not stand still. His own officers were restless, and in mid-April 1775 the ministry informed him that he would have no more troops, and that he must act. Accordingly Governor and General Thomas Gage set into motion a secret plan to seize the Provincial Congress's military supplies stored twenty miles west of Boston at Concord. Because Concord was four times farther away than Mystic, the operation would be difficult. But Gage had good intelligence about the objective and the route to it, and so he believed the job might be quickly done with a minimum of disturbance to the inhabitants. He wished to avoid touching off another Powder Alarm.

The commander of the expedition, Lt. Col. Francis Smith, did not learn the objective of his sortie until he opened his sealed orders on the night of April 18. But Patriots had already guessed where the troops who had been bustling around Boston were headed. Concord was an obvious target; the only question

---

22. John Andrews to William Barrell, Boston, Jan. 29, 1775, Massachusetts Historical Society, *Proceedings*, 1st Ser., 8 (1864–1865):398–399.

was whether the troops would take the longer land route through Roxbury and Brookline, or whether they would save a few miles by crossing the mouth of the Charles River to Charlestown and proceeding from there. Despite Longfellow's fanciful account, when Paul Revere, the Whigs' courier, learned that the troops were assembling around the rowboats on the banks of the Charles, it was he who sent the sexton of the Old North Church up the church tower with two lanterns to signal the Provincial Congress's executive body, the Committee of Safety, which was waiting in Charlestown. Immediately the committee sent a rider to warn Concord. A little while later Revere and William Dawes would set out. Even though there were British scouting parties out patrolling the roads to intercept messengers, several riders would succeed in raising the alarm all the way to Concord and beyond. This time it was no rumor of destruction that would later be erased. The British were marching against the stores of the Provincial Congress and might even be aiming to seize its leaders, Samuel Adams and John Hancock, and its treasury.

Meanwhile the British raiding party got off to a late start and then delayed its march from Charlestown. Though the raiders passed through Menotomy (Arlington) in the dark, it was already light by the time they reached Lexington, six miles east of Concord. Here they met a militia company of nearly seventy men—fathers and sons, uncles and nephews, cousins, in-laws—standing assembled on the common to "observe" the British. When the redcoats drew within musket range, they were commanded not to fire, but to surround and disarm the militia. Simultaneously Captain John Parker ordered his militiamen to disperse. As they turned and scattered, overanxious soldiers pulled their triggers, and a brief, pointless massacre ensued. Eight militiamen were killed, more were wounded; only a handful returned the British fire. But in those chaotic moments the war began. The British would skirmish again around the North Bridge at Concord and later, after destroying a small quantity of supplies, head back to Boston. But that afternoon as they retraced their steps, the blood they had so impulsively shed that morning would haunt them. The corpses in Lexington were real, not imagined, and among militiamen, the urge for revenge and vindication overflowed. As the redcoats marched east, the woods and pastures, the fieldstone walls, the barns and sheds and villages were no longer peaceful. Snipers were everywhere. For each militiaman hit by the infantry at Lexington, twenty-five redcoats would bleed before the troops, through the shrewd intervention of a relief column, finally made it back to Boston. By nightfall on April 19, nearly three hundred of the king's soldiers and almost one hundred colonists lay dead or wounded. Massachusetts was at war with Great Britain.

The long months of waiting were over. Within a few days tens of thousands of militiamen from Massachusetts and the neighboring colonies poured into the Boston area, surrounding the capital so thoroughly that General Gage and his troops were helpless to act. Within three weeks the Continental Congress reconvened at Philadelphia, and by mid-June it was organizing a Continental army to defend Massachusetts and the other colonies. On June 15 John Adams, to the chagrin of his Braintree boyhood friend John Hancock, nominated George Washington as commanding general. A Massachusetts-Virginia alliance had been forged in Congress that would form the cornerstone of the national union.

But before Washington had time to set out to organize the army, there was more news from Boston. On June 17 General Gage, now reinforced by Generals Howe, Clinton, and Burgoyne and one thousand troops, decided to attack the colonial emplacement that had just been set up on Breed's Hill, just to the south of Bunker Hill in Charlestown, overlooking Boston. General Howe directed the frontal assault by the redcoats up the hill. Twice they fell back under the murderous fire of the outnumbered but well-fortified defenders. On the third attempt Howe's troops succeeded, though only because the provincial militiamen had run out of powder. As the Yankees retreated, they left behind over one thousand British casualties, more than twice their own casualties. Howe had gained his objective, the high ground at Breed's and Bunker hills, but at a dreadful cost. More officers died that day than in the whole remainder of the war. Gage's reinforcements were entirely spent, and British military morale plummeted. Even before Washington's arrival the

New England militia had shown that it could meet Britain's best in a pitched battle. The ardor of April 19 was confirmed by the battle of Bunker Hill.

Now a new period of waiting began in Massachusetts as imperial politics gradually caught up with events. The practical demands of creating a durable army, trained and equipped, still remained to be filled; while a final round of petition and negotiation with the king was attempted by Congress. In Pennsylvania and New York especially, influential men were eager for a reconciliation with Britain and fearful of the conflict and chaos independence might generate. Until these major colonies became reconciled to independence, political strategy dictated a pause, although by this time people in Massachusetts were generally ready, even eager, to cut loose from Britain.

As Boston entered its second winter of British occupation, it had become a Tory refuge. In the countryside outspoken friends of Britain were treated with suspicion and hostility. They feared for their lives, even though relatively few were molested. What frightened them particularly was the recognition that power was now entirely in popular hands. As friends and kinsmen of Governor Hutchinson's circle, and as admirers of English standards of society and government, they had always put their trust in elite, hierarchical rule. Consequently the county conventions and the expansion of popular rule manifested in town meetings and Whig committees of correspondence, safety, and inspection that investigated and punished suspected Tories, often led them to panic. Anarchy and mob rule seemed to flourish. Fearing the worst, they fled to the safety of British troops.

Their fears, while exaggerated, were certainly not groundless. Tories were being purged from all positions of trust and became easy targets of private and public animosity. Some were publicly humiliated, occasionally with pine tar and feathers, and their property was often subjected to vandalism. Popular authorities did not go out of their way to protect Tory rights, and in some localities they led the charge against them. Britain and its sympathizers had become "the enemy" as Massachusetts mobilized for full-scale war.

The occupation of Boston, and Massachusetts, ended finally

in March 1776. Cooped up in a garrison town, surrounded by far more numerous American troops, the army had been immobilized since the Bunker Hill battle. Still the British refused to leave, until Washington's troops, supplied with cannon captured ten months earlier at Fort Ticonderoga, threatened Boston by mounting the artillery on Dorchester Heights. Once again the British were forced to act. General Howe prepared to attack the Heights, but bad weather intervened, and Howe, thinking back on the losses he had sustained assaulting Breed's Hill, changed his mind. To preserve his army he would leave Boston for the friendly port of Halifax. Within two weeks Boston was "liberated," a disheveled town, where looting and vandalism by the troops and an outbreak of smallpox cast a pall that even the jubilation of Continental soldiers could not dispel. Except for some coastal marauding a few years later, no more front-line warfare occurred in Massachusetts.

In July the Congress caught up with Massachusetts and declared independence. The news of it "diffused a general Joy" in the province. Massachusetts's opposition to British measures now achieved sublime vindication. One patriot, a descendant of a Pilgrim who had sailed into Plymouth harbor with Bradford that snowy night in 1620, proclaimed that "every one of us feels more important than ever; we now congratulate each other as Free men." [23] Independence was heady news.

Thomas Hutchinson, who learned of the Declaration a month later, read it with a sense of exasperation and personal bitterness. The calumnies and distortions he had tried to eradicate now reigned triumphant in America. Defeated and angry, he composed a polemical reply to the Declaration of Independence that he humbly laid at His "Majesty's feet." [24] Writing from his own sense of Massachusetts, he denied that Americans ever "were a *distinct* people from the kingdom." Politically, he maintained, the relationship of the colonists to England was

23. James Warren to John Adams, Boston, July 17, 1776, *Warren-Adams Letters*, 1:261.

24. Words inscribed in the copy Hutchinson sent to King George. Quoted in Bailyn, *Ordeal of Thomas Hutchinson*, p. 357n.

"just the same before the first Colonists emigrated as it has been ever since." Bradford, Winthrop, and all their successors had always been subject to "the Supreme Legislative Authority," Parliament.[25] The problem, he reiterated, was that bands of unprincipled, demagogic agitators had conspired to poison the minds of the people against England in order to achieve separation. In Hutchinson's mind the reality of a loyal, monarchy-loving English population overseas had been transformed into a nightmare of democracy, anarchy, and treason. He would never grasp the fact that the Massachusetts of his youth, for all its provincial imitation of England, had always possessed a profound attachment to individual autonomy and toward authority that was grounded on consent.

John Adams, the provincial lawyer of yeoman stock, knew better. Yet Adams also knew that independence was only a beginning. At the moment of jubilation in Philadelphia after Congress had voted the Declaration of Independence, he invoked the central concerns of the Massachusetts Yankee culture, even as he celebrated: "It may be the Will of Heaven that America shall suffer Calamities. . . . If this is to be the Case, it will have this good Effect, at least: it will inspire Us with many Virtues, which We have not, and correct many Errors, Follies and Vices, which threaten to disturb, dishonour, and destroy Us." Hutchinson saw Massachusetts as having been overrun with viciousness. Adams saw vice and virtue locked in a struggle and immediately raised his voice for reform:

> the new Governments . . . will require a Purification from our Vices, and an Augmentation of our Virtues or they will be no Blessings. The People will have unbounded Power. And the People are extremely addicted to Corruption and Venality, as well as the Great. . . . I must submit all my Hopes and Fears, to an overruling Providence, . . . unfashionable as the Faith may be.[26]

---

25. Malcolm Frieberg, ed., *Thomas Hutchinson's Strictures Upon the Declaration of Independence* . . . (London, 1776; Boston, 1958: Old South Leaflet No. 227), p. 10.

26. John Adams to Abigail Adams, Philadelphia, July 3, 1776, *Adams Family Correspondence*, L. H. Butterfield, *et al.*, eds., 2 vols. (Cambridge, Mass.: Harvard University Press, 1963), 2:28.

Now that the British were gone and independence was theirs, exhortations to moral reform would ring throughout the new state. The time had come to try to create a government true to the Revolution and to their past, one which liberated individuals and simultaneously upheld communal ideals.

5

A Republic of Virtue or Liberty?

*I*N Massachusetts on a summer's day in 1776 it was easy to support independence. One's own life, one's liberty and property were immediately at stake. Nearly everyone agreed that ancestral birthrights, bequeathed by heroic Puritan forefathers, must be transmitted intact to the next generation and to all posterity. Defense against British oppression provided people with an appealing basis for consensus. But creating a new government and a new society was a far more complicated and controversial undertaking than asserting independence. Though people were eager to denounce British tyranny, many still clung to British conceptions of political and social order. Others, more rooted in Yankee ways, hoped to create an austere *American* republic in which simple manners and individual political liberty were pre-eminent. All agreed that the state of Massachusetts must be a republic, but whether it should be ruled by the best people for the interests of all or governed by ordinary men responsive to popular wishes remained a central issue for two generations. Rhetorically, the contest between the few and the many became a debate between virtue and liberty, the two most broadly appealing ideals in Massachusetts public life.

These were recurrent themes from the late 1770s, when the Berkshire Constitutionalists pressed for more responsive government, through the 1780s when Shays's Rebellion erupted in Hampshire County (which then included Hampden and Franklin

102

as well), and on into early decades of the nineteenth century, when the conflict became routinized and finally diluted in the electoral contests of Federalists and Jeffersonian Democratic-Republicans. Moreover the operations of the independent Commonwealth of Massachusetts awakened regional and religious conflicts that the royal government had effectively contained. Its new majoritarian political structure encouraged—even required—debate. Its tradition of an active, widely patronized press and its heritage of voluminous, articulate public debate made Massachusetts a key American forum for the issues of the day.

When the war began in Massachusetts, economic activity had already been gravely disturbed by the blockade of Boston and the patriotic boycott of English trade prescribed by the Continental Congress. During the summer of 1775 militia service and enlistments in the Continental Army added to the burden as thousands of able-bodied men worked with rifles instead of plows, hoes, and harvest tools. Although the year following Lexington and Concord was the peak year of military activity for Massachusetts people, the financial drain continued throughout the war, ruining thousands of families and driving thousands more into serious debt. For farmers and tradesmen who had always lived frugally, close to the margin, the combination of high taxes and time lost for military service produced extensive hardships. In thousands of homes where fathers and sons were killed or disabled, the stress of war was even more intense. In April 1775 doing battle with redcoats was a glorious adventure, but as the years dragged on, the war became a malignant, demoralizing force. The social and economic side effects of a long war were profound on an agricultural and commercial society that lacked the insulation of great surpluses.

One crucial source of discontent was the fact that the war conspicuously enriched some people while it was impoverishing others. Armies, after all, have to be supplied, and the heavy taxes raised out of the pockets of all found their way finally to the pockets of those who were advantageously involved in supplying the troops. The most numerous beneficiaries of wartime economic conditions were prosperous market farmers who were scattered all over Massachusetts, though concentrated in the east and in the Connecticut Valley. Crop prices rose more rapidly than production costs, so farms large enough to produce substantial surpluses yielded unusual profits. From 1777 onward there were repeated public complaints about exorbitant farm prices and the readiness of farmers to withhold their crops from market until they could get the best price. The majority of farmers lacked sufficient land and labor to benefit from the high prices, since other costs were also rising. But the number who did prosper was significant, and in the 1780s enlarged and sometimes newly constructed Georgian houses would become durable monuments to the selective agricultural prosperity generated by the war.

Even more conspicuous were the mercantile fortunes that the war created. Opportunities abounded for merchants whose connections in the countryside enabled them to become conduits in the supply network, as well as for those who were associated with the patriot leaders. Moreover the departure of Tory merchants from Boston and the North Shore ports created a vacuum that their competitors rushed to fill. In addition from 1776 onward New York trade was interrupted by British occupation, so Massachusetts merchants enjoyed renewed profits from transatlantic and coastal commerce. When the French arrived in 1778, they brought with them naval supply contracts that made a handful of merchants rich. Thereafter privateering became a spectacular, if hazardous, source of wealth. The Cabots and Lees of Beverly, the Derbys of Salem, and the Bostonians John Codman, Stephen Higginson, and Thomas Russell were among more than a score of merchants whose fortunes were founded on capturing British merchant vessels.

Because their assets were always in motion, these fortunate merchants were far less drained by taxation and inflation than were farmers and tradesmen. Watching the changes, Robert Treat Paine, a delegate to the Continental Congress, observed that "the course of the war has thrown property into channels, where before, it never was, and has increased little streams to overflowing rivers: and what is worse, in some respects by a method that has drained the sources of some as much as it has replenished others.'' [1] Because the arbitrary economic consequences of the war impoverished some, strained many, and enriched a few, the divisiveness of wartime political questions was intensified. Policies respecting taxation, currency, and price controls were bound to have unequal effects. In time of heightened anxieties, when people worried not only about their immediate economic well-being but also about the survival of the United States and the establishment of an equitable republican government, Massachusetts's political structure and the men who controlled it faced their severest test.

Contrary to the expectations of Thomas Hutchinson and other Tories, Massachusetts did not collapse into anarchy when it became an independent state. One major test came in the summer of 1776 when the Provincial Congress successfully reopened the courts that had been closed for two years since the enactment of the coercive Administration of Justice Act. The authorities acted gingerly, recognizing that debtors and their kinsmen might be happier to see the courts remain closed.

A second major test of Massachusetts's political equilibrium came when the General Court sought permission from the electorate to draft a new constitution, since the legitimacy of all government was doubtful now that the Massachusetts charter was void. During the autumn of 1776 people all over the state weighed the issue, and a majority finally rejected the proposal. While the reasons varied, the consensus was that the General Court contained so many inexperienced members and was so burdened with day-to-day affairs that it should not be entrusted with the awesome responsibility of drawing a constitution. In any case, many people believed, a constitution would require popular ratification, not merely legislative enactment. The decision to delay the creation of a constitution did not unleash an orgy of disorder, nor did it incapacitate the provisional government.

The fact was that the presence or absence of anarchy was

---

1. Paine to Elbridge Gerry, Boston, April 12, 1777, in James T. Austin, *The Life of Elbridge Gerry,* 2 vols. (1828; 1829; New York: DaCapo, 1970), 1:220–221.

contingent on local government during the war as it had been during the colonial era. In the towns, the co-operation of citizens was based on tradition, shared ideas about the rules of politics, and personal trust. The fact that town meetings, like the state government, could not control prices did not produce alienation. Towns were highly responsive if not always effective, and local administration was normally flexible. People who really needed tax abatements generally got them. Families whose survival was threatened because husbands or sons were off in the army received town aid. Draft quotas were filled by paying bonuses to volunteers, by taxing those who had cash to create bounties that attracted landless young men. Except for the raising of troops and supplies, state government was remote. Every town seemed to have its own constitution, written in the minds of its inhabitants and preserved in the multitude of precedents contained in the town records. Maintaining order was the routine achievement of the people in nearly three hundred communities around the state.

Yet the statewide issues of taxes, inflation, and the administration of justice were lively and divisive. The interests of merchants and prosperous market farmers, chiefly located in the eastern counties, were not the same as those of the semi-subsistence farmers who were most numerous and influential in Worcester, Berkshire, and upland Hampshire towns. As time went on, the framing of a state constitution became entwined with these economic questions since their resolution was contingent on who was represented in the General Court. Ultimately the most controversial question for constitution writers would be representation. More than any other, this issue generated highly self-interested maneuvering for competitive advantage.

One consequence was delay. In most states constitutions were rapidly drafted and approved during the first years of the war. But in Massachusetts the call for a constitution was not only rejected in 1776, but even when the House of Representatives did draw up and approve a constitution in early 1778, the voters turned it down. The explicit reasons given for opposing the 1778 constitution varied widely. The weakness of the governor and the failure to create a strong, independent upper house were criticized in eastern Massachusetts. In the west the fact that property qualifications for senators and the governor were proposed was as objectionable as the fact that poor men would be disenfranchised from voting for these offices. Moreover, the compromise on representation that had been negotiated aroused widespread criticism. Eastern towns complained that by allowing a representative for every town, regardless of population, sparsely settled communities would enjoy undue influence and the whole legislature would be so large as to be unwieldy. Western communities, for whom the cost of sending a representative had often seemed prohibitive, complained at the provision that each town must be responsible for the travel and *per diem* costs of its delegates. Actually divisions of interest, partly economic and partly regional, were so acutely felt that it is unlikely that any constitution would have achieved broad support in 1778.

Independence from Britain had not dissolved the social bonds of civil order in Massachusetts towns, but it had destroyed the network of royal patronage that had furnished a major source of inter-county political integration for provincial government. Until the 1780s, when a new gubernatorial patronage network slowly emerged, there were few concrete, particular loyalties that bound the leaders of all the counties together. Instead, certain legislative issues, a few family linkages, and a generalized patriotism for Massachusetts and the United States furnished the means of cohesion. Single-minded patriotic ardor quickly receded after Independence, but it remained a potent source of corporate unity, within communities and in the state at large.

Consequently, even though there was considerable dissatisfaction with the provisional government and widespread warweariness, Massachusetts was not restive. By 1779 there was so much self-confidence in the American cause that loyalists who had fled in 1774 and 1775 were beginning to drift back to their homes. Although they were widely excluded from public office, only the most prominent remained targets of acute hostility. Most of the loyalists were able to retain their property and regain a measure of acceptance. Confiscation laws only affected major crown appointees and others who had left behind substantial debts. In the latter case property was seized and sold not for vengeance, but to satisfy creditors. Old standards of equity in government endured.

It was in the spring of 1779 that the townspeople voted to hold a special convention to draft a constitution. It would be more expensive than having the legislature do it, but many believed it would also be more productive. In September the convention opened at Boston. Its members, drawn from almost every part of the state, included the major Revolutionary leaders. John and Samuel Adams and John Hancock, as well as rising figures such as Benjamin Lincoln and Caleb Strong, played active roles in the convention. Ultimately it was John Adams, the key political and legal theorist among the old Patriot group, who drafted the new constitution. Drawing on the most enlightened political science of the day and on Whig ideals, Adams designed a modern governing structure that enshrined the traditional ideals of the Bay Colony.

A firm believer in the guiding powers of correct rhetoric, Adams opened the constitution with a preamble recalling that of the Declaration of Independence which he had worked on three years earlier. The purpose of government was "to secure the existence of the body-politic; and to furnish the individuals who compose it, with . . . their natural rights and the blessings of life." Explaining precisely what was meant, Adams defined the body politic in terms reminiscent of the Mayflower Compact and Puritan political thought. "Formed by a voluntary association of individuals," he said, the body politic was "a social compact, by which the whole people convenants with each citizen, and each citizen with the whole people, that all shall be governed by certain laws for the common good." [2] In theory, corporate and individual good merged, although it was clear that common interests superseded those of individuals.

The first section of the constitution consisted of a declaration of rights in which the basic elements of free republican govern-

2. Oscar and Mary F. Handlin, eds., *The Popular Sources of Political Authority: Documents on the Massachusetts Constitution of 1780* (Cambridge, Mass.: Harvard University Press, 1966), p. 441.

ment were spelled out. Procedural rights protecting citizens from government oppression were enumerated, together with Whig safeguards including a free press, free assembly, and the right of the people "to keep and bear arms for the common defence." [3] In several instances particular British offenses of recent years, such as the Quartering Act, were forevermore prohibited. Corporate power would be supreme, but not absolute. Individuals were the source of government, and their rights would be guaranteed.

At the same time the people, through their government, were empowered to create a religious establishment "for the support and maintenance of public protestant teachers of piety," and to direct inhabitants to attend services, provided they could "conscienciously [*sic*] and conveniently" do so.[4] Taxes raised for religious support would be paid to whichever local denomination each taxpayer preferred, provided he attended a local church; otherwise the sums raised would go to the majority church in the town. Protestant religion was so generally regarded as a public good that individual rights of conscience were recognized only within the framework of regular church attendance. For Baptists, Methodists, and Quakers, whose numbers had grown since the Great Awakening, the multiple religious establishment of this constitution represented a long step toward disestablishment and full religious liberty in a state where Winthrop's commonwealth was still widely revered, and where the Congregational clergy and its seminary, Harvard College, enjoyed public financial support.

The main body of Adams's draft was the "Frame of Government," laying out the powers of the legislature, the executive, and the judiciary, and the boundaries between the branches.[5] The form of government, which anticipated the federal Constitution of 1787, had to compromise the most divisive political issues, especially the matter of representation. Here the solution was to give something to nearly everyone. The upper house of

3. Handlin and Handlin, *Popular Sources,* p. 446.
4. Handlin and Handlin, *Popular Sources,* pp. 442–443.
5. Handlin and Handlin, *Popular Sources,* p. 446.

the legislature, the senate, would be chosen annually, as were all elective officers, and apportioned according to equal tax districts. The rich and populous counties of Suffolk and Essex would each have six senators, while others would have one to five senators. Nantucket and Martha's Vineyard would share a senator. Senators themselves must own land of at least £300 value or personal property and real estate worth a minimum of £600. Their electors, too, must meet a property test, so the senate was explicitly meant to represent the principle that one's stake in government was partially proportional to wealth.

The lower house carried the same relatively low property test for electors, but its actual composition was clearly intended to represent all regions and the common mass of people. Every incorporated town would have one delegate, regardless of its size, although future towns would have to possess at least 150 taxable men (about 700 people) to be represented. Larger towns could have more delegates according to a formula that, while discriminating against the people of large towns, still provided Boston with six representatives. One key complaint of small towns distant from Boston, that the expense of representation hit them unfairly because of transportation costs, was met by the stipulation that in each session one round-trip journey to the legislature would be paid for every delegate out of the state treasury. Although in its property tests for voters as well as delegates the House of Representatives retained a modicum of the elitism of the colonial past, it was designed to be broadly based and close to the people.

In contrast, John Adams and the convention chose to elevate the governor's office. Unique among all officials, the governor was given the title "His Excellency." He must also be a rich man, owning a Massachusetts freehold worth at least £1000, and he must "declare himself to be of the christian religion." [6] His powers, largely modeled on those of his colonial predecessors, included calling and dismissing the legislature, commanding the state's military forces, and vetoing legislation. Notwithstanding their unfortunate experiences with Governors Bernard

6. Handlin and Handlin, *Popular Sources,* p. 456.

and Hutchinson, the Revolutionaries in Massachusetts, unlike those in most states, did not create a weak governor. Experience since 1775, as well as John Adams's application of political theory, demonstrated the necessity for a vigorous executive. Since each term of office was limited to a year, the possibilities of executive abuse appeared to be curtailed.

The constitution of 1780, which was as deliberately and rationally devised as political circumstances would permit, was conceived within a vigorous tradition of representative government. Moreover the corporate values of the Massachusetts Bay colony were adapted to the new era. The presumption of a close link between high social status and public office endured in the governor and the senate. The public commitment to a society of sober morals was underwritten by retaining a modified Congregational religious establishment. Revolutionary republicanism, as it was understood in Massachusetts, was consistent with the Puritan heritage.

Public support for education, a major feature of the General Court's program under Winthrop in the 1630s, was recognized as critical for the new commonwealth and written into its constitution. Where the objectives had once been public piety and clerical training, the new constitution asserted that "the encouragement of arts and sciences, and all good literature, tends to the honour of God, the advantage of the christian religion, and the great benefit of this and the other United States of America." [7] Harvard College and the public schools must be maintained. There was no need for, and little sense of, a break with tradition.

Yet underlying these formal, institutional continuities with the past, a new vision was evident. The secular utopianism of the Revolution was explicit in the injunction that

> it shall be the duty of legislatures and magistrates, in all future periods . . . , to cherish the interests of literature and the sciences, and all seminaries of them; . . . to encourage private societies and public institutions, rewards and immunities, for the promotion of

7. Handlin and Handlin, *Popular Scources,* p. 465.

agriculture, arts, sciences, commerce, trades, manufactures, and a natural history of the country.[8]

The constitution pointed toward a Massachusetts that would be increasingly enlightened, advanced, and productive.

In March 1780 the convention completed work on the constitution and sent it out to the towns, urging them to ratify it. In an address to their constituents the delegates admitted that this was not "a perfect System of Government: This is not the Lot of Mankind." Yet they urged that the proposal be viewed carefully and sympathetically since, they asserted, it was the product of careful deliberation and repeated compromise. Recognizing that some provisions might be controversial, they explained the reasoning behind the new protestant religious establishment, the property requirements for suffrage, and the system of legislative apportionment. The tone of the entire address from "Your Delegates" to their "Friends and Countrymen" was mild and ingratiating.[9] Nearly all of those who had spent months laboring over the document were eager to see it accepted. Their commitment to the constitution of 1780 was chiefly responsible for its ultimate success.

Townspeople did not blindly defer to their leaders and shower their handiwork with accolades. In town after town a querulous individualism marked the evaluation of the document. As the convention had anticipated, the complaints clustered around the religious establishment, voting qualifications, and apportionment. Why not complete liberty of conscience, some argued, while others fretted over the fact that the Congregational monopoly was broken, so the orthodox must now compete. In the poorer towns of Worcester County and farther west, there were many who found outrageous the disfranchisement of citizens, including Revolutionary soldiers, because of their poverty. In populous eastern towns some complained that they were underrepresented in an overlarge assembly because of the inclusion of delegates from every single town. But there were also more idiosyncratic criticisms against the creation of certain offices like

8. Handlin and Handlin, *Popular Sources,* p. 467.
9. Handlin and Handlin, *Popular Sources,* pp. 435, 434–440.

that of lieutenant-governor and Governor's Council, against the wording of particular oaths, against the distribution of specific powers among officials. Collectively the towns' review of the constitution illustrated not only the penetration of Revolutionary ideology among the people, but also the individualistic, unsystematic way in which they had combined it with older ideas and local political expectations. The ratification process revealed the absence of a coherent, integrated outlook toward state government. Individualism had not degenerated into the chaos of every man for himself; but there were hints of the spirit of every town and every interest group for itself. At the state level, independence had destroyed an effective traditional system of political integration, the patronage and deference once commanded by the provincial government of colonial days.

While the ratification of the constitution revealed the absence of statewide political integration, it successfully marked the beginning of a new era. For the convention evaluated the returns on the constitution of 1780 as approval, however narrow, and they moved to establish the new government without further delay. An election was quickly called, and in October 1780 John Hancock, the overwhelmingly popular choice, was inaugurated as the first governor of the Commonwealth of Massachusetts. Out of all the turmoil of resistance to Britain it was he, not one of the Adamses, who emerged as the central figure in Massachusetts public life during the crucial decade of the 1780s.

John Hancock had been born in the North Precinct of Braintree in 1737, just two years after his father, the Reverend John Hancock, Jr., had baptized Deacon Adams's son John. But unlike his schoolmate John Adams, young Hancock was plucked out of Braintree soon after his father died by his wealthy uncle Thomas. By this time Thomas Hancock, the second son of "Pope" Hancock, the Lexington pastor, had made a fortune in trade and, childless, was eager to adopt his nephew and make him his apprentice and heir. Later on the now wealthy youth would be educated at Harvard as his forbears had been.

When he was graduated at the age of seventeen, he immediately went to work for his uncle. After nine years he became a partner, and at Thomas Hancock's death in 1764 he became the sole proprietor of the business. Within the next several years Samuel Adams would draw him into Boston and provincial politics. By late 1774 when he was elected president of the Provincial Congress and chairman of its Committee of Safety, Hancock had become the most prominent Whig in Massachusetts. His national stature was similarly elevated; indeed it was as president of the Continental Congress that Hancock seized the opportunity to display his bold signature on the Declaration of Independence. But in spite of long service in Congress Hancock never achieved the national role he coveted as commander of the Continental army. Still, he was pleased to return to Massachusetts as His Excellency, the governor of the Commonwealth.

At home Hancock had created a broad following among people from all regions and walks of life. From the 1760s onward he had displayed his wealth in a generous, public-spirited way, providing employment and a variety of charitable donations including the gift of Bibles to struggling congregations. As a member of the inner circle of Massachusetts Whigs, he kept his purse always open to the patriot cause. During the war Hancock made himself conspicuous among Boston merchants by donating firewood to the poor and willingly accepting Massachusetts and Continental notes in payment for debts. Hancock was unique among his peers in that he actively cultivated popularity as a means of enhancing his political stature. By breaking the political code of republican gentlemen and courting the people, he became the target of their private scorn. But Hancock's use of his wealth, together with his sensitivity to tides of opinion, ultimately elevated his career in Massachusetts beyond that of his early mentor Samuel Adams and his rivals John Adams, James Bowdoin, and James Warren. Hancock was the all but unanimous popular choice for governor in 1780. Thereafter he was re-elected with seventy- to ninety-percent majorities every time he ran until his death in 1793.

As his colonial predecessor Thomas Hutchinson had done, John Hancock managed personally to exercise an integrating influence on state politics. He was better known personally throughout the state than any other leader; his private and public patronage, together with his reputation as a sterling patriot—one who had been singled out for punishment by the British in 1775, enabled him to blunt the edges of regional and interest-group conflict during the early 1780s. Yet Hancock, for all his patriotic glitter and political maneuvering, did not lead in solving the problems of taxation and finance, and in time these came to a head. Hancock's response was to retire from office in 1785, claiming reasons of health. His successor was his erstwhile electoral challenger James Bowdoin, now allied with Samuel Adams and James Warren.

Bowdoin, in contrast to Hancock, wanted to resolve Massachusetts's financial crisis, whatever the cost in popularity. His approach, which appealed to creditors and mercantile interests broadly, was to raise taxes to pay off the war debt over a fifteen-year period. For farmers who were already having trouble meeting their taxes because of the slump in farm prices, the prospect of additional direct taxation was alarming. Since Bowdoin was also deaf to cries for the relief of debtors, tension mounted until in 1786 a rebellion broke out in Hampshire County.

Hampshire and Berkshire had never been thoroughly integrated into provincial or state politics due largely to geography. Patterns of trade and settlement in the west ran north and south along the river valleys, connecting the area almost as closely to Connecticut as to Massachusetts. During the colonial era government patronage had tied county notables to the royal government, within the western towns people had typically deferred to the leadership of the regional elite. But the Revolution disrupted both of these sources of cohesion, so social and economic tensions came to focus on the shortcomings of state fiscal policy, a policy that more nearly met the needs of eastern merchants and tradesmen than of farmers who were semi-self-sufficient.

Indeed, the Bowdoin administration's policies combined with the depressed economy to make thousands of farmers all over the state—in Worcester County and even in the eastern counties of Middlesex and Bristol, restive. But in central and eastern

Massachusetts the breadth and depth of alienation were less acute, and allegiance to the state government was stronger. When Daniel Shays, Luke Day, and a handful of other Revolutionary veterans organized armed resistance to the courts of Massachusetts, they would have sympathizers throughout the commonwealth, but not supporters.

The insurgents of 1786, like those of 1774, began with a county convention to formulate common grievances and call for their redress. Meeting in late August at Hatfield in the central part of Hampshire County, delegates from fifty of the fifty-seven towns met to identify the "many grievances and unnecessary burdens now lying upon the people" that were sources of "great uneasiness" and "discontent." [10] When they finished, they had specified no less than seventeen complaints. Several aimed at the constitution of 1780. The senate and the courts of Common Pleas and General Sessions, which had thwarted debtor relief, should be abolished. The system of representation was no good, and all officers of the government, they argued, should be annually elected and made dependent on the house of representatives, instead of a fee system, for their support. These were the constitutional issues.

Most of the grievances, however, were wholly questions of policy. The table of fees for using the courts was unfair. The system of taxation and appropriation was no good because it operated "unequally between the polls and estates, and between landed and mercantile interests." [11] The refusal to issue paper money and other fiscal matters were distressing. Government policy was wrong-headed and, these farm representatives believed, discriminatory. Why, after all, must the General Court meet in Boston instead of a site farther west? A populist tone ran through all the Hampshire complaints. The people were fed up with officials and especially lawyers.

The delegates from Hampshire wanted a special legislative session to be called to deal with their grievances, and the wheels

10. George R. Minot, *History of the Insurrection in Massachusetts* . . . (Worcester, 1788), p. 34.
11. Minot, *Insurrection,* p. 35.

to be set in motion for constitutional revision. In the meantime, just as conventions had done a decade before, they called on the people to "abstain from all mobs and unlawful assemblies." [12] But having delivered a frontal assault on the legitimacy of the Massachusetts senate and the courts, the convention had not encouraged a mood of restraint. Within a week a crowd of over a thousand armed men seized the courthouse at Northampton and so, for the time being, abolished the objectionable courts of General Sessions and Common Pleas.

Governor Bowdoin proclaimed their actions treason, but official threats did not curb popular discontent. In early September a crowd of several hundred men occupied the courthouse in Worcester and blocked proceedings there. When it began to appear that farmers in Middlesex and Bristol in the east as well as those of Hampshire, Berkshire, and Worcester might resort to arms to close the courts, Governor Bowdoin began to take military action to assure the maintenance of the state government. To protect the Supreme Judicial Court which was scheduled to meet at Springfield in late September Bowdoin ordered 600 loyal Massachusetts militia troops to occupy the courthouse there. When more than a thousand insurgents arrived, led by Daniel Shays, it proved impossible to transact business, and though Shays may have been chagrined that government troops occupied the courthouse first, there was no question that his show of force had intimidated the supreme court into retreat. The judges retired east from Springfield, wholly abandoning their original plan to go on to Berkshire.

By early October the General Court, meeting in emergency session, had begun to consider both the insurrection and the grievances that lay behind it. Some members favored immediate suppression of the rebellion, but the majority, sympathetic to at least some of the complaints, and wanting to hear and consider the numerous petitions that had poured in from scores of towns, blocked swift or vigorous repression. The house of representatives wished to end the uprising by conciliating the insurgents with reform legislation. At the end of October, however, the

12. Minot, *Insurrection,* p. 37.

Shaysites issued a call for a second county convention in Hampshire and also invited towns to prepare for war, requesting that provisions be laid in and that, as in 1774, men should "stand ready to march at a moment's warning." [13]

When news of these measures arrived in Boston, the governor's hand was strengthened. The assembly passed a riot act and temporarily suspended the right of habeas corpus. At the same time the General Court provided exemption from prosecution under the act to all insurgents who would swear allegiance to the state and act accordingly by the first of January, 1787. The determination to suppress the rebels was joined with the desire to conciliate them, and so, in addition to relief acts dealing with taxation, lawsuits, and court fees, the General Court took steps to reassert its authority with a forty-five-page address to the people of Massachusetts, explaining and justifying the operations and expenses of government. The court took the position that "misinformation" was chiefly responsible for the wide popularity of the rebel movement. Using clear, step-by-step terms, the court presented a financial accounting of its stewardship to the public, hoping to silence rumors of government extravagance. The address also lectured the people on the vices of paper money, likening demands for it to the Israelites' call to Aaron "to make them a calf." Ultimately the General Court maintained, the government was being made a scapegoat "as if *they* had devoured them [the people]," [14] whereas the fundamental sources of unhappiness lay within the people themselves.

The climax of the address was an appeal by the official leadership of Massachusetts society for a reformation of morals that would create a rebirth of republican virtue. Since American independence corruption had made alarming headway:

. . . habits of luxury have exceedingly increased, the usual manufactures of the country have been little attended to. That we can buy goods cheaper than we can make them, is often repeated, and is even become a maxim in economy, altho' a most absurd and

13. Minot, *Insurrection*, p. 64.
14. *An Address from the General Court to the People of the Commonwealth of Massachusetts* (Boston, 1786), pp. 4, 34.

MASSACHUSETTS

A photographer's essay by Ted Polumbaum

Photographs in sequence

destructive one. While these habits continue, the wisest Legislature will not be able to remove our complaints . . . we have indulged ourselves in fantastical and expensive fashions and intemperate living. . . . Without a reformation of manners, we can have little hope to prosper in our public or private concerns. . . . That virtue which is necessary to support a Republic, has declined; and as a people, we are now in the precise channel, in which the liberty of States has generally been swallowed up. But still our case is not desperate; by recurring to the principles of integrity and public spirit, and the practice of industry, sobriety, economy, and fidelity in contracts, and by acquiescing in laws necessary for the public good, the impending ruin may be averted, and we become respectable and happy. . . . In such a cause we may hope, that the God of our fathers, who has defended us hitherto, will prosper the work of his own hands, and save the fair structure of American liberty from falling into ruin.[15]

Massachusetts's leaders hoped that ultimately, if the people were exhorted to follow the banner of virtue and to support *their* government, the rebels could be effectively isolated and would quickly seek the promised indemnity. To assure thorough circulation of the message, the senate ordered that the address be read to town meetings by town clerks and to congregations by the ministers on Thanksgiving day. Hereafter insurgents would be on notice that in attacking the government they were attacking the rights of individuals subsumed in the corporate rights of the body politic of Massachusetts.

The effects of this remarkable republican homily from the representatives to their constituents are uncertain. In rebel towns it never had a hearing, nor did it abate the willingness of Daniel Shays to pressure the courts with armed men. Finally Governor Bowdoin decided it was best to delay further court sessions until January. Postponement would give insurgents time to reconsider their resistance, while allowing government troops time to assemble and prepare their attack. Bowdoin recognized that as the cold winter set in, the rebels would be undermined by the scarcity of food and shelter. By the beginning of the new year,

15. *Address from the General Court,* pp. 33–35.

1787, he was confident that the courts, supported by troops, could reopen.

In mid-January Governor Bowdoin gave orders to General Benjamin Lincoln, a Worcester native, to move west in command of the entire militia. After a three-day march from the outskirts of Boston, Lincoln's troops arrived in Worcester on January 22 in time to witness the opening of the courts the following day. As Bowdoin had hoped, the firm show of force had intimidated the rebels, so no opposition of any sort was raised. Now Lincoln and his men moved west to Hampshire County.

Before they arrived, however, blood was shed at Springfield. There Shays, together with Eli Parsons and Luke Day, had collected about 2,000 troops. They planned to use their superior numbers to force 900 government troops under General Shepard to abandon their position at the arsenal overlooking Springfield village. If the Shaysites succeeded, they would establish effective control of the country and occupy a strong position in any future negotiations with the government. On January 25th, Shays made his move, although more in a symbolic than a tactical manner. Not fully believing Shepard's troops would fire, he ignored all warnings from Shepard and marched a column of troops to within two hundred, then one hundred yards of Shepard's encampment. Now Shepard ordered his artillerymen to fire over the insurgents' heads, but when they still kept coming, Shepard ordered the cannon to fire at the center of the approaching column. The cannonballs succeeded where all previous political maneuvers had failed. Shays's troops broke ranks and fled, leaving three of their own Massachusetts men dead, the first victims of this civil war.

The "victory" of Shepard's government troops exposed the weakness of the insurgent movement. For while farmers and tradesmen had shouldered arms against the commonwealth, their intentions were reformist, not revolutionary, and they were ambivalent about how far they should go in pressing their resistance. They did not mean to commit treason by taking up arms; they merely intended to mount pressure on the governor and legislature. When these authorities, represented by Shepard's and Lincoln's armies, showed they were ready to fight, the rebels had second thoughts. Within the week Shays, whose troops had reassembled twenty-five miles northeast of Springfield at Pelham, pressed for a settlement based on a general pardon. In a letter to General Lincoln and in a petition to the legislature, the Shaysites admitted that "we have been in errour, in having recourse to arms, and not seeking redress in a constitutional way," and they asked the General Court "to overlook our failing," to accept the innocence of their intentions, and to grant a pardon in exchange for laying down their arms.[16] A single skirmish had brought them to the edge of surrender.

But Lincoln, and the General Court, rejected these terms since the Shaysites remained in arms. The rebels had missed their opportunity to surrender before January 1 in exchange for a pardon; now it was said that they sought to dictate it at gunpoint. When, early in February, Shays unexpectedly moved his men across the Worcester County line to Petersham, Lincoln acted decisively. In an overnight march through a snowstorm, he led his militiamen thirty miles from their encampment at Hadley to Petersham where the exhausted militia surprised the rebels. Shays and the other leaders escaped across the state line to the north, but the rest of the rebels, after being disarmed and swearing an oath of allegiance, went quietly home. There was no battle, no formal surrender, only collapse. Elsewhere, in Worcester, Hampshire, and Berkshire, there would be a few more confrontations in the coming months—two rebels were killed and thirty wounded at Sheffield on February 27th—but the rebellion was broken. The legitimacy of the commonwealth, which even the rebels ultimately accepted, had been vindicated.

The political and psychological wounds of this civil war were slow in healing, however, and memories of the rebellion exercised a profound influence on Massachusetts public life for a generation. Nothing could have more powerfully impressed people with a realization of the difficulty of satisfying diverse constituencies within a republic. Shays's rebellion was the most immediate object lesson in the fragility of republican government,

16. Minot, *Insurrection,* p. 127.

and it helps to account for the special excitement which controversies over the French Revolution would have in the Bay State during the 1790s. After 1800 the citizens of Massachusetts would come to accept the idea of opposition as routine in party competition at the ballot box. But recognition of the legitimacy of political opposition within a competitive structure required a new perspective for people all over New England and the United States.

In 1787 Massachusetts returned to the security of re-electing John Hancock to the governor's chair. After his death in 1793, Hancock's successor would be none other than his ally Samuel Adams. Each in his own way, the two old Revolutionary heroes helped to unify state politics. Neither possessed an organized following, but memories of their Revolutionary exploits attracted broad support.

At the town and county level the aftermath of the rebellion was divisive, as the victorious "friends of government" settled scores with former rebels by excluding them from office and by administering the laws of property and indebtedness harshly. In many instances young Shaysites moved on, emigrating to New Hampshire, New York, and Vermont. Indeed with each passing year the turnover in local populations caused by migration to the north and west, as well as movement from agricultural to commercial towns, generally reduced the bitter heritage of the rebellion.

Nevertheless the deeper issues of the revolt remained alive. For in the autumn of 1787 townspeople elected delegates to the convention that would meet in January 1788 to ratify or reject the United States Constitution drafted the previous summer at Philadelphia. The debate over the federal Constitution was in some ways an extension of the controversies that had racked Massachusetts so recently and went to the heart of republicanism. Centralization was set against government close to the people. The interests of merchants, manufacturers (including artisans), market-oriented farmers, and creditors seemed in conflict with those of the semi-subsistence upland farmers who had supported the insurrection. Everyone wanted a republic of virtue, but would national government, providing secure credit and conducted by a cosmopolitan elite be more conducive to virtue than the confederation, where state governments were essentially autonomous? In a sense the old questions of Winthrop's day were being posed in different terms. The vision of corporatism and an elevated magistracy was embodied in the Constitution. Opposition to it traded on the same concern for individual liberty and anti-statism that Puritans had also voiced. Now the issues were framed in the secular language of political science. The covenant became a constitution and the voice of the majority assumed a quasi-divine authority.

When Massachusetts's ratifying convention met in early 1788, a narrow majority of its members opposed the new federal Constitution. Whatever the political and commercial benefits of national union, many greeted it with suspicion. The discussion surrounding the new proposal reiterated many of the arguments that had been expressed during the Revolutionary crisis. Would liberty be secure if a distant national authority was created with the power to tax? Could liberty be safe if officials were elected for two- to six-year terms of office, instead of being subject to the recall mechanism of annual elections? Would the people of Massachusetts retain the autonomy that was a legacy from their ancestors as well as from their own recent past? Many citizens were alarmed because in contrast to Massachusetts's own constitution, this new Constitution carried no religious ·requirements for officeholders. Infidels and free-thinkers might someday gain control of the government. A decade later, when Thomas Jefferson sought election to the presidency, this anxiety would intensify opposition to his candidacy in Massachusetts.

In time, however, the Federalists succeeded in persuading some of the delegates to change their minds. Most important, Samuel Adams and Governor John Hancock, whose followings overlapped, both decided to support ratification. They became convinced that the federal Constitution did contain sufficient structural safeguards to warrant support, and they both were eager for the commercial and diplomatic advantages that a vigorous national government could provide. Both men, deeply enmeshed in the fate of Massachusetts, were also veterans of the

Continental Congress. They knew and convinced others that the political and economic interests of Massachusetts and the United States were complementary. In contrast to state leaders in New York and Virginia, Adams and Hancock ultimately brought decisive support to the federal cause.

Within a few years their judgment seemed vindicated by a new surge of prosperity. Every part of the state flourished as agricultural prices rose and trade and manufacturing expanded. Merchants and sailors had not only regained access to their old markets in the Atlantic and Caribbean, they had opened new ones from the Baltic to the ports of China. After 1793, when Europe entered a decade of recurrent warfare, Massachusetts became more prosperous than ever before. Everything people produced found a profitable market, and with cash in their pockets farmers and tradesmen, as well as merchants and lawyers, became consumers of store-bought goods on an unprecedented scale. In a republican society the urge for luxury and display was somewhat chastened, finding expression in the elegant understatement of classic architecture and the English decorative styles of Adam and Hepplewhite. For the first time classical columns and pilasters gleamed white among the clusters of ox-blood clapboard saltboxes in country villages. In the port towns, from Newburyport and Salem south to Hingham and Plymouth, elegant town streets displayed the new, self-conscious urbanity bred by the cosmopolitan experience of successful interstate and international trade.

The few who were wealthy, like Harrison Gray Otis, the Boston merchant and real estate developer who built not one but three city mansions over a period of years, seemed to revel in their sterling and silk. The many, who were fortunate if they had some pewter and a few coin-silver spoons, now tasted amenities they had seldom known. Cane sugar was preferable to a steady diet of the homemade maple variety. Imported cotton and woolen textiles supplemented homespun. Newspapers and pamphlets found broader markets than ever before. Voluntarily, eagerly, the people of Massachusetts ceded the economic independence of the old semi-subsistence life in favor of the interdependence of a more specialized, commercial society.

This shift, reminiscent of the change that had occurred in the 1730s and 1740s, also generated anxiety and conflict, both religious and secular. The sense that a revered past was being supplanted awakened a keen desire to preserve old virtues. In both religion and politics a rhetoric emerged that shared some of the concerns of the Great Awakening. A social mobilization, raising the consciousness of inhabitants in religious and civic affairs and engaging their active participation, was sustained by the prosperity of the federal era.

The religious mobilization had two major thrusts. The most profound and wide-ranging was the collection of activities included in the movement called the "Revival," or Second Great Awakening. Congregationalists turned in the direction of heartfelt piety, emphasizing conversion with renewed vigor. As in the 1740s, some churches split, with scores assuming the name of "evangelical Congregationalists." Baptists, whose evangelical views put them in a permanent state of revival, enjoyed a wave of growth in numbers and prosperity.

At the same time there was also an "awakening" of sorts in the orthodox clergy. As a result of the constitutional provisions of the new government in the commonwealth, clergymen found themselves thrust into an uncongenial, competitive, religious environment. On one hand they were beset by lay preachers and Baptists in their parishes, while on the other, a new rationalistic deism was spreading. Some of the clergy tried to bend with prevailing circumstances, either becoming revivalists themselves or else moving in the direction of Unitarianism, a religion that was peculiar to eastern Massachusetts. More often, however, the orthodox clergy dug in, mounting rhetorical counterattacks. By the 1790s, when traces of the Deism promulgated by the French republic cropped up in Massachusetts, the ministers' tone was shrill, apocalyptic, almost hysterical. Irreligion and vice, evident in public indifference to established clergymen, led them increasingly to form associations among themselves and to seek political allies.

They found their allies within their own congregations. Deacons as well as other parishioners worried about the erosion of their churches' financial base of support, in addition to larger

questions of social morality. The secular establishment of selectmen, justices of the peace, lawyers, and merchants were
often among their parishioners, and men in these positions were
also fearful of the violent disorders of Revolutionary France
and, more immediately, distressed by the decline in customary
respect due to social leaders like themselves. Here, too, the
republican structure of government was partly to blame since it
had created a fertile climate for electoral competition. At the
same time dynamic economic growth was shuffling local hierar-
chies of wealth. For the majority of Massachusetts people the
political outlook known as Federalism seemed to provide the
most reassuring answers.

The presidential election of 1800, which pitted Massachusetts's own John Adams against the Francophile Virginia
Deist, Thomas Jefferson, mobilized Federalism on a broad
scale. The now ancient Samuel Adams, who remained the
staunch Congregationalist he had ever been, vainly tried to defend Jefferson against malicious vituperation in the press and
from the pulpit. But Adams no longer possessed the health and
strength to make a difference, and his old "Puritan republicanism" was becoming anachronistic. The new Republicans in
Massachusetts were friendly to Deists and Baptists—they were
champions of complete freedom of religion—and they were
tinged with anticlerical sentiments. Consequently Republicans
were a vocal, but generally weak, minority during the early
years of the nineteenth century.

Federalism became the new source of integration in Massachusetts public affairs. Pledged to sustain the orthodox religious establishment and to defend the interests of commerce
and manufacturing tradesmen, it commanded great support in
eastern Massachusetts and in the more prosperous, commercially developed towns to the west, particularly in the Connecticut Valley. The Republican minority, which stood for more
open opportunities in religion and economic life, enjoyed its
strongest appeal among the poorer farming towns where Shaysites had once been numerous. Yet the Republicans also commanded support among some artisans and merchants in eastern

towns. Massachusetts was becoming decidedly more heterogeneous in a variety of ways.

The willingness to accept diversity, however, came slowly. For Baptists and other minority denominations, Federalist hegemony meant that full religious equality awaited the 1830s. Minorities, whether religious or political, were much quicker to recognize the necessity of pluralism than were the majorities who still cherished the ideal of uniformity. Congregationalists understood that they would never regain the dominant position they had held in the past; yet they fought a rear-guard action to retain the advantages they still possessed. Federalists, permanently defeated at the national level, still believed they might preserve the commonwealth as a right-thinking enclave. Organizing both inside and outside the legislature, they developed a party structure that reached down to the towns and to precincts within them. By means of their Washington Benevolent Societies they created popular membership associations including thousands of citizens. Although nominally nonpartisan, these societies were instruments of Federalist views. Since most people saw themselves as patriots rather than partisans, membership in a society explicitly devoted to the principles of George Washington was satisfying.

In time the competitive nature of public life became accepted, even ritualized in party politics. Though the rhetoric of religious and secular party conflict remained intense as the issues were refought year after year, the effect of the words diminished. Conventions developed within which the purpose of invective was no longer to destroy the opponent, but rather to arouse one's friends to action. The contestants learned to speak to their own constituencies instead of wasting their effort preaching to opponents who were deaf to their arguments. Within a decade of Jefferson's first election this general acceptance of inflated public rhetoric signaled the emergence of a new era in which diversity and competition would supplant uniformity and unity as reigning public ideals.

The Massachusetts Federalists, self-proclaimed champions of virtue, were a reluctant vehicle of this transition from the colonial past stretching back to Winthrop and Bradford. They won most of their electoral battles with the Republicans, but they lost the war. Like the Puritan magistrates, the Federalists were devoted to the moral and material leadership of men of learning, piety, wealth, and leisure, in the interests of all. The Puritan ideal of a stable, orderly, uniform society, in which people knew their places and behaved accordingly, was also a Federalist ideal. But by the early nineteenth century it was only a dream. Reality required the few to court the many if they hoped to gain their favor. Reality required that competition, within the majoritarian provisions of republican government, determine which persons and policies would rule. Ultimately Massachusetts would be a republic of liberty because liberty was public business, and virtue had become a religious, and therefore private, matter. The commitment to virtue remained powerful, but it was no longer a central objective of the state. For the present, the perennial tension between corporate and individual good was being resolved in favor of individuals. The corporate good, the job of the state now, was to promote liberty for individuals. The preservation of virtue would be their responsibility.

6

The Hive of Industry

⌀Y 1860, little more than a quarter-century after the death of John Adams, Massachusetts had been transformed. The raw young minutemen who marched off to battle on April 19, 1775, now lay in graveyards all over the Bay State and scattered throughout the United States. By the time Abraham Lincoln led the new Republican party to its landslide victory in Massachusetts, romantic legends of the colonial past were springing up, replacing living memory. The old predominance of agriculture and waterborne commerce endured into the first decades of the nineteenth century; yet changes were accumulating. Political continuity with the colonial past had been broken in the 1770s. After 1800 the economy of Massachusetts took on a new character. The population of the state doubled, then tripled, even though the eastern district—Maine—became a separate state. Urban life became predominant. After two centuries, farming was decisively surpassed by manufacturing as the chief occupation and leading source of income in Massachusetts.

The religious and ethnic homogeneity that had prevailed during the eighteenth century, preserving a link between the Revolutionary generation and Winthrop's Bay colony, yielded to diversity. Innovation and variety became characteristic of religious and social life as well as of economic activity. The ideals of uniformity and orthodoxy in religion and politics were overshadowed as competition became the ruling principle in the

129

marketplace of Massachusetts. The vision of the Puritan commonwealth, in which the corporate good defined individual liberty, was reversed. Now it was the thirst for individual liberty that was paramount, defining the public good. Just as the immigrant newcomers to Massachusetts had done, the grandchildren of the minutemen departed from the paths of their forefathers. They were creating new monuments in the Massachusetts landscape—factories, railroads, cities—while they learned to live in unfamiliar surroundings with people who held different views.

The sharp growth in the population of Massachusetts after 1780 demanded a transformation of the economy. Had people remained chiefly dependent on agriculture, they would have sunk ever more deeply into poverty. Prior to the Revolution, during the middle decades of the eighteenth century, Massachusetts had witnessed a marked slowdown in population growth that was significantly related to the near-saturation of productive land. But after 1780, and especially in the decades after 1820, the population grew swiftly, at rates comparable to the most dynamic periods of colonial settlement. Moreover, even though the state was not growing so rapidly as the new nation, the sheer numbers were staggering, given the size and physical character of the state. In 1780 the population had stood at 270,000 people. By 1820 the figure had grown to more than half a million, and in 1860 it reached 1.2 million. The population density had risen from thirty-three persons per square mile in 1780 to 153 persons in 1860. Massachusetts was the most thickly settled state in the union, save only for tiny Rhode Island.

The growth of Massachusetts's population was closely connected to a general pattern of urbanization that was not simply tied to a few cities like Boston or Worcester or Springfield. All over Massachusetts, communities with no more than two or three thousand people at the time of the Revolution grew to five, ten, even twenty thousand by 1860. Because water transportation was largely confined to the eastern counties, eastern Massachusetts enjoyed the most spectacular growth, from Fall River and New Bedford north to Gloucester, Lowell, and Newburyport. Yet inland towns also grew dramatically. Worcester, connecting with Providence by means of the Blackstone River and canal, grew twelvefold, from 2,100 people in 1790 to 25,000 in 1860. Along the Connecticut River, Springfield, Hadley, and Northampton became urban centers, as did Adams and Pittsfield in Berkshire. Here the shift to industrial production arrested an exodus from the region, which, between 1810 and 1820, had caused a decline in the population of Berkshire and the smallest statewide growth rate (11 percent) of the nineteenth century, less than one-third of the national rate.

The urbanization of Massachusetts took several forms. Along the seacoast, old colonial ports had long possessed a quasi-urban character. Many of their inhabitants had always engaged in some branch of commerce, the fisheries or the building, furnishing, and maintenance of shipping. Here the diversity of occupation, wealth, and social background characteristic of a commercial city such as Boston had been visible by the time of the Revolution. Yet though the people of such north-shore towns as Newburyport, Gloucester, and Marblehead, or the south-shore ports of Hingham and Plymouth, might trade in faraway places, they were more insular than they were cosmopolitan. Their greatest passions were aroused by parochial questions, like the threat of contagion from the Marblehead smallpox hospital, the operation of which in the 1770s led to riots among neighbors who carried bitter grudges years later. Even after 1800 in Salem, at that time the most populous and urbane community next to Boston, the great national division between Federalists and Jeffersonians was transformed into a village feud by the fierce rivalries of the Derbys and the Crowninshields. Urbanization certainly was already more advanced in port towns than in the farm hamlets and county seats of the interior. But after 1800 the economic and social diversity in settlements, as well as awareness of the world beyond town and state, would grow so as to make such communities truly urban.

In these port towns urbanization was primarily dependent on commerce. The prosperity generated by trade with the warring European nations before 1807 expanded their economies, and employment and population grew accordingly. But Jeffersonian policies, beginning with the Embargo of 1807 (which stopped American trade with England and France), undermined their growth. Shipbuilding and supply, major industries, came to a virtual standstill. The Federalist mood found expression in irate polemics and ironic verse:

> Our ships all in motion once whitened the ocean,
> They sailed and returned with a cargo;
> Now doomed to decay, they have fallen a prey
> To Jefferson—worms—and embargo.[1]

In order to persuade the European powers to recognize the principle of free trade, Jefferson effectively stopped transatlantic commerce, a severe setback to maritime Massachusetts.

It was not until 1815 that commerce could resume on the global scale of the previous decade, and by then critical changes had occurred. American merchants were no longer middlemen and carriers for a Europe locked in warfare. English competition was intense and successful. Henceforward the port towns would regard the years before the embargo as a halcyon era; and it would be a decade before they returned to comparable levels of activity. On the north shore, Newburyport and Salem would never regain their commercial importance. Nor would Plymouth on the south. Only the commercial eminence of Boston would be enhanced as a centralization of overseas trade developed in the 1820s and 1830s. The urbanization of the lesser port towns might have halted entirely had they not emulated their inland neighbors and become sites for manufacturing.

The rise of industrial enterprises in the interior of Massachusetts was connected directly to the fate of agriculture. So long as farming prospered, few men looked elsewhere for their bread. But from the middle of the eighteenth century onward, more and more farm communities were suffering from a long-term, though intermittent decline. Their populations grew, but the quantity of arable land was fixed, and its productivity was diminishing. The initial response was migration to vacant lands.

---

1. Newburyport, 1808. Quoted in Samuel Eliot Morison, *The Maritime History of Massachusetts, 1783–1860* (1921; Boston: Houghton, Mifflin, 1961), p. 187.

People went first to the northern half of Connecticut and to central and western Massachusetts. After the Revolution they went north into Vermont and New Hampshire, and into Maine. By 1800 a stream of settlers was again heading west, now into the Mohawk valley in New York and beyond into Ohio. Massachusetts's role as exporter of literate, industrious Yankees was established.

Migration, however, was only one solution. The evidence suggests that many farm boys and girls were so strongly committed to their families and their communities that they preferred to sink or swim in Massachusetts. It was this attachment of ordinary people and of merchant capitalists to their native commonwealth that would transform the social and economic landscape of the state within the lifetime of the post-Revolutionary generation. Declining agriculture would stimulate the creation of new transportation facilities, new industries, and specialization in nearly every sphere of activity. These developments exploited existing concentrations of labor and created new ones.

In farming communities, whether county seats or meeting-house villages, industries typically began on a tiny scale. Grist mills and sawmills operated by two or three men had long taken advantage of the water power available in almost every township. Now a paper mill was added, or carding and fulling mills to process homegrown wool were begun. This industrial activity usually processed local farm products such as grain, hides, and fleece, or it supplied common articles of consumption like iron, farm tools, nails, and pins. Most often the industrialization began almost imperceptibly, requiring little capital and employing only small numbers.

Simultaneously people found themselves driven, by lack of other opportunities, to engage in cottage industries, not only spinning, weaving, shoemaking, basket-making, and fashioning wooden implements, but also making wheels and wagons, clapboards and shingles, barrels and pottery. In the past these occupations had been for the hours left over from farming and food-processing, during the winter season. Now, with many farms dwindling in size or having excess labor, they assumed

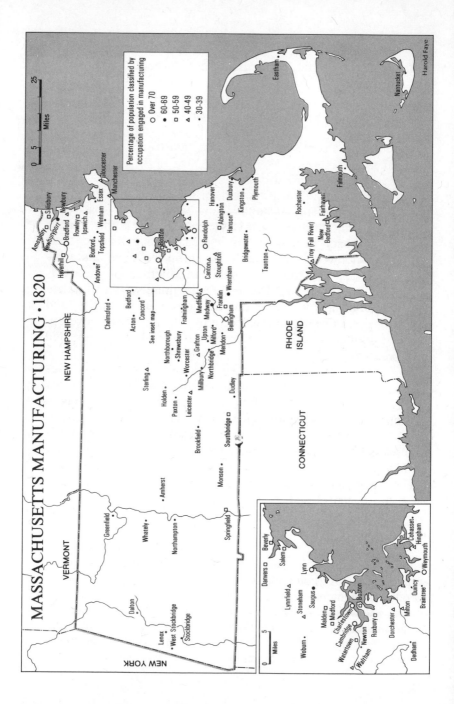

MASSACHUSETTS MANUFACTURING · 1820

Harold Faye

Percentage of population classified by occupation engaged in manufacturing

○ Over 70
● 60-69
□ 50-59
▲ 40-49
· 30-39

Miles
0 5 25

VERMONT

NEW HAMPSHIRE

NEW YORK

Dalton
Lenox
West Stockbridge
Stockbridge

Greenfield
Whately
Northampton
Amherst

Monson
Springfield

CONNECTICUT

RHODE ISLAND

Brookfield
Southbridge
Dudley

Holden
Paxton
Leicester
Worcester
Sterling
Northborough
Shrewsbury
Grafton
Millbury
Upton
Northbridge
Milford
Mendon
Bellingham

Chelmsford
Acton
Bedford
Concord

See inset map

Framingham
Medfield
Medway
Franklin
Wrentham

Salisbury
Amesbury
Newburyport
Haverhill
Bradford
Newbury
Rowley
Ipswich
Wenham
Boxford
Topsfield
Andover

Gloucester
Manchester
Essex

Boston
Randolph
Canton
Stoughton

Hanover
Abington
Duxbury
Hanson
Kingston
Plymouth

Bridgewater
Taunton

Troy (Fall River)
New Bedford
Fairhaven
Rochester
Falmouth

Eastham
Nantucket

Inset map

Miles
0 5

Woburn
Danvers
Beverly
Salem
Lynn
Lynnfield
Stoneham
Saugus
Malden
Medford
Charlestown
Cambridge
Watertown
Waltham
Newton
Dedham
Roxbury
Dorchester
Milton
Quincy
Braintree
Weymouth
Cohasset
Hingham
Boston

new importance, often becoming the chief source of cash. By the first decades of the nineteenth century industry was unobtrusively preserving a veneer of agricultural prosperity in the countryside. Had people been relying on the soil alone, fewer houses would have been neatly painted and fewer of their inhabitants decently clothed.

The more people turned to market production, even on this small scale, the more thoroughly they became enmeshed in the world of commerce. The costs of transportation assumed enormous importance—every dollar spent on transportation meant a dollar lost to the producer. And if inland people wanted to buy what they did not produce, they must pay the freight. For this reason turnpike and canal building and, after 1830, railroad building enjoyed widespread interest and a measure of public support. The locations of these facilities, their crossings and termini, were magnets producing concentrations of population. Market-agriculture and market-industry thirsted for cheap access to customers. As urbanization developed at village crossroads and water sites, it was magnified by new and improved transportation.

But large-scale, conspicuous industrialization and urbanization required large-scale capital expenditures, and it was not until these were forthcoming in the decades after 1810, that dramatic changes took place. The chief sources of this capital were the merchants of Boston and the other port towns. Already in the 1790s they had begun to invest in turnpikes to expand their access to farm and forest products. Later, when Napoleonic warfare and Jeffersonian policy interfered with their trade, they began to consider investments in factories. Yet because industrial profits were small compared to trade, in spite of equivalent risks, there was no rush into industry. Merchant capitalists did not shift their interests until a handful of the boldest and most farsighted among them had demonstrated the immense opportunities for secure, profitable investment in textiles.

The basic technology of textile mills had already been imported from England into Rhode Island and had shown some limited success by the first years of the new century. As a result a boom in cotton-spinning mills had occurred before the onset of the War of 1812. In Massachusetts these tiny mills, each employing several people, were erected in towns that lay along the Merrimack River in Essex, the Charles in Middlesex, the Somerset (now Taunton River) in Bristol, and the Blackstone in the southeast quarter of Worcester County. From an economic standpoint their impact was minimal, and in the entire state they employed scarcely one hundred people. Yet they provided a beginning in the development of a wide pool of mechanics familiar with the rudiments of mill construction and machinery, and they inspired some wealthy men with a vision of far more substantial and sophisticated industrial possibilities.

The most important of these men was a merchant, a native of Newburyport, Francis Cabot Lowell. By 1810 Lowell was well established in Boston and had accumulated substantial reserves of capital. But the uncertain climate of trade made him restless, and in 1810 the thirty-five-year-old Lowell took his wife and children to England for an extended vacation that was supposed to strengthen his health. In England, where the Lowells resided for two years, Francis Lowell became an industrial tourist, exploiting his mercantile connections to gain access to a wide range of Lancashire and Scottish textile operations, from the smallest one-room mill to the great, four-story brick factories where power looms wove hundreds of yards daily. When Lowell returned to Massachusetts in 1812, he had worked out a plan to create a single factory in which he would house all the varied processes required to turn raw cotton into finished cloth. He would need $100,000 in capital, one-sixth of which ($15,000) he was prepared to invest himself. He raised the remaining sum from a small circle of fellow merchants, including his brother-in-law Patrick Tracy Jackson, who was eager to manage the company. With his investment of $20,000, Jackson became the largest single stockholder in the new Boston Manufacturing Company. Lowell and Jackson, who had known each other since boyhood in Newburyport, worked closely together to provide the impetus for innovations that would transform the American textile business and act as a catalyst for the industrialization and urbanization of Massachusetts.

Jackson selected a site six miles west of Boston along the

Charles River, at Waltham, for the great experiment. He bought out an existing paper mill, its land, and its water rights, and it was here that Lowell, with his chief mechanic Paul Moody, created the factory and its machines. Moody was a native of Newbury who had worked as a weaver, in a nail factory, and who had recently worked in Amesbury constructing carding machines for the dozens of small carding mills that were springing up. Like Jackson and Lowell, he was a person of proven abilities in his mid-thirties.

Building and equipping the new factory occupied much of 1813 and 1814, so it was not until after the War of 1812 had ended that the Waltham mill began to produce for the market. Now the English were flooding America with their textiles, and the small mills that had so recently flourished became idle. Postwar reconstruction compounded their problems, and many went bankrupt. The economic climate was so gloomy that from 1817 through 1820 only six new factories were incorporated in the entire state, less than two per year. In 1817 Francis Lowell, the founder of the Boston Manufacturing Company, died, but under Jackson's gifted leadership and Moody's careful and inventive supervision, the Waltham mill succeeded. Sales volume grew tenfold from $3,000 in 1815, the first year of operations, to $34,000 in 1817. It then multiplied ten times more in the next five years, with annual sales reaching $345,000 in 1822. By this time a second, larger mill had been erected. The capital assets of the company had swelled from the initial $100,000 to over three-quarters of a million dollars, and annual dividends were running between 12 and 28 percent. The Waltham mills proved conclusively that even under adverse economic conditions large-scale mills, where all fiber-processing, spinning, and weaving operations were integrated, made money.

In 1812 and 1813 Lowell had solicited only a half-dozen others to join the Boston Manufacturing Company. One of them, Nathan Appleton, a prosperous Boston merchant from New Ipswich, New Hampshire, had been only a reluctant participant. Lowell had asked him for $10,000, but since he had lost earlier investments in cotton manufacture, Appleton had only subscribed $5,000 in what he then believed was a risky venture.

A decade later, with Waltham's profits soaring, Appleton was only too glad to open his purse when Patrick Tracy Jackson approached him with a visionary scheme for the creation of an entire city of mills. Waltham had been good for the Boston Manufacturing Company, and the water site Jackson had arranged there had fully met the original requirements. But their mills at Waltham were enclosed by the existing small-scale industrial and farming settlements, the water power was limited, so there was little opportunity for expansion. By 1820 Jackson realized that what he, Lowell, and Moody had done at Waltham could be multiplied elsewhere almost indefinitely. He wanted to begin at once, and with the backing of Appleton and the Boston trading house of the Scotsmen Boott and Sons, he set about opening a new era in Massachusetts industrial and urban history.

At Waltham the new mills and their dormitories for one hundred, then two hundred mill girls, had substantially altered the face of the town. Still they were augmenting an ongoing process of industrialization and urbanization, and their workers remained a minority among the townspeople. The scale of the Waltham mills, while larger than any others, was not so great that it overwhelmed existing patterns of social and political life. The town had absorbed the mills rather than the reverse. But when Jackson and the newly organized Merrimack Manufacturing Company bought the Pawtucket Falls site in northeast Chelmsford, they set out to transform a pastoral landscape.

Chelmsford, a town of 1,500 people in 1820, twenty-five miles northwest of Boston, was much like a hundred other farming communities. Two-thirds of its inhabitants were farmers, producing the wide range of grains, meats, fruits, and dairy goods that were commonly found on farms which fed themselves while also selling for the market. The Merrimack Canal, built in the 1790s to augment Newburyport's lumber supply for shipbuilding and its provisions for trade, ran through Chelmsford, so it was a more market-oriented town than most in Middlesex and Worcester counties. But its mixture of farming with small industries (employing 31 percent of its adults) made it typical in other respects. Chelmsford village, located in the central part of the town a mile south of the Merrimack and several miles from the Pawtucket Falls site, had its meetinghouse, a few stores, shops, and dwellings. Jackson and the new Merrimack Manufacturing Company did not seek to disrupt it. Their mill city would rise on the open land adjoining the falls and the canal.

Moody and Jackson learned of the site in 1820 and quickly set about acquiring land and water rights. In 1821 they bought up farms and several small mills as well as the existing canal, which ran a mile and a half around the falls. In the following year Jackson's dream became visible. Moody and Jackson began by building a dam across the river and widening and deepening the canal. The latter task required fifty tons of gunpowder for blasting and $120,000, more than the entire capital that founded the Waltham mills. In 1823 these jobs were completed as was the erection of two mill buildings. Machinery for them had already been constructed at the Waltham factory and was installed as soon as the buildings were finished. On September 4, 1823, production began. Moody, who had overseen its construction, called the mill wheel "the best in the world," exclaiming he had never seen "machinery start better." [2] Immediately work began on a third mill, and two more were started the next year. In 1825 the machine shops were moved from Waltham to the new location, where they were housed in a large, five-story brick building. Under Jackson's leadership merchant capital was flooding in. The following year, 1826, the four-square-mile area containing the water site and the surrounding real estate was set off from Chelmsford as a new town, named for the deceased founder of the Boston Manufacturing Company, Francis Cabot Lowell. This first company town, whose population reached 3,500 in 1828, would prove an important model of urbanization for Massachusetts and the United States in the nineteenth century.

In contrast to Waltham, the creation of Lowell required a full

2. Reported by Kirk Boott. Quoted in George Sweet Gibb, *The Saco-Lowell Shops: Textile Machinery Building in New England, 1813–1949* (Cambridge, Mass.: Harvard University Press, 1950), p. 67.

range of urban development to provide housing and amenities for a labor force that was drawn from far and wide to an essentially vacant location. At Waltham it was chiefly local men who were employed to construct buildings and their machinery. Moody, Lowell, and Jackson had supervised the carpenters, masons, and smiths already residing nearby. But the enterprise at Lowell would have overwhelmed the local labor supply, holding back the pace of development. Consequently Jackson imported workers from the British Isles, from rock-strewn farms, and from lesser mills—including five hundred Irish laborers to work on the dam and canal and, a few years later, hundreds of mechanics to build, assemble, and maintain the machines that were used locally and sold to mills from nearby New Hampshire southward to Rhode Island and Connecticut. In addition to dormitories for mill girls, the company built row housing for families, and stores. Indirectly it built schools, churches, and other public buildings. As *the* real estate developer for Lowell, the company fulfilled Jackson's dream of a spacious, fireproof brick city on a gridiron plan, where efficiency, order, and regularity ruled.

Lowell was truly an instant city. In 1836, ten years after it was set off as a town, it was formally incorporated as a city with mayor, alderman, and common council. By now the population had grown to nearly 18,000, and the diversity and cosmopolitanism characteristic of an urban center were evident not only in the complexity of its economic life, but in Lowell's five newspapers and five religious denominations. The city's religious composition, like its economic base, dramatically illustrated the profound departure from the colonial past. Now there was a Catholic church and a Universalist church, as well as two Methodist, three Baptist, and three Congregational chapels and meetinghouses. What was happening in Lowell, the urbanization based on industry, was far more rapid and intense than in other towns. Yet the direction was the same almost everywhere in Massachusetts during the first half of the nineteenth century.

The pace of industrialization and urbanization depended on a wide variety of circumstances. In Worcester the construction of the Blackstone Canal, financed by Rhode Island merchants to expand their commercial hinterland and completed in 1828, provided a major impetus for economic development. Here, no one business was dominant as cotton and woolen mills flourished in the 1830s together with shoemaking, machine shops, paper milling, foundries, and coach making. At Springfield the first major industry was the United States Arsenal, whose gun production thrived during the War of 1812. Later, in the 1820s, Jonathan Dwight, Jr., and his brother Edmund, scions of a powerful dynasty of Springfield merchants, bought the water rights and real estate that lay along the south side of the Chicopee River, four miles south of Springfield Village. Copying the model of Patrick Tracy Jackson and the Merrimack Manufacturing Company, the Dwights formed the Boston and Springfield Manufacturing Company, raising its $500,000 capital from Springfield and Boston merchants including several who were already investors in Waltham and Lowell. Although the scale never matched that of Lowell, the company created a mill village that had 2,000 people by 1835, a decade after production began. These major textile enterprises, together with the armaments and paper industries, which in the 1830s employed over two hundred workers each, gave Springfield an unusually broad base of large industries together with a wide range of smaller ones.

The combination of local and outside investment capital seen at Springfield was common. Thousands of small enterprises in Massachusetts were financed locally, and scores of these, as they grew, attracted support from capitalists in Boston and the other cities. Large-scale enterprise was seldom totally financed by local investors. The all-pervasive industrialization of the state did depend chiefly on local ingenuity, thrift, and continuous reinvestment. In Massachusetts during these decades, even the most agricultural town had more industry than the traditional gristmills, sawmills, and tanneries. An 1837 survey shows that woven palm-leaf hats or pocketbooks, wallets, scythes, buttons, or pins were commonly produced in those few towns that did not possess at least one cotton, woolen, or paper mill. Everywhere the pressure of a rising population on a declining agriculture forced people to use their wits to devise new modes of production.

By 1860 Yankee ingenuity had carved a record of thousands of small successes, dozens of which were truly spectacular. Massachusetts, in addition to leading the nation in shoemaking and textiles, contained industries representing practically the entire spectrum of American manufacturing from A (artificial limbs) to Z (zinc oxide). Indeed, of the six hundred industrial, commercial, and agricultural occupations listed in the United States census of 1860, people in Massachusetts were engaged in more than three-quarters of them. From the standpoint of employment and volume of business, however, there were six areas of activity that dominated the industrial economy: leather goods; textiles; machine-building; metalworking; the extractive industries (forest, fishery, and quarry products); and consumer goods.

Boot and shoemaking, which employed more than 60,000 people in 1860, more than 28 percent of the state's entire industrial labor force, had a long history. Farmers in Lynn, a poor Essex township just to the south of Salem and Marblehead, had built up a large cottage industry of shoemaking before the Revolution, and in succeeding decades Lynn shoes became a standard item in Atlantic trade. By 1860 shoemaking had grown into a vast factory industry with over 25,000 workers in Essex County, 20,000 more in Middlesex and Worcester, and another 15,000 in Plymouth and Norfolk counties. In addition, the demands created by shoe manufacture had led to the development of major leather-processing shops nearby. The boot and shoe trade had such far-reaching influence in the industrial economy that Massachusetts's prosperity rose and fell with it.

In dollar volume, textiles were even more important than shoemaking. Although cotton and woolen mills, being far more intensively capitalized and mechanized, employed fewer people overall, still, with more than 50,000 workers, these mills accounted for nearly one-quarter of all industrial employment. Located in every region from Essex and Bristol west to Berkshire, cloth and carpet manufacture was more broadly diffused

across the state than shoemaking. Middlesex County, the home
of Lowell, possessed the greatest concentration of textile workers (13,000), followed by Essex (9,000), Hampden in the Connecticut Valley (7,000), and Bristol (6,000). By 1860, however, the trend both in shoemaking and textiles was toward
concentration in fewer companies with larger factories. Local
dependence on a particular industry was fast becoming the rule
in many towns.

Machine-building was highly important, not only for the
mechanization of the shoemaking and textile industries but of
other industries in Massachusetts and all over the United States.
By 1860 Massachusetts was one of the leading states in the
production of machinery and machine tools. Although the
growth of machine building was directly tied to textiles and
shoemaking, its origins lay in the colonial era.

Every colonial town had its mill and its blacksmith. The
woodwork required to build a water wheel, power transmission
gears and shafts, as well as home spinning wheels and looms,
had made some carpenters into mechanics, just as elaborate iron
crafting had done the same for blacksmiths. These men built the
cotton and carding mills of the 1780s and 1790s, and the machinery inside them. Using wood for the structural members and
iron at points of pressure and friction, they adapted the skills
and designs of the agricultural past to make machines that had
been invented by the more advanced English textile industry.
By the early years of the nineteenth-century, demand for such
machinery had grown so rapidly that two- and three-man machine shops began to appear first in Rhode Island and then in
Massachusetts. It was in such a shop in Amesbury that Francis
Lowell found Paul Moody, and in constructing the machinery
for the Waltham mills they intensified the pace of machine
building dramatically. Later Moody created and ran the great
machine shop at Lowell, which possessed a wide variety of
drills, lathes, and equipment for cutting, stamping, and hammering. By the 1830s cast-iron was replacing wood in machine
frames, and within two decades machine building would become chiefly a metalworking craft. Because of the high capital
investment and the concentration of highly skilled labor de-

manded, machine building tended to be, as at Lowell and New-ton Upper Falls, directly tied to a textile company or, as in Lynn, connected to a shoemaking firm.

Yet independent machine shops also emerged. Usually they were small, specializing in simple, widely used devices and in the production of particular parts used in other factories. Some-times they built machines that performed a single operation in a complex manufacturing process. In a few cases such small shops grew in size and sophistication to become major suppliers to an entire industry. The Whitin Machine Works, located in Northbridge twelve miles southeast of Worcester on the Mum-ford River, was among the most important and outstanding ex-amples of the indigenous development of machine building. Beginning in 1831 as an offshoot of the Whitin brothers' cotton mill, by the 1840s it became their chief source of profit on the strength of John C. Whitin's patented cotton-picking machine, which was the best in the cotton industry. In the following dec-ade Whitin was employing over five hundred men in his new brick factory, and his workers were producing a full line of cot-ton textile machinery. Business acumen, a ready supply of skilled workers, and Whitin's fortunate location near both the Rhode Island and eastern Connecticut textile mill markets en-abled his enterprise to prosper without infusions of merchant capital.

By 1860 machine shops like Whitin's employed only a frac-tion of the men engaged in metalworking industries. The old co-lonial crafts of the clockmakers and the smiths—gun, silver, and iron—provided the skilled men who, by 1860, had rendered these crafts obsolete while creating new ones. Paul Revere's od-yssey from artist in silver to industrial pioneer, reveals one way in which the transformation to industrial metal work occurred.

At the time of the Revolution Revere had already risen to the pinnacle of his craft in America. After the war, however, he turned his back on the expanding luxury market in silver table-settings and tea services. Instead he and his son Joseph Warren Revere started a foundry in which he could tinker with metal-lurgy. Revere's first important product was church bells; by the 1790s he was casting them in abundance. Revere also produced marine hardware and developed new techniques for machine-drawing and hammering copper and bronze so that the bolts, spikes, and fittings he manufactured undersold English imports. In 1795 Revere won the contract to outfit two United States frigates being built at Boston, and he was able to supply all the necessary parts save one—the copper sheathing for their hulls—which was imported from England.

In 1800, at the age of sixty-five, Revere set out to remedy this lack by establishing a rolling mill. A native of Boston who had spent his entire life there, he was now forced to leave in order to obtain water power. The site he selected in the newly incorporated town of Canton, was a dozen miles south of Boston's North End shipyards. Here, on the Neponset River, he transformed an old slitting mill into the first American rolling mill. Within a year he was producing sheet copper for marine use and for roofing. Revere's copper would not only sheathe American shipping, it would also cover the dome on Charles Bulfinch's Massachusetts State House and the roof of Benjamin Latrobe's New York City Hall. Within a few years Revere would be making copper boilers for steam engines, including the one used on Robert Fulton's first successful steamboat. In later decades when steam engines came into wide use, the technical skills in forging and working copper and brass developed at Canton would help sustain their manufacture in Massachusetts.

Revere was one silversmith who turned from decorative to practical metal work, but most silversmiths stayed with silver, enjoying the popular demand for consumer luxuries that upward aspirations and commercial prosperity nourished. Here, however, the craft was transformed by the desire to meet the burgeoning market for table silver, jewelry, and Victorian ornament. Initially, in the first years of the nineteenth century, craftsmen and their apprentices turned to nickel silver to satisfy their customers. But brittannia ware, an amalgam of antimony, copper, tin, lead, and zinc, was imported from England and undersold it. In the 1820s a Taunton silversmith succeeded in making brittannia metal in his own shop, and from this discovery grew the Reed and Barton factory, which recruited and trained local people. By 1860, when over one hundred men and women worked side by side with Henry Reed and Charles Barton, the silversmith's craft had been subdivided out of existence. Some people specialized in design, others in casting, rolling, pressing, spinning, and soldering; and the final appearance was created in separate polishing, plating, and engraving operations. Reed's standards of craftsmanship were the highest in the industry, but while his product surpassed the work of a journeyman silversmith, it would never match the aesthetic heights of a Revere. For the decorative arts like silver and cabinetmaking the new mass production had costs as well as benefits.

When it came to wholly utilitarian goods, however, mass-produced articles equaled or exceeded the standards of old-time artisans. Factories in Bristol and Worcester counties made cutlery and edged tools—scythes and axes, hoes, shovels, and plow blades—that were cheap and durable. Machine-made wire, nails, spikes, and other hardware were equally satisfactory and had the additional advantages of uniformity and, increasingly, standardization. Metalworking shops were never on a scale comparable to the great textile mills, but they did concentrate labor around water-power sites.

The extractive industries—quarrying, lumber, and fishing—made a smaller impact on urbanization. Towns did not grow into cities because of local quarries, forests, or fishing grounds. Quarries, like those at Quincy, were worked by small teams of men and animals who, after blasting and cutting the stone, hauled it to a railway or a barge. Because transportation costs were so high, no quarry could serve an extensive area, and so the common pattern was for small, localized quarries for marble, granite, and slate.

The pattern for lumber was similar, although for different reasons. Timber trees were scattered through much of central and western Massachusetts and were most often logged by farmers during the winter. Centralization of milling, except to a degree along the Connecticut River, was not feasible. Consequently the dispersion of sawmills characteristic of the colonial era continued. But the mills grew in size and in the complexity of their operations as circular saws, planers, and other milling machinery came into use. Still, few mills had as many as a dozen employees. It was pulp-paper mills, just beginning in the 1860s, far more than lumber mills, that would create large factories and urban concentrations.

Even more than forest industries, fishing was tied to its colonial origins. On the North Shore, Gloucester and Marblehead, fishing centers for two centuries, remained fishing ports as their role in sea-borne commerce declined. Fishing also remained important in the town of Plymouth. On thinly populated Cape Cod, fishing was, next to farming, the chief occupation. Cod and mackerel supported about two thousand families, almost one-third of the population. Primacy in whaling, once belonging to Nantucket and Martha's Vineyard, had passed across Buzzard's Bay to New Bedford. Like other forms of fishing, whaling was entering a decline, but in 1860 it still supported 50,000 people in southeastern Massachusetts and the islands. In New Bedford, supplying the whale ships and processing and distributing their catch provided the employment to generate major urbanization, and its population exceeded 10,000 by the mid-1830s. By 1860, New Bedford and the adjoining textile city of Fall River formed one of the great urban areas in the entire United States, both ranking among the top twenty-five manufacturing cities in the nation.

The production of consumer goods, items like clothing, home furnishings, musical instruments, books, reflected the radical change in American ways of life between 1800 and 1860. These were the years when semi-self-sufficient farming all but disappeared, and the ideals of bourgeois comfort and amenities characteristic of the Victorian age supplanted the rustic simplicity that religious beliefs and economic realities had forced on the majority of the people from Winthrop's day to John Hancock's. But Massachusetts produced consumer goods for the national market as well as for home consumption. As a result, though consumer industries were located in every corner of the state, they were concentrated in the most commercially accessible areas—in Boston and its environs and along the railways that now connected Massachusetts to neighboring states.

The range of such industries was almost endless, buttons and bedsteads, cigars and spectacles, stove polish and perfume, candy and combs. Virtually anything money could buy was being produced in the state where, two centuries before, sumptuary laws had required frugality. In farming areas some of these were still cottage industries; farm wives wove straw baskets and bonnets. In Boston, the hub of commerce, politics, and administration, production of consumer goods had become the leading occupation.

No one regarded Boston as a factory city, nor was it dominated by large-scale industries in the manner of Lowell, Chicopee, or Fall River. Yet as early as 1820 the census had shown a majority of its workers employed in production rather than trade. At that time, in the early decades of the century, shipbuilding remained the largest single industry, and most of the others catered directly to the needs of trade, like barrel making, or else to the urban market. Boston itself grew rapidly after 1790, breaking out from the commercial plateau that had held the population close to 16,000 for two generations since the 1730s. By 1800 Boston grew to 25,000, and in the 1830s, when the population shot past the 60,000 mark, Boston was being transformed into an immense city. By 1860 its population exceeded 180,000, ten times its size in 1790.

Most of the people who produced for the consumer market labored in small shops with half-a-dozen or a dozen co-workers. Ready-made clothing, for which the chief equipment was the scissor, the needle, and the sewing-machine, made small demands on space and so was well suited to Boston and other cities. Furniture, too, was a labor-intensive product that did not require much space, and which benefited from proximity to market. Boston's role as a cultural center for New England and the United States was also reflected in its industries. In 1860 close to one thousand men were at work making musical instruments, mostly pianos, for the national market. An even larger number was occupied with printing and bookbinding. In some ways industrial Boston was old-fashioned, dominated by artisan craftsmen whose wares recalled the eighteenth century.

Yet there were some products, such as steam engines and

sewing-machines, that represented the most advanced technology. Indeed even the Boston-built clipper ships, whose glory would fade quickly after 1860, were the swiftest, most advanced vessels of their day. While technological skills were widely dispersed across the state, they were nowhere more abundant or sophisticated than at Boston.

There was one Boston industry, the construction of fireproof safes, that suggested Boston's emergence as a white-collar city of banking and insurance. Although outpaced by New York, Boston had developed as a key center for money management. As it had in New York and Philadelphia, the eighteenth-century experience in insurance and banking, combined with the local concentration of commercial capital, had produced the basis for vast enterprises that by 1860 made Boston, with its army of black-coated clerks, a national financial capital. Even though most investments remained at home in Massachusetts, immense sums went south and west to finance the cotton trade, railroads, and commerce.

The calculating, rational viewpoint that pervaded capitalism in Massachusetts did not distinguish it from other places in the north. Yet in Massachusetts this spirit was part of a general outlook that was, there more than anywhere else, sustained by a panoply of organized activities devoted to progressive improvement. Financiers computed risks and returns with the object of maximum profit, while all around them people with other objectives were investing their efforts in human capital—schools and colleges, lyceums and libraries. Massachusetts's innovative economic development rested on a literate population that was committed to improvement through education.

The heritage of public investment in primary and higher education stretched back to the first generation of settlement in the Bay Colony, but the explosion of interest in education during the first half of the nineteenth century was in response to a fresh enthusiasm for popular education sustained by the new republicanism and the evangelical spirit of the Second Great Awakening, as well as more practical motives of upward mobility. Moreover, in contrast to Puritan education, which had emphasized tax-supported, formal grammar and college training to prepare clergymen and magistrates to supervise the people, the desire for education now encompassed the entire population. Formal schooling, both public and private, as well as informal access to learning and books, shared equally in the new education movement.

In the eighteenth century the chief route to elite status had been the Latin schools that were publicly maintained in prosperous villages in every county. From there, one sought admission to Harvard. As time went on, classes at the college grew larger, and more and more of its graduates chose to pursue careers in law and commerce for the sake of personal advancement rather than the public good. By 1800 the idea that education opened the doors to wealth and prestige was firmly established.

The common English schools of eighteenth-century farming towns provided their students with practical skills in reading, writing, and arithmetic, but they did not lead to Harvard. Popular education provided only the bare essentials for a pious and productive life. Yet after the Revolution the desire for elite schooling expanded. The same people who were seeking prosperity in the marketplace and displaying it in pilastered and pedimented houses all over the commonwealth wanted opportunity for their children. Yet most towns were not so prosperous that farmers were ready to support a grammar school out of taxes. The solution was the private or quasi-private academy, by which aspiring parents with sufficient cash joined together to expand the opportunity for further education. Scores of academies sprang up after 1790, sometimes preparing students for college, but more often providing the terminal education for would-be republican gentlemen and their wives. Ultimately most of them were replaced by or merged with public high schools, but during the first half of the century, and beyond, they educated thousands of men and women.

The same kinds of aspirations broke Harvard's monopoly on collegiate education. In 1790 a college was founded in the northwest corner of the state at Williamstown, supported by the bequest of Colonel Ephraim Williams (a local hero of the French and Indian War), by local subscriptions, and by a state lottery. Thirty years later, notwithstanding Harvard's opposi-

tion, a more centrally located college was created by Connecticut Valley leaders at Amherst. Sustained by the prosperity of
the valley towns, Amherst quickly grew into a major institution
with several hundred students. In 1837 in the neighboring town
of South Hadley, a schoolteacher named Mary Lyon founded
still another college, Mount Holyoke Female Seminary, designed "to give a solid, extensive, and well-balanced English
education. . . . which will prepare ladies to be *educators*." [3]
Supported by the donations of nearly two thousand people from
about ninety Massachusetts towns, and aided by two Amherst
College professors, Lyon opened her seminary with more than
one hundred students. This was the first college anywhere in the
United States devoted to women's education, and the first
created for the purpose of training teachers.

Mary Lyon, who came from Buckland, a poor farming town
in the hills of nearby Franklin County, had grasped two of the
dynamic forces that were operating in Massachusetts and
throughout the north: the liberation of women from exclusively
domestic roles; and the growing desire for high-quality primary
education for every child. Mary Lyon began her teacher-training
seminary in precisely the year that the General Court created the
office of state superintendent of education, a post filled by
Horace Mann, a lawyer and state senator who was to become
the nationwide leader of the movement to improve the common
schools.

Horace Mann came from the town of Franklin on the Rhode
Island–Massachusetts border, and he attended college at Brown,
the Baptist college in Providence. For him, the orientation of
existing schools represented a threat to republican society.
Mann complained that common public schools were run by
local boards at minimum expense—for classrooms, teachers, and
books—and that as a result a meager literacy was the most they
could provide. In his view the public schools were the crucial
nurseries of a republican citizenry. Their morale should be high,
they should be well equipped, and their instructors should be

3. From the catalogue, quoted in John Warner Barber, *Historical Collections* . . .
of Every Town in Massachusetts (Worcester, 1841), p. 339.

moral and cultural models for whom teaching was a genuine vocation rather than a stop-gap between college and a career in law or trade. High standards of performance should be the rule rather than the exception.

In the dozen years Mann held office, he waged a successful uphill struggle to lengthen the school year, raise teachers' salaries, and create normal schools to train teachers. His support came largely from educated leaders in eastern Massachusetts, including industrialists and financiers, who shared his goal of uplifting the common people and educating them for industrial society. From their perspective, public education was a crucial source of public order, and their patronage expressed their desire to influence the values and culture of the masses. But Mann also drew on the spirit of evangelical Protestantism, which, during the 1820s and 1830s, had led to the founding of well over one hundred Sunday schools. Mann's concern for practical, civic, and moral education, combined, gave his appeals broad support even though they did cost money and did tend to centralize power in the state board of education at the expense of localities.

Popular belief in education beyond reading, writing, and arithmetic was the driving force behind the voluntary, adult-oriented educational efforts of the period. Beginning in the 1790s there was a great burst of library founding, more than forty in that one decade alone. Generally these were subscription libraries founded by many of the same people who interested themselves in academies. But as time went on, most libraries became broadly accessible, and by 1860 many were entirely public. By this time lyceums, local lecture-and-discussion clubs, were going full force in scores of towns. These lyceums, conceived by a man from Millbury, near Worcester, Josiah Holbrook, joined the ideas of self-help and expert instruction with the belief in the uplifting effects of social intercourse. Initially confined to men, who each discoursed on his own specialties to his fellows, lyceums quickly became open to everyone from the age of fourteen up. Mechanical and scientific subjects made room for history, geography, and literature as the lyceums became agencies of general knowledge and culture. Education was not simply for children; it was for everyone.

Education in its broadest sense—the acquisition and exchange of knowledge—became one of the leading forms of recreation for people as the specialized, industrial economy gave them more leisure time. For people with Puritan antecedents, recreation that was more cerebral than physical, more uplifting than exhausting, and oriented toward words rather than actions, was appealing. Among all classes and occupations, the demand for reading matter was intense. It was satisfied in the first instance by newspapers, by 1860 scores of them.

The Massachusetts press was the oldest in the nation, the first book in America having been printed at Cambridge in 1640, and the first newspaper, the *Boston News-Letter,* in 1704. By the middle of the nineteenth century, New York was established as the leading national center of publishing, but Boston remained important especially for literary and learned publications. As early as 1815 the *North American Review* had become the most notable literary periodical in the country. Later, in the 1840s, Margaret Fuller and Ralph Waldo Emerson had edited the *Dial,* a transcendentalist journal. In the following decade the *Atlantic Monthly* appeared under the direction of James Russell Lowell. These magazines emanating from Massachusetts were among the principal vehicles of literary culture in the United States.

Most people, however, were reading political and religious newspapers rather than the best literary journals. What was wanted was a continuous supply of information—including "news," essays, and advertising—so all over Massachusetts print shops responded. Generally people took papers that reinforced their preferences in a world where their own beliefs were increasingly assaulted by contending viewpoints. For as the industrialization and urbanization of Massachusetts proceeded, daily encounters were more often heterogeneous, with people whose ethnicity and class differed, and who held competing views on politics and salvation.

Some heterogeneity had been part of Massachusetts life at least from the Great Awakening. But the rapid pace of commercial and industrial developments after 1800 helped to expand its range and penetration dramatically. The experience of Lowell, a heterogeneous community growing up on the site of Congregational, Yankee Chelmsford, differed in degree but not in kind from the emerging pattern of experience all over the commonwealth. Religious uniformity yielded first to diversity and then to economic development, which sustained immigration, extended the range of social variation.

The splintering of Congregational orthodoxy, which began in the eighteenth century, destroyed Congregational hegemony early in the nineteenth century, and reduced it to a minority religion long before the Civil War. The explosive growth of Baptist and Methodist groups drew common people away from the old establishment, while clergymen and deacons were themselves dividing over the issue of trinitarianism. In eastern counties Unitarianism frequently triumphed, and the Harvard of the Mathers emerged as the capital of the new creed. Yet here, too, a split developed, and a more popular, emotional Universalism grew up alongside the refined rationalism of Unitarians. Immigration, chiefly from the British Isles, reinforced these patterns, bringing new adherents to a dozen different sects.

When the massive Irish immigration began in the 1840s, Roman Catholicism, until then a small denomination whose worship was confined to Boston, became a mighty force. Within the period of one generation Catholics became the largest single denomination in Boston, and the fifth largest in the state. As of 1860 the concentration of Irish natives was greatest in Boston (Suffolk County), comprising about one-third of the entire population. But the Irish had also spread out from Boston. Nearly one-quarter of the people in Middlesex and Norfolk counties were Irish-born, and farther away in Essex and Bristol, and even in Hampden and Berkshire, in the west, almost one-fifth of the inhabitants had come from Ireland. Although people were also coming from Scotland, England, and Wales as well as continental Europe, the predominance of the Irish was so pronounced as to make them almost synonymous with immigrants.

The experience of these Irish country people and the heritage of the Catholic church favored uniformity, yet as a minority in

Massachusetts they immediately reinforced the trend toward cultural pluralism. They did not necessarily like dealing with Yankee Protestants on a daily basis, and many Yankees were hostile to them. But the expanding industrial economy had room for a quarter of a million immigrants in the 1840s and 1850s, and quickly put tens of thousands of Irish men and women to work in construction, in factories, and in domestic services.

The Massachusetts Irish had come to stay. Their presence brought a whole new dimension to the development of pluralism, since Yankees widely regarded them as fundamentally "different" from other white people, and believed that the Catholic church was the religious embodiment of tyranny and corruption. A decade before the great migration of the 1840s, Yankees had rioted against Catholics, destroying a convent two miles from Boston in Charlestown. In the past, anti-Catholicism had been an accepted element in the religious and political ideologies that dominated the colonial and Revolutionary eras. Until the 1840s pluralism developed within the boundaries of Protestantism, indeed the Constitutional tie between Congregationalism and the state had only been severed finally in 1833. Now, in the 1840s and 1850s, the boundaries were being pressed outward to include Catholics.

Although there were no more riotous attacks on Catholics, Massachusetts had entered a period of the sharpest conflict and social anxiety it had known since the Revolution. Simultaneously its people and their institutions were forced to adjust to industrialization, urbanization, ethnic and religious diversity, and to increasing disparities of wealth. The order and equilibrium of the eighteenth century vanished with disconcerting speed and finality well before 1860. At the same time, Massachusetts's role in national government was receding from the pinnacle of the Revolutionary crisis. John Adams, whose wartime credentials placed him on a footing with Washington and Jefferson, had been the only Massachusetts man to gain election to the presidency in the electoral college, and his son John Quincy Adams, who served in the 1820s, had been the only other president from Massachusetts. During the decades from Independence to 1860 Massachusetts's rank in population had declined from third among the states to seventh, with a corresponding decline in her congressional strength. In 1790 the delegates from Massachusetts had comprised thirteen percent of the House and seven percent of the Senate, but in 1860 their numbers had dropped to four percent and three percent respectively. While Massachusetts society was under strain from within, state leaders recognized that her influence in national government was shrinking.

Yet this seeming "eclipse" of Massachusetts in national affairs concealed the new role that its people were playing in leading Americans to confront the central social and political issues of the nineteenth century. Because Massachusetts became industrial and urban before the rest of the nation, and because its people were facing the challenges of competition and pluralism, the tensions in Massachusetts society anticipated those of the nation at large. In formal political terms, perhaps, Massachusetts was lagging, but in adapting to a dynamic, heterogeneous world, Massachusetts was in the vanguard. It was in the Bay State that the key social and political issues of the day were being tested—questions of race and ethnicity, of education and social responsibility, of economic development and individual rights. The old problem of reconciling individual and corporate goals emerged again as the Massachusetts of old, where farmers, fishermen, tradesmen, and merchants were bound together in a deferential, congregational society, was transformed into an urban, industrial commonwealth.

7

Missions to the Nation

$\mathcal{T}$HE first half of the nineteenth century in America was an age of paradoxes. Physical expansion, economic development, and material prosperity nourished boundless optimism, while at the same time evangelical preachers proclaimed to millions of eager listeners that depravity and corruption lurked everywhere. Perfectionist optimism flourished alongside millenarian gloom. Americans celebrated individual self-assertion and autonomy, while they urged others to conform. Libertarian beliefs echoed from pulpits and platforms, as did eloquent apologias for the virtues of both chattel slavery and wage labor. Individualism and corporatism prospered, as did commitments to egalitarianism and hierarchy. America was a society where contradictory impulses fed repeated conflicts.

In the minds of contemporaries these were struggles between fundamental truths, commanding loyalties that erased the boundaries between states. When the future of the nation, perhaps all mankind, was at stake, one's attachment to a single locality was overshadowed. It was in this context that Massachusetts, like other states, began to lose its particular identity. More than in most places, the people of the Bay State became involved with the general issues that excited concern. Indeed Massachusetts emerged as a nursery for the missionaries of a hundred causes. The dollars-and-cents commercial and industrial energies of Massachusetts people, which sent their products all over the United States, found a counterpart in the religious and social activism that spread their ideas and doctrines across the continent. Massachusetts was the metropolis of New England during the era of that region's cultural imperialism. Though Massachusetts's distinctiveness was waning, its people put their stamp on the culture of the American republic.

They were concerned with everything. Some embraced highly controversial, divisive causes like abolition, temperance, and women's rights, while others pursued objectives that were broadly appealing: improved education, moral reform, and higher standards of public health and personal hygiene. Advocacy of a cause was always clothed in benevolence, but traces of partisan, denominational competition showed through. Advocates of every ideal were propelled onward by a spirit of optimism. Even the most apocalyptic visionaries raised their voices, confident that people could act to save themselves and their fellows. The promoters of prison reform and therapeutic care of the physically and mentally handicapped represented the quintessential merger of the optimism and altruism that were widely evident. Such movements transcended Massachusetts, but they were shaped by people who had not only been born and raised there, but who had begun their public careers confronting the failings of their native commonwealth. Their criticisms of American society began at home, in the state where rapid social and economic changes made the contradictions between individual and collective goals, between new aspirations and old values, especially acute.

The sensitivity to the faults of this world as well as the belief that people must actively intervene to erase them, had both secular and religious origins. The republicanism of the early national era was profoundly moralistic, and virtue—private and public—was one of its fundamental tenets. The United States, if it possessed virtue, would become a utopia of liberty, justice, and social happiness; so the good citizen was obliged to cultivate improvements in a public as well as a personal way. The second Great Awakening, which emerged in the 1790s and endured for several decades, prescribed a kind of piety that was parallel to this civic virtue. Moreover the Awakening generated a contagious energy and immediacy to the drive for virtue. In peacetime, as patriotic fervor waned, the ambition for salvation more than took up the slack. Gospel piety, even more than patriotism, propelled people to seek out others, exhort, and persuade them to support virtuous causes.

Like the first Great Awakening, the evangelical movement of the early nineteenth century had no political boundaries. In Massachusetts the movement had no central leader nor any particular geographic source. Everywhere the second half of the eighteenth century had witnessed a decline in religious concern and a tendency toward a placid Arminianism, where ethical conduct and sober respectability were sufficient for grace. In the more cosmopolitan towns in eastern Massachusetts, this turn away from orthodox Calvinism had become a trend, and even before 1800 a liberal (in the sense of nonsectarian) Unitarianism was evident in a handful of congregations. In Massachusetts, the second Great Awakening was an effort to reverse this trend, to re-establish Divine will, conversion, and faith as the essence of Christianity. Whether Congregational, Baptist, or Methodist, this was the crucial objective.

The conflict between religious liberals and conservatives lasted for generations and was fought in thousands of communities across the United States, and hundreds in Massachusetts. But the single most important battlefield in the Bay State was Harvard College, still the seminary for Congregational Massachusetts. The struggle began in 1803 when David Tappan (uncle of the later abolitionists Arthur and Lewis Tappan) died, thus vacating the Hollis Professorship of Divinity. By this time the faculty of Harvard and its trustees were evenly divided into orthodox and Unitarian factions, and the Hollis professorship promised to tip the balance decisively one way or the other. For two years the professorship remained vacant as the battle raged in college halls and drawing-rooms. Finally, in 1805, the Unitarians triumphed, naming one of their own, the Hingham pastor Henry Ware, to the post. Pressing their advantage, they replaced the acting president, who was orthodox, with another Unitarian. Defeated, the Calvinist trustees and faculty resigned from the college in a storm of protest, and Unitarianism became the new Harvard orthodoxy. Until the Civil War and beyond, Harvard would remain the principal beacon of the "Christian Enlightenment" in America and the school for numerous social commentators and reformers.

The orthodox retreated from Harvard, but they were not defeated. Although their resources were dispersed, their supporters were numerous and intensely devoted. Within two years they had created a rival theological college at Andover, financed chiefly by people from Newburyport, Salem, and Andover. In 1808 they admitted the first class, housed in a new four-story brick building. From the outset they flourished, and so by the 1820s the school was expanded to accommodate more than sixty students, drawn from several colleges, principally Williams, Yale, and later Amherst. Andover became a center of the awakening in Massachusetts and a focal point for a whole range of missionary endeavors.

The New England Tract Society, founded at Andover in 1814, was to serve as a training ground for numerous efforts on behalf of virtue. English evangelists had already demonstrated that distributing tracts by the millions was both practical and effective. The New England society, renamed the American Tract Society in the 1820s, was built on the premise that "god has made every man responsible for the use or abuse of his personal influence," and everyone was "sacredly bound to employ it in doing good." Cheap tracts enabled all Christians to do the work of salvation actively. For people who were personally diffident, for one who lacked "the talent of talking to those he meets with, especially to strangers, on subject of religion," the tracts offered *"an easy way of doing good."* [1] The movement to place uplifting homilies in the hands of the masses was led by clergymen who were often distribution agents, but the dues-paying members who enlisted in the cause were mostly laymen—merchants, shopkeepers, lawyers, teachers, and middle-class farmers and artisans. A mood of pious condescension toward those who were too ignorant or too poor to provide themselves with the gospel pervaded the movement.

1. *Publications of the American Tract Society* (n.p., 1824), pp. 6, 9.

The problems of infidelity, obviously, were not unique to Massachusetts, and the objectives of the founders were national in scope. But the motivation for the society and the methods it adopted were closely related to the growing commercialization and urbanization of the state. More people were "free-floating" in society, unattached to any church. As commerce and travel expanded and village populations rose, the pious became more aware of profaneness in the behavior and beliefs of others. At the same time the expanded commercial network and the ready access to the printing press made the idea of mass distribution of tracts feasible. In a few years thousands of people in Massachusetts, both men and women, would be contributing their pennies, dimes, and dollars to a cause which relied on a Christian cosmopolitanism that had been almost unknown in eighteenth-century communities.

In one sense, however, the national and even global objectives of Massachusetts organizations like the Tract Society and the later American Bible Society and the Sunday School Union were highly provincial in that virtue in Massachusetts became the standard for people everywhere. Winthrop's old vision of Massachusetts as a city upon a hill was revived and extended so that not only would Massachusetts become the model to be admired and emulated from afar, but its citizens would personally sally forth to awaken those who slumbered, whether in New York, Ohio, or China. Such missionary activities spawned in the Second Great Awakening would influence the character of abolitionism, temperance reform, and many purely secular endeavors.

The viewpoint of religious liberals was more thoroughly cosmopolitan. With their headquarters at Boston, the commercial hub of New England, the Unitarians were appropriately tolerant and urbane. Their foremost leader, William Ellery Channing, was a native of the sophisticated, pluralistic seaport, Newport, Rhode Island. Channing had come to Harvard for college in the 1790s, and after a brief period as a schoolmaster in Richmond, Virginia, returned permanently to Boston in 1803 as pastor of the Federal Street church. From this prestigious pulpit Channing came to exert a profound influence on young reformers and intellectuals in eastern Massachusetts. Many of them—Ralph Waldo Emerson and Theodore Parker, Horace Mann and Charles Sumner, Dorothea Dix and Thomas Wentworth Higginson—regarded him as their mentor for a time, and after his death in 1842 Channing was described as "the *saint* of the Unitarians." [2] Channing's ideas were complex, but at their core lay a simple faith in the necessity of supporting universal truths that were, by their nature, good. Reason and morality permitted mankind to distinguish good and evil, and it was men's responsibility to be moral agents. Though the inspiration was different from Cotton Mather's, the injunction was the same, to do good.

Both the Christian conservatives and the liberals placed great confidence in the individual's ability to grasp the truth and to develop self-discipline. Moreover, even though the Calvinists were pessimistic about the essential nature of humanity, they were hopeful that untold millions could be saved by God's grace. In this setting nearly everyone was taught at an early age to make his own moral judgments, and pressed to develop an active conscience, no matter what his denomination, social class, or community. The missionary generation of antebellum Massachusetts was nurtured in an era of strong partisan identities in politics and religion. The willingness to advocate one's beliefs, to stand up and be counted, was a normal requirement of growing up.

Missionaries and reformers were born in all parts of the commonwealth, from the eastern district of Maine to Berkshire County. Yet for most of them Boston was a major site of their activities. Boston, after all, was the seat of state government and possessed the greatest concentration of population and wealth. It was also the chief communication center for New England. Moreover Boston's rapid growth during the first half of the century made its problems of poverty, crime, and drunkenness especially conspicuous. Some of the causes espoused by reformers were universal and had no particular connection to urban or industrial development, but because Boston was increas-

---

2. Ernest Renan, quoted in Daniel Walker Howe, *The Unitarian Conscience* (Cambridge, Mass.: Harvard University Press, 1970), p. 20.

ingly becoming the central metropolis, it was a place to launch movements and was a magnet for them.

Dorothea Lynde Dix, born in the frontier town of Hampden, Maine, in 1802, was descended from prominent Boston and Worcester families, but her own parents were poor, and she learned to endure hardships early. Her mother suffered chronically from poor health, and her father, who had no head for business, became an itinerant Methodist preacher who was frequently away from home. Until she was twelve, Dorothea Dix often had charge of her two younger brothers, but then her grandmother Dix intervened, and Dorothea moved to Boston to live with her. Two years later she was sent to live with a great-aunt at Worcester, and it was here that her talents began to emerge. In her great-aunt's barn, at the age of fourteen, Dorothea opened a school to teach poor children their abc's. Although she was herself largely self-taught, Dix would later make a career in Boston as a schoolmistress. Her first published writings would be a children's textbook in science and a collection of poetry designed for children. Then, in the late 1820s, she became governess in the family of her new pastor, William Ellery Channing. Under Channing's influence, Dix became an author of liberal devotional writings for youth, and in the 1830s she opened a school of her own in Boston. In 1836, however, she suffered a nervous breakdown and so was forced to give up the school. When her doctor prescribed travel, she visited the British Isles, staying with Channing's acquaintances. It was here that she first became seriously aware of humane methods of caring for people who were mentally disturbed. Dix returned to Boston the following year and, supported by her grandmother's legacy, spent several years visiting friends, traveling, and "resting."

Dix's "conversion" to the work of a reformer occurred in 1841 when, at the request of a Harvard divinity student, she volunteered to teach a Sunday school class to the women in the East Cambridge jail. Here she discovered disturbed women who were treated cruelly although they were guilty of no crime. Dix identified with these forlorn souls, and she was outraged. Immediately she took the matter to the Middlesex Court, and to

Channing's friend Samuel Gridley Howe, who supported her cause in the press. Here Dix won her first victory, and the jail was renovated, the better to accommodate the mentally ill.

For Dorothea Dix this was all new and exciting, but actually others had been working for a generation to provide not merely humane conditions, but genuinely therapeutic care for people who suffered with mental sickness. In 1818 a private hospital, McLean, had been opened at Boston, and in the same period Louis Dwight's Boston Prison Discipline Society had been working to improve conditions in jails and in the treatment of inmates, and to separate the poor, the sick, and the juveniles from criminal convicts. During the years when Dix was running her school, Horace Mann was leading the movement in the General Court to create a state mental hospital, and in 1833 it was opened at Worcester. Six years later it was already overcrowded, so Boston established its own lunatic asylum. Thus Dorothea Dix, who discovered the cause of the mentally ill in 1841, was a latecomer to a movement that had scored major advances in Massachusetts and several other states.

Yet it was Dix who transformed the cause into a national campaign by her contagious zeal, her audacity, and her masterful appeals to public opinion. Encouraged by Howe and Channing, Dix began by making a thorough personal inspection of every jail and almshouse in the entire commonwealth. For eighteen months she traveled from town to town making herself the unrivaled expert on the actual conditions that prevailed. Then, in 1843, she presented the legislature with a devastating written report on what she had found—cruelty, degradation, and disease. Weeks later the General Court voted the funds to expand Worcester State Hospital, in spite of arguments that such a policy represented a further unwarranted expansion of the state government and its budget at the expense of the towns.

With this victory, Dorothea Dix became something of a celebrity among reformers, and she was soon in demand in other states. In 1844 and 1845 she extended her investigations to Rhode Island, New York, and New Jersey, in each case preparing a muckraking report that called on the legislatures of those states to follow Massachusetts's example and create (or expand) a state mental hospital. Her *Remarks on Prison and Prison Discipline in the United States* (1845) was widely read, and during the next several years Dix was active in southern states—Kentucky, Maryland, Mississippi, Alabama, Tennessee, and North Carolina—as well as northern ones—Pennsylvania, Ohio, and Illinois. Though she could never singlehandedly arouse a legislature to action, her influence was formidable, and in 1848 she set her sights on the creation of a national trust to finance a program to care for disturbed people throughout the country. The public lands were being used to finance schools and railroads, Dix argued, so why not mental hospitals? In time the scheme won support, passing both the House and the Senate in 1854. But President Franklin Pierce, echoing the arguments that had been heard in Massachusetts and elsewhere, asserted this would be an improper extension of national powers. The problem, he said, belonged to the states, and he vetoed the bill.

Dix was sadly defeated, and as she had twenty years before, she returned to Europe. Now, however, she needed no introductions from Channing. Soon she became involved in promoting the cause in Scotland and all over the Continent, from France to Russia and even into the Ottoman Empire. Before she returned to America, Dix had pressed her views on a wide array of dignitaries, including Pope Pius IX. No one from Massachusetts, and no American woman had ever possessed such a far-reaching influence in the United States and abroad.

Yet by the late 1850s the American effort on behalf of treatment for the mentally ill was largely spent. Even in Massachusetts the public hospitals had become custodial welfare institutions for the indigent, rather than centers of medical treatment. Dix and her colleagues had eliminated the worst physical abuses, and they had succeeded in liberating their charges from jails, but they could not fulfill the promise of therapeutic care. It was beyond the reach of taxpayer support and also largely beyond the capability of psychiatric medicine. The state mental hospitals that were Dix's legacy—she was directly involved in the creation of over thirty around the country—were a distinct improvement over local cellars and outbuildings, but lacking the capacity for treatment, they gradually became prisons of a sort, where society hid its least fortunate people from view. Dix's crusade had been founded on the optimism of her generation, a faith that flourished in the early decades of the century.

Samuel Gridley Howe was just a year older than Dorothea Dix, but his upbringing and his gender gave him a very different start. In contrast to Dix, Howe began with opportunities. He was born into a well-to-do Boston family and educated at the Boston Latin School. He would have attended Harvard: however, his father, who was fed up with stuffy Federalists, broke with convention and sent Samuel to Brown, where he was a contemporary of Horace Mann. Upon graduation in 1821, Howe returned to Boston to enroll in the Harvard Medical School. But he did not pursue a medical career in the usual way. Indeed Howe quickly distinguished himself as the archetypal romantic, at least for a Massachusetts Yankee. When his studies were complete, he did not open an office on Court Street, he enlisted on behalf of the Greek war of independence from Turkey. Sailing to the Mediterranean, he became a soldier and surgeon who for six years fought with and cared for the Greek and Polish revolutionaries, also leading a fund-raising drive in Massachusetts and throughout the United States so that the cause of independent republicanism could triumph in distant lands.

When Howe returned to Boston at the age of thirty, he had had his fill of swashbuckling heroics and the destructiveness of warfare. Possessing independent means, he turned to philanthropy at the most intimate level by creating a school for six blind children in his own home. Before departing from Europe he had studied treatments for the blind that were being used in England, France, and Germany, and so had begun to prepare himself. During the next forty-five years Howe would continue his work with blind children, developing techniques that would be employed all over the country.

Initially he created a system of raised lettering that allowed his students to learn the alphabet and then to read. In these early years Howe was eager to demonstrate that blind children actually could be taught to read, and so he exhibited the children's achievements to gatherings around the state. Thomas Handasyd

Perkins, a wealthy merchant-capitalist who witnessed one such exhibition, was so impressed by Howe's work that he offered to donate his mansion for use as a school, provided Bostonians would raise $50,000 to sustain the institution. The appeal of Howe and the children was so moving among the Boston bourgeoisie that Perkins's terms were quickly met, and the school expanded, becoming the Perkins Institute.

It was here in 1837 that Howe scored the most remarkable success, teaching Laura Bridgman, an eight-year-old who was not only blind but also deaf and dumb, to communicate. When she was brought to Howe, she knew only a primitive, home-made sign language that conveyed her most basic needs and responses like "yes" and "no." But Howe, defying the prevailing view that anything more was impossible, set out to teach her the alphabet, and then to label common household objects with raised lettering so that Laura could connect words that she could not hear with objects she could not see. For months they worked on it, and Laura came to master the system, but only in a mechanical way. At last, however, "the truth began to flash upon her: her intellect began to work: she perceived that here was a way by which she could herself make up a sign of anything that was in her own mind, and show it to another mind." Howe and Laura were ecstatic: "At once her countenance lighted up with a human expression: it was no longer a dog or a parrot: it was an immortal spirit, eagerly seizing upon a new link of union with other spirits!" [3] Laura Bridgman had rewarded the physician whose therapy rested more on humanitarian faith than on scientific knowledge.

In contrast to Dorothea Dix, whose achievements in Massachusetts launched a national career, Howe stayed rooted in the commonwealth although his influence and example were widely recognized. In the mid-1840s he actively worked on legislation to improve systems of training for the deaf, collaborating with Horace Mann. At the same time Howe took up the cause of mentally retarded children—idiots, as they were then called.

---

3. Howe's report, quoted in Oscar Handlin, *The Americans* (Boston: Little, Brown, 1963), p. 225.

As an investigator for a state commission Howe visited sixty towns and personally examined hundreds of afflicted children. His final report appealed to the legislature to provide for the children with kindness and decency. In 1848 Howe's efforts led to the creation of a state program for retarded children at the Perkins Institute. He also worked to provide foster homes for juvenile delinquents. For Samuel Gridley Howe no human being was beyond redemption.

The final decade in Howe's odyssey of good works was spent as president of the Massachusetts Board of State Charities as well as head of the Perkins Institute. As board president Howe was to lead in establishing rational, systematic policy and administration for the congeries of public welfare institutions that had been created in the state during his lifetime to care for people who were sick, disabled, poor, and criminal. By now Howe's enduring optimism had become old-fashioned, and a snobbish, pessimistic determinism that linked mental illness, poverty, crime, and breeding was coming into vogue. Incarceration, "to protect society," was the new policy, which Howe could never really accept. For Howe the good of each individual, even blind, dumb Laura Bridgman, defined the corporate good. Howe hated large, bureaucratic, custodial institutions. He believed that "the care and treatment of the dependent and vicious classes" should be diffused throughout society, in homes and workshops, churches and schools. "We should enlist," Howe argued, "the greatest number of individuals and families in the care and treatment of the dependent"; public institutions should be kept small and used "only in the last resort." [4] Penny-pinching legislators all around the United States would pervert Howe's intentions, and use his words to justify skimpy budgets. After the Civil War, Howe's romantic optimism, grounded on personal commitment and faith in mankind, had become anachronistic in social-welfare programs. When Samuel Gridley Howe died in the centennial year of 1876, some of the utopian hopes of the Revolutionary era died with him.

---

4. Quoted in Gerald N. Grob, *The State and the Mentally Ill* (Chapel Hill, N.C.: University of North Carolina Press, 1966), pp. 190–191.

Both Howe and Dix had fought uphill struggles for decades against the inertia of old habits and institutions and against people who believed they were impractical and naive. In political forums they had been met with resistance from those who begrudged the cost of reform and those who believed that government had no business assuming responsibilities that could be left to private individuals and agencies. Yet however controversial their proposals, their objectives—the care of mentally ill and physically disabled people—did not assault popular sensibilities or prevailing values. Their reforms operated within a broad consensus of charitable attitudes, and so they never excited harsh antagonisms. Other Massachusetts missionaries were less fortunate. When they came to espouse the rights of women and the liberation of slaves as part of the fulfillment of individual rights promised by the Revolution, they were treading on the personal values and interests of millions of their fellow citizens, so they aroused bitter, even violent hostilities. What was needed to maintain their advocacy was a powerful inner sense of the truth and the reinforcement, psychological and material, of some like-minded people. In the Bay State they found what they needed, and as the Pilgrims and Puritans who first settled Massachusetts had done, they proceeded according to their own unpopular convictions.

One of the most vigorous, effective pioneers of the women's movement was Lucy Stone, who was born in 1818 at West Brookfield in the western part of Worcester County. Her family was comfortably well off, by local standards; her father, the son of an officer in the Revolution and in Shays Rebellion, ran a farm and a tannery with his wife and eight children. Lucy was raised as an orthodox Congregationalist, and she was a pious child. However, in her early teens she began to question particularly the doctrine that men should rule over women. She suspected the Bible was being misinterpreted, so she resolved to learn Greek and Hebrew to enable her to judge the question for herself. But since her father believed such subjects were not fit for a girl, she had to content herself with English schooling, and at the age of sixteen she took a job as teacher in a local district. Lucy Stone used her earnings to further her own education at academies in the neighboring town of Warren and in Wilbraham, about twenty miles west. When she was twenty-one, she was ready to enter Mount Holyoke Female Seminary at South Hadley. Stone studied there for several years and then, seemingly the perpetual student, she moved to Ohio to enter Oberlin College in 1843. The journey was justified because at Oberlin, the first coeducational college, Lucy Stone could pursue her biblical studies. Oberlin itself was a western outpost of a whole range of Yankee causes, especially evangelical piety and abolitionism. Since Stone had been a reader of abolitionist writings for the past decade, Oberlin's climate of opinion was congenial.

At Oberlin Stone learned Greek and Hebrew and realized her ambition to re-examine scriptural statements on the relations of the sexes. Her conclusion, that absolute sovereignty over women distorted the true gospel, fed her feminism and fostered her challenge to the limitations that even Oberlin placed on women. At the time of her commencement in 1849, when she became the first Massachusetts woman to graduate from a classical college, Stone refused to prepare a public address, since the authorities insisted that one of her male colleagues would have to deliver it, as it would be inappropriate for a woman to speak to a public meeting.

A few months later Lucy Stone's career in public speaking began when her brother, a minister at Gardner in the northern tier of Worcester County, took the radical step of inviting her to speak from his pulpit. Now William Lloyd Garrison, who had met Stone at the Oberlin commencement, took her on as a lecturer from the American Anti-Slavery Society. Because of her gender, she drew crowds as a curiosity; at the same time her earnest rhetoric was persuasive. Stone's emphasis, however, quickly moved from the cause of slaves to the ideologically related question of women's rights. As she put it: "I was a woman before I was an abolitionist. I must speak for the women." [5] Within a year she was an active feminist, taking a

---

5. Quoted in Louis Filler, "Lucy Stone," *Notable American Women, 1607–1950,* Edward T. James, *et al.*, eds., 3 vols. (Cambridge, Mass.: Harvard University Press, 1971), 3:388.

leading role in calling the first National Women's Rights convention, which met at Worcester in 1850. It was here that Stone met her contemporary Susan B. Anthony, a native of Adams in Berkshire County. Anthony was not yet a committed feminist, and Stone's oratory had a powerful effect on her.

A few years later, in the 1850s, Lucy Stone was dismissed from her orthodox church because of her controversial speaking career on behalf of women and abolition. Soon after, she became a Unitarian. When she married in 1855, it was the Unitarian abolitionist Thomas Wentworth Higginson who performed the radical ceremony in which Stone and her husband, Henry Blackwell, protested the marriage laws of Massachusetts, which subjected a wife and her property to the control of the husband. As a symbol of her independent identity, Lucy Stone did not take Blackwell's name, although their daughter Alice, born two years later, did.

During the Civil War, Stone curtailed her public career to devote herself to the nurture of little Alice. As the child grew older, Stone returned to her career of promoting women's rights, which, now that blacks were enfranchised, centered on the suffrage. In 1869 she settled in the Dorchester section of Boston, and spent the rest of her life there, serving as an executive of the American Woman Suffrage Association and, with her husband and daughter, publishing the *Woman's Journal*. Between them, Lucy Stone and, after her graduation from Boston University in 1881, Alice Stone Blackwell made their journal into the oracle of the women's movement for half a century.

The feminist cause that Stone proclaimed was not a distinctly Massachusetts movement. Yet a roll call of its major figures includes a disproportionate share of Massachusetts people: the author Lydia Maria Child; the lecturer Abby Kelley Foster; the essayist and critic Margaret Fuller; and the physician Harriot K. Hunt. For if the majority of women in Massachusetts, as elsewhere, accepted their subordination to men in varying degrees, many did not. They believed that their own individual, independent identity must be realized. As long ago as 1776 a member of their grandmothers' generation, Abigail Adams, had issued a warning. "Remember the Ladies," she said, for "if perticuliar care and attention is not paid to the Laidies [*sic*] we are determined to foment a Rebelion, and will not hold ourselves bound by any Laws in which we have no voice, or Representation." [6] In Massachusetts, where the Revolution was recalled with reverence, women found encouragement for proclaiming the libertarian message of those heroic times. The united front of men and women who had always in the past asserted traditional female subordination, cracked. Men joined women in advocating civil rights for their mothers, their sisters, their daughters.

The question of women's rights, after all, was not considered in isolation from the whole range of reform objectives. The drive for women's suffrage and property rights gained momentum in the wake of the movement to eliminate property requirements for voters, to end the religious establishment in Massachusetts (which was done in 1833), and to abolish imprisonment for debt. The successes of these reforms left women and blacks as the last two legally subordinate classes, and their causes were linked actually as well as theoretically. Lucy Stone, though she felt herself a woman first and an abolitionist second, had first taken to the lecture circuit for the American Anti-Slavery Society, and she remained committed to the abolition cause. Stone's sisters in Massachusetts feminism—Child, Foster, Fuller, and Hunt—were all abolitionists. Indeed the two most prominent male feminists were William Lloyd Garrison and Wendell Phillips. Though very different from each other, these two men whose careers intertwined epitomized the independent, assertive, self-righteous spirit of the missionaries who emanated from Massachusetts in the antebellum era.

Garrison, the son of an immigrant sea captain, was born at Newburyport in 1805. Three years later his father deserted the family, and little William was placed under the care of the orthodox Deacon Barrett for a Christian upbringing. From the age of nine onward the boy was apprenticed out to tradesmen, first a shoemaker, then a cabinetmaker, and finally a printer. As a

---

6. Letter to John Adams, Braintree, March 31, 1776, *Adams Family Correspondence*, 1:370.

"printer's devil" Garrison showed real aptitude, and at the age of thirteen he was taken on as an apprentice by a local newspaper. Working for the *Newburyport Herald,* Garrison rose to become a full-fledged journeyman in a trade that was rapidly expanding but which was nevertheless overcrowded. At the age of twenty-one he left the *Herald* to become the editor of the Essex County *Free Press,* one of the thousands of short-lived American newspapers of the era. Garrison soon moved on, going in 1828 to Boston, where he briefly edited a reform paper, the *National Philanthropist,* and then on to Vermont. This peripatetic career, common among young printers who wanted to run their own paper, landed Garrison in Baltimore in 1829. It was here in the slave state of Maryland that he realized his calling as an abolitionist, working as coeditor of the *Genius of Universal Emancipation* with the Quaker Benjamin Lundy. Together they were jailed for libel, beginning Garrison's war with conventional politics.

William Lloyd Garrison was not long in prison, and after he got out, he went back to Boston. At Boston he found support among black people for a new abolitionist paper. In Massachusetts, where slavery had been outlawed by the constitution of 1780, the issue of abolition was quiescent. The cotton textile industry thrived on the product of slave labor, and few people were disposed to challenge the status quo in the slave states. Indeed urban development and rising race consciousness were proceeding in tandem in the Bay State. Increasingly, formal patterns of segregation curtailed the freedom of blacks. Their discontent, and their subscriptions, sustained Garrison in his new vocation as editor of the *Liberator.*

On January 1, 1831, standing *"within sight of Bunker Hill and in the birthplace of liberty,"* Garrison demanded the immediate abolition of slavery. Rejecting the colonization movement that he had once supported and condemning all forms of gradualism, the twenty-five-year-old Garrison declared:

> I *will be* as harsh as truth, and as uncompromising as justice. On this subject, I do not wish to think, or speak, or write, with moderation. No! no! Tell a man whose house is on fire to give a moderate alarm; tell him to moderately rescue his wife from the

hands of the ravisher; tell the mother to gradually extricate her babe from the fire into which it has fallen;—but urge me not to use moderation in a cause like the present. I am in earnest—I will not equivocate—I will not excuse—I will not retreat a single inch—AND I WILL BE HEARD. The apathy of the people is enough to make every statue leap from its pedestal, and to hasten the resurrection of the dead.[7]

For the first time, a white Massachusetts native took up the crusade that David Walker, a black second-hand clothes dealer in Boston had been preaching for several years. Garrison's energy, commitment, and skill would soon make him the principal leader of a movement that eventually transformed American attitudes toward slavery.

In the *Liberator* Garrison lamented public apathy, but within a year or so, that apathy was replaced by active antagonism. Garrison, not content with just a newspaper oracle, led in the formation of the New England Anti-Slavery Society organized at Boston in 1832 in emulation of the flourishing American Trade Society. Speakers, agents, pamphlets, subscriptions, would spread the message throughout New England and the nation. The evangelical spirit, as well as its techniques, infused abolitionism. Grounding their appeals on Christian principles as much as on the ideals of the Revolution, the abolitionists effectively challenged the status quo with verbal assaults.

Outside Massachusetts, in the South particularly, a repressive response was almost immediate. Incendiary attacks on the established order were intolerable, and in Congress the effort began to bar the United States mails to abolitionist writings and to ban abolitionist petitions to the House and Senate. The chief defender of abolitionists in Washington was John Quincy Adams, the ex-president who returned to Congress to represent a southeastern Massachusetts district. Adams, not yet an active abolitionist, vigorously defended the republican principle of free speech. But from the abolitionist standpoint things got worse before they got better.

The worst year was 1835. By then the New England Anti-

7. *The Liberator*, I, p. 1.

Slavery Society had joined with the American Anti-Slavery Society in a national propaganda campaign that included mass mailing as well as full-time paid agents. Violent protests against abolitionist agitation were endemic all across the United States, and in Massachusetts crowds at Lynn and Boston nearly killed the visiting British advocate George Thompson and William Lloyd Garrison. The "Garrison mob," as it was later called, began by breaking up a small meeting of the Boston Female Anti-Slavery Society that gathered on the afternoon of October 21, 1835. Garrison had been invited to address this group of thirty women at the *Liberator*'s building on Washington Street, but a crowd of young men invaded the hall and finally succeeded in grabbing Garrison, notwithstanding the effort of Mayor Theodore Lyman, a Harvard-educated Jackson Democrat, to extricate him. Garrison was dragged through the streets to the site of the Boston Massacre. Here he was stripped to his underwear, but though he was verbally abused, several burly men protected him from being physically beaten. Ultimately Mayor Lyman returned with constables and they wrenched Garrison away, driving him by horse and carriage at breakneck speed to the Leverett Street jail for safekeeping. The next morning Lyman and several other officials persuaded Garrison to leave Boston for several days "to tranquillize the public mind." No effort was made to arrest any of those who had led the crowd or attacked Garrison. Garrison himself believed that the episode was "planned and executed, not by the rabble, or the workingmen, but by *gentlemen* of property and standing,' " and "evidently winked at by the city authorities." [8] Garrison's suspicions were plausible; only two months earlier Mayor Lyman had led a meeting at Faneuil Hall, at which the mercantile elite of Boston chastised the efforts of abolitionists and proclaimed support for the constitutional guarantees that protected slavery in the South. Abolition seemed to challenge social, political, and economic arrangements that enjoyed wide support in Massachusetts.

8. George M. Fredrickson, ed., *William Lloyd Garrison* (Englewood Cliffs, N.J.: Prentice-Hall, 1968), p. 45.

Yet the abolition cause continued to win converts. In 1837 the abolitionist editor Elijah P. Lovejoy, a native of the frontier town of Albion in the old eastern district of Maine, was killed defending his press in Alton, Illinois; and fellow abolitionists instantly elevated him to martyrdom. In Boston William Ellery Channing, among others, petitioned Mayor Samuel A. Eliot and the aldermen for permission to use Faneuil Hall to protest Lovejoy's death. After initially rejecting the petition, the authorities yielded. When the meeting came to order, both the friends and foes of abolition were represented, and after Channing addressed the assembly on the importance of free speech, the attorney general of Massachusetts, James T. Austin, issued a rejoinder. Lovejoy's right to free speech, he said, was no more legitimate than Parliament's right to tax the colonists; and so the men who killed Lovejoy were great patriots, the equals of those Massachusetts sons of liberty who had gloriously dumped the tea in Boston Harbor. Lovejoy was merely pitiful, Austin declared: he "died as the fool dieth." [9] When the attorney general sat down he was loudly cheered.

But Austin did not have the last word. Wendell Phillips, a twenty-six-year-old lawyer with some prior experience in platform oratory, rose to answer him. Phillips's heart pounded with indignation when Austin "asserted principles which place the murderer of Alton side by side with Otis and Hancock, with Quincy and Adams." Pointing to their portraits which hung around the hall, Phillips exclaimed, "I thought those pictured lips would have broken into voice to rebuke the recreant American, the slanderer of the dead. . . . For the sentiments he [Austin] has uttered, on soil consecrated by the prayers of Puritans and the blood of patriots, the earth should have yawned and swallowed him up." Phillips went on to explain that the patriots of 1776 had battled to defend constitutional rights, whereas Lovejoy's assailants fought to destroy the constitutional right of free speech. "James Otis," he said, "thundered in this Hall when the King did but touch his *pocket*. Imagine, if you can,

9. Louis Filler, ed., *Wendell Phillips on Civil Rights and Freedom* (New York: Hill and Wang, 1965), p. 6.

his indignant eloquence, had England offered to put a gag on his lips.'' Insisting on the abolitionists' share of the Revolutionary heritage, Phillips concluded that ''when Liberty is in danger, Faneuil Hall has the right, it is her duty, to strike the keynote for these United States.'' [10] The people of Massachusetts possessed a historic responsibility to cleanse the nation. When Phillips sat down, he had created a new career for himself as spokesman for Garrisonian abolition and advocate for the oppressed.

Like Dix, Howe, and Garrison, Phillips came to his calling indirectly. Born in 1811 as the eighth child in a prosperous Boston merchant family, young Wendell enjoyed all the advantages of wealth, talent, and health. At the Boston Latin School he won the prize for declamation and then went on to Harvard College, from which he was graduated in 1831. After three years' training at the law school with Supreme Court Justice Joseph Story, he entered practice in the conventional way on Court Street. But since Phillips's family provided him with independent means, he had no need to embroil himself in the technicalities of writs and pleadings on behalf of other people's money. After Phillips married the daughter of a rich merchant, Ann Terry Greene, who was herself an ardent member of the Boston Female Anti-Slavery Society, his direction became clear. "My wife made me an out-and-out abolitionist," he recalled. "Wendell, don't shilly-shally!" Ann Phillips decreed.[11]

The masthead of the *Liberator* proclaimed the evangelists' motto: "Our Country is the World, our Countrymen are all Mankind"; and Garrison, recognizing Phillips's superb oratorical gifts, quickly pressed him into service as a key voice in the crusade beyond the boundaries of the Bay State. During the next twenty-five years Phillips would spend most of his time traveling throughout the northern states giving free lectures on abolition. Phillips also earned substantial fees (which he plowed back into the cause) by lecturing on history, philosophy, literature,

10. Filler, *Wendell Phillips,* pp. 3, 8, 9.
11. Quoted in Richard Hofstadter, *American Political Tradition* (New York: Random House, 1954), pp. 141, 143.

and art on the lyceum circuit from Maine to Missouri. On these occasions he was warmly applauded, but when he mounted the platform to attack slavery, the greetings were more mixed. Phillips was heckled and mobbed again and again in the 1840s and 1850s—so much that he became a shrewd manipulator of crowds. Proud to fight the good fight, he could not be intimidated. His opponents lamented, partly in scorn and partly in despair, that "Wendell Phillips is an infernal machine set to music." [12]

Phillips did not shilly-shally, and he was radical. As early as 1842 he followed Garrison in publicly cursing the Constitution of the United States as a covenant with slavery, and arguing that political separatism was better than joining in evil. Both Garrison and Phillips recognized the "unrealistic" character of their attack on the Union of 1787, but their realities were truth and virtue, and they *would be heard*. In 1840 they were both willing to see the American Anti-Slavery Society split over the ideological issues of women's rights and pacifism, to which they were committed. For men who were in some sense disciples of Channing, the expedients of the moment and the survival of a particular organization were always subordinate to their perceptions of truth. And however impractical they may have been, however "counter-productive" their decision literally to burn the Constitution at a Fourth of July rally at Framingham in 1854, it was the intensity and sincerity of their commitment, rooted in individual judgment, that gave them their moral force. In a struggle that Garrison and Phillips believed concerned ideological absolutes, pragmatism had limited appeal.

This romantic streak in Massachusetts abolitionism was becoming more and more evident in the 1850s. The Fugitive Slave Act of 1850, which placed federal marshals in the role of slave catchers and enlisted the compliance of every state, led to subversive activities among the enemies of slavery. The Worcester and Boston clergymen Thomas Wentworth Higginson and Theodore Parker, among others, were prepared to use violence in defense of liberty, just as Parker's grandfather had done when

---

12. Hofstadter, *American Political Tradition,* p. 143.

he assembled the militia on Lexington green in 1775. Grandfather Parker had said that morning: "If they mean to have a war, let it begin here." [13] His musket hung in the Reverend Mr. Parker's study, and his sentiments inspired the abortive attempt in Boston to liberate the captured slave Anthony Burns in 1854, the supplying of arms to Yankees who joined the civil war in Kansas in 1856, and the sponsorship for John Brown's effort to start a slave rebellion by capturing the U.S. arsenal at Harpers Ferry.

When the Civil War began in 1861, Garrison and Phillips discovered that their abolitionism was deeper than their pacifism, and they supported the Union cause. They and the abolition-tinged Massachusetts Republican party led by Senators Charles Sumner and Henry Wilson, and Governor John A. Andrew, pressed Lincoln and the Congress toward emancipation. Higginson, following the thrust begun at Harpers Ferry, gained permission to lead the first regiment of black troops in late 1862. By the following year, with the president formally committed to emancipation, abolitionists began to exult. Their impact on events had been indirect, except for Harpers Ferry, and had the Confederacy yielded early in the war, slavery would have been preserved. But though abolitionists were never a majority controlling public policy, their role in destroying the moral legitimacy of slavery had been decisive.

Garrison and Phillips in Massachusetts, and others elsewhere, were soldiers in a second American Revolution founded on the principles of the first. "Life, liberty, and the pursuit of happiness" would be the right of all Americans, not a particular class. As the war ended, Phillips hardly paused to catch his breath before marching onward in the struggle for equality for blacks, for women, and for working people. Although the target of abolition had been slavery alone, the movement had relied, as shown by *Uncle Tom's Cabin,* on cultivating empathy for the unfortunate. Now the old reformers, Dix, Howe, Stone, Garrison, and Phillips, as well as new ones like Clara Barton (of Ox-

---

13. Quoted in Henry Steele Commager, *Theodore Parker: Yankee Crusader* (Boston: Beacon Press, 1960), p. 4.

ford, in Worcester County), tried to press the whole range of humanitarian and libertarian reforms to fulfillment.

They were met, however, by powerful opposition and widespread indifference. An ideology of "Christian Capitalism" that was wedded to individual and corporate profit-seeking, as well as pragmatic popular desires to "get ahead," combined to elevate the selfish pursuit of gain. Concern for others was shouldered aside in favor of economic interests throughout the United States. In Massachusetts these attitudes had been growing for more than a generation. They were rooted in the Yankee commercial tradition and in the justifications that had surrounded the economic development which transformed the state between 1800 and 1860. At the same time Massachusetts was the breeding ground of reform missionaries, it was also a center for capitalist ideology. In 1837, the year when Phillips rose to prominence in abolition, his old mentor, Justice Story, was sitting in judgment on the Charles River Bridge case. If the bridge at Concord was a shrine in the crusade for liberty, then the bridge from Boston to Cambridge became a landmark on the road toward democratic, laissez-faire capitalism. During the antebellum era, in addition to altruistic causes, people from Massachusetts were becoming missionaries for a capitalism clad in Christian robes.

Harvard became the college of capitalism. From the 1820s onward, Boston businessmen established their supremacy over the administration and even the faculty. Josiah Quincy, the ex-mayor of Boston, was appointed president, ending the long line of clergymen who had led the college in the past. Faculty members who were strenuous on behalf of reform causes became unwelcome in the eyes of the trustees, and in the year of the "Garrison mob" one professor was fired after publishing a pamphlet endorsing abolition. Financially, Harvard became dependent on the munificence of great capitalists like the Appletons, Cabots, Lawrences, and Lowells, who valued classical and scientific learning, but resented any threat to their Whig social, political, and economic views. Being elitist in principle as well as practice, such men would never resort to the "vulgar propaganda" of the advocates of temperance, women's rights, or abolition; but they did underwrite professorships and text-books. These men were the sponsors of Francis Bowen, the Harvard professor whose book, *The Principles of Political Economy* (1856), was dedicated to "A Highly Honored Class, THE MERCHANT PRINCES OF BOSTON, Who Have Earned Success By Sagacity, Enterprise, and Uprightness In All Their Undertakings." [14] For a generation of American college students, Bowen's *Political Economy* was a standard text.

Francis Bowen, born in Charlestown in the same year as Wendell Phillips, 1811, did not enjoy Phillips's advantages. After attending school in Boston and taking a term at the Phillips Academy in Exeter, New Hampshire, he became a publisher's clerk, then briefly taught school before entering Harvard. After graduation in 1833 he returned to Exeter to teach mathematics. In 1839 Harvard hired Bowen as a tutor. When John Gorham Palfrey gave up as editor of the *North American Review* a few years later, the Whigs who financed the *Review* brought Bowen in as editor. This was the platform from which Bowen launched his career as philosopher, litterateur, and spokesman for Christian capitalism.

Ten years later his distinguished record for wide-ranging, socially approved scholarship was rewarded by appointment to the Harvard faculty as Alvord Professor of Natural Religion, Moral Philosophy, and Civil Polity. As professor of natural religion, Bowen enjoyed wide latitude with respect to theology, and indeed his intellectual orientation was far more secular than religious. A careful and critical reader of contemporary British and French commentators on economics and politics, Bowen was nonsectarian in approaching secular questions, and as a critic of France and Britain he had an outlook that was distinctly democratic, or, as he would have put it, "republican." The huge concentrations of wealth overseas, the inheritance laws and customs that held these intact, were disfunctional in Bowen's eyes. "Capital and land," he maintained, "are not mere instruments for the production of wealth . . . ; they are also necessary means for the support and happiness of the whole na-

14. Francis Bowen, *The Principles of Political Economy* (Boston, 1856).

tion; and in this capacity, like rain and fertilizing agents for the soil, they produce the more effect the more evenly they are distributed.'' [15]

Yet Bowen was not an advocate of an even distribution, of leveling. In his view the divinely ordained ''natural'' laws of economics dictated that wealth be accumulated according to the talent of particular entrepreneurs to employ it productively. Inherited wealth ranked below earned income, which was an instrument of general prosperity. Bowen proclaimed a democratic capitalism in which small capitalists could band together to form corporations for large projects, and in which all were free to accumulate (or dissipate) wealth. His highest encomiums went to the *nouveaux riches:* ''the most natural and sensible way of deriving personal gratification from newly acquired wealth, and of making a show of it in the eyes of the world, is to give largely to public charities. The sums which are contributed here [in the United States] by individuals for the support of schools, colleges, churches, missions, hospitals, and institutions of science and benificence, put to shame the official liberality of the oldest and wealthiest governments in Europe.'' Bowen's apologia for new wealth was forthright. In Boston six million dollars had been given in donations from 1800 to 1850 and, Bowen asserted, everyone knew ''that the most numerous and magnificent gifts and bequests are made, not by men who have inherited their fortunes, but by those who have amassed them by their own exertions.'' [16]

The moral philosophy sustaining Bowen's views was a bland, beneficent Christianity. It was morally right for some to acquire great property and others to suffer in misery. The law of private property was a Divine absolute. When a man sought his own profit, this was not destructive self-seeking, because individual gain also benefited the community, ''lending aid to thousands of human beings whom he never saw.'' Bowen claimed that: ''we are all servants of one another without wishing it, and even without knowing it; and we are all co-operating with each other

15. Bowen, *Principles of Political Economy,* p. 545.
16. Bowen, *Principles of Political Economy,* pp. 545, 546.

as busily and effectively as the bees in a hive." [17] Economic laws, like Christian principles, were natural laws, and all operated in harmony. The economic transformation of Massachusetts, its industrial and urban development, was fundamentally good. Great capitalists were instruments of progress. Reformers who interfered with them were challenging nature as God in His wisdom had created it. People like Garrison, Phillips, and Lucy Stone, or even Dorothea Dix, who denounced the *status quo* were, in their ignorance, retarding the fruition of Christian progress. Here the foundations were laid for the "gospel of wealth" that would sustain the Republican Party, and many Democrats, in the post-Civil War era.

The people who dwelled in Massachusetts had never been more divided in their attitudes, objectives, and ideals than on the eve of the Civil War. Some, both Irish and Yankee, were ethnic provincials, and some were cosmopolitan friends of mankind. Some believed the history of Massachusetts demanded that they actively pursue the selfless ideals of the Puritan and Revolutionary past, while others took their inspiration from the Yankee ingenuity that had brought prosperity to the thin, stony soil and rocky harbors of the state. As an industrial society emerged, remnants of the older commercial and agricultural order lingered, and those who earned their bread from industry and its economic by-products did not always shed the views of their agrarian youth, whether it had passed in Worcester County or County Cork. From earliest times, the people of Massachusetts had been struggling with the tension between self-assertion and corporate goals. Now people from the "Bowen school" of capitalists argued that individual economic self-assertion led to the fulfillment of collective goals, but at the same time they denied the legitimacy of collective efforts by legislatures and unions to interfere with one minority class, the entrepreneurs, who claimed to know better. In contrast, reformers of every kind were active interventionists, seeking to impress their individual moral certainties upon the whole society through persuasion and legislation.

17. Bowen, *Principles of Political Economy,* p. 27.

To a large degree Massachusetts missionary activists were talking past their opponents rather than to them. Their proselytizing, after all, knew no bounds; and it was far more effective to try to convince people who were uncertain or indifferent, than to confront people whose minds were made up. Massachusetts, like the nation at large, had become a plural society where contradictory views flourished. But the people of the commonwealth, like people in other states, were not yet pluralistic, not yet prepared to accept the legitimacy of beliefs and opinions that they did not share—so they were tense and competitive.

In some ways the Civil War and the Republican party's hegemony thereafter provided means for subsuming differences and creating a semblance of unity. The lines of public conflict were simplified, but sharp differences remained. In the decades following the war, the divisions that had been shifting and amorphous in the 1830s and 1840s became definite and durable, solidifying around religious, ethnic, and class-based organizations. Massachusetts, early to industrialize and urbanize, also led the way in the emergence of the major elements in the politics and social structure of industrial America.

8

The First Stages
of Pluralism

OR Massachusetts, as well as for the United States, the Civil War marked a division between two eras. After the War the old missionary zeal lingered, but its force was spent. Veterans of past battles, such as Lucy Stone, Wendell Phillips, and Thomas Wentworth Higginson (who lasted until 1911), still found audiences for their reforming oratory; but though some people were willing to hear their arguments, the romantic, idealistic faith of their day, in people and society, had become anachronistic. The dominant spirit throughout the United States between the Civil War and the First World War was self-aggrandizement.

The setting was more competitive than ever; people who enjoyed privileged social positions and inherited wealth found rivals among "new" men of industry and commerce. Farmers and small businessmen, craftsmen and factory workers, were also in competition. Although the rise of large corporations was beginning to introduce monopolistic elements into the nation's economy by the end of the century, most people lived in a world where competitive self-seeking was necessary and legitimate. Old reformers and new ones challenged the Adam Smith-Herbert Spencer philosophy that glorified individual pursuit of self-interest. But though reformers denied the standard asser-

185

tions that ubiquitous rivalry enhanced the common good, the people who lived in North Shore Italian villas and Back Bay brick mansions, as well as those who lived in bleached clapboard farmhouses, in mill dormitories, and in the alley-way shanties of East Boston, all knew that competition was a fact of life, and they looked out for themselves first, and often last. Ironically it was not just the poor or aspiring, but even the most highborn and wealthy who felt insecure in the dynamic social and economic environment of late nineteenth-century Massachusetts.

Some rhetorical commitment to the old ideal of disinterested service for the common good survived and exercised an influence on the language of public affairs and benevolence. But true believers were few in number, and they were generally located at the periphery of power. The old idea of an objective, disinterested definition of the public good, the ideal that magistrates had been righteously seeking from John Winthrop's day to John Adams's, was being transformed. Now the common good would be defined in relation to the interests of individuals banding together as groups. As a mass society developed, people became submerged politically into collective categories; social class, denomination, and ethnic background became primary identities, commanding substantial loyalty in public affairs. "Is it good for men of property, or working men, or Catholics?" people asked themselves. "Class" loyalty, broadly construed, outweighed loyalties to particular towns and to the commonwealth. Patriotism, nourished by the Union cause and by the process of naturalization among immigrant citizens, became chiefly national. The importance of state and locality paled in comparison to class and nation.

With society divided among competing groups, Massachusetts politics became pre-eminently the art of coalition-building. The Democratic and Republican parties fulfilled this role by acting as brokers among contending groups, and by arduously locating common denominators. More than ever before, the political parties functioned to bring a measure of harmony and coherence to a society that was more deeply and variously divided than at any time in the past. This was a world of public affairs that could no longer be guided by seeking rigid adherence to absolute principles. If an alliance, however unlikely, worked, it was a good one. Pragmatism, the doctrine that practical consequences must be the test of ideal principles, became the operating standard in public life. Harvard philosophers, chiefly Charles S. Peirce and William James and the Harvard jurist and man of action, Oliver Wendell Holmes, would provide the theoretical foundations that gave legitimacy to such mundane realities of decision-making in Massachusetts.

The Civil War left the Massachusetts Democratic party in ruins. A full decade after 1865 would pass before the Democrats succeeded in winning a congressional district. In the 1850s the issue of slavery expansion had begun to deplete Democratic ranks seriously, as Know-Nothing and then Free-Soil candidates attracted Yankee farmers, tradesmen, and industrial workers. The battle to preserve the Union converted most of them, and even many Irish immigrants, into Republicans. The majority enthusiastically supported the war and contributed substantially to the Union triumph. Consequently, the Democrats' long, uphill struggle began from deep in the valley of odium. Merchant advocates of free trade, people who lived by southern commerce, and Irish immigrants provided their nucleus of support. Ultimately the resurgence of the Democrats as competitors in a two-party system would be founded on the latter constituency. For as the Irish became Irish-Americans, they made their home in the Democratic party. They became the most loyal and powerful bloc within it; and if they could not dictate policy and select candidates themselves, by 1880 they possessed a decisive veto in party councils. The rebirth of the Democrats was linked to the emergence of the Massachusetts Irish.

Before the Civil War the Irish escaping the potato famine had been the most vulnerable, impoverished people in the commonwealth. Pre-famine Irish immigrants had been few in number, and they had been largely assimilated into society. The first president of that exclusive Boston club, the Massachusetts Historical Society, had been James Sullivan, and the key leader in the creation of Lowell had been Patrick Tracy Jackson. But when poor Irish men, women, and children began to pour into Massachusetts by the tens of thousands in the late 1840s, they alarmed Yankee natives and awakened their prejudices. The burning of the Ursuline Convent in 1834 foreshadowed the hostilities they faced.

In the 1840s and 1850s Massachusetts was not physically or psychologically prepared for a mass migration. Since the 1630s there had never been one. Boston, the center of new arrivals, was already overcrowded, its population having grown by nearly fifty percent in the decade before 1845. Then, beginning in 1846 and for a decade thereafter, owing to proximity and the patterns of Atlantic trade, Irish farm people flooded into Boston at the rate of one thousand per month, a migration six times larger than that which had peopled southern New England with Europeans in the 1630s. Even if they had all been prosperous, educated Protestants, their arrival would have strained the social order. The fact that they were poor, often illiterate, and Roman Catholic, encouraged an ethnocentric Yankee reaction. Many feared for the survival of middle-class Protestant values in public life.

Because most Irish came to America poor, they became the subordinates of native whites rather than their rivals in the economy. Taking whatever jobs they could find, however poorly paid, back-breaking, or onerous, they struggled for survival. Immediately their presence expanded the ranks of menial labor and domestic servants; and ultimately, with the help of general white prejudices, they would crowd blacks out of their traditional service jobs. By the early 1850s, when the migration was at its height, the Irish were spreading all over the state. The great mill towns provided thousands of factory and construction jobs, but immigrants also found work in smaller communities. They labored on railroads and highways, they were teamsters, stable-hands, and hired help for farmers. By seeking out all available jobs, Irish people turned up in virtually every township in the state within less than a decade. In Boston, where successive arrivals made crowding most intense, thousands died from infectious diseases. But elsewhere, from a physical standpoint, the incorporation of the newcomers into Massachusetts was easy.

Culturally, however, the division was sharp, durable, and the source of severe strains. Whether or not they practiced them systematically, Yankees had been nurtured on the Republican virtues of a sober, independent citizenry in which middle-class ideas of industry, frugality, cleanliness, and punctuality were held to be the correct standards of Massachusetts citizenship. Insofar as immigrant workers and their families failed to conform, they were subject to an aversion based as much on class as on ethnicity. Victims of poverty, the Irish were blamed for it by insular natives.

Anti-Catholicism had an even longer heritage in the popular culture of the commonwealth. The Puritans had defined their religion largely in opposition to Rome. The ceremonies of liturgical worship were misleading superstitions in their judgment. Latin services and priestcraft concealed Christ's gospel rather than illuminating it, and celibacy was unnatural. For a century at least it was generally held that the Catholic ecclesiastical structure was tyrannical and in league with monarchy around the world to subvert free, constitutional government. The Pope himself was called anti-Christ, and lurid tales of political, financial, and sexual corruption had long provided Protestants with a kind of pious pornography. Being both poor and Catholic, the Irish were obvious targets of group hostility.

Smug jokes, often imported directly from England, about "Paddy's" drinking, fighting, and irrational, spontaneous passions helped informally to reinforce Yankees' sense of superiority. "What is the greatest invention since the wheel?" asked one riddle. The answer was "the wheelbarrow, because it taught the Irishman to walk on two legs." [1] Such humor, closely connected to the endless "Coon" jokes made at the expense of blacks, helped to make vicious, degrading stereotypes part of everyday experience. Although the Know-Nothing party dominated state government for only a brief period in the 1850s,

1. Oral tradition.

the sentiments that made its investigation of Catholic educational institutions such as the College of the Holy Cross seem legitimate lived on in public life. Throughout the post-Civil War decades, hostility to Irish Catholics was an undercurrent in the Republican party, which came to the surface whenever public and parochial schools or Boston politics were discussed. In the 1890s the American Protective Association, a Protestant lobbying group, would revive elements of the Know-Nothing message explicitly. Wealthy leaders in commerce and industry disdained vulgar nativist politics—they welcomed cheap labor—but they too saw the Irish as depraved. The Yankee elite viewed all outsiders to their ranks with condescension, but the Irish were the mudsill of society in the 1860s and 1870s.

The vitality of Yankee bigotry was partly a response to Irish success in Massachusetts. Time, service to the Union cause during the war, and their own ambitions and talents changed the circumstances of the Irish in the generation after 1865. The massive migration of famine victims slowed as conditions in Ireland moderated. People who had begun by taking any job for any pay thriftily accumulated savings, founded their own modest businesses, and bought homes. Deprived for centuries of any political voice, they quickly grasped the opportunities that local and state politics presented. For although they had spread all over the face of the commonwealth, patterns of employment, income, prejudice, and perhaps also preferences, had segregated the Irish in particular neighborhoods in Boston and the mill cities, especially Fall River, Haverhill, Holyoke, Lawrence, Lowell, and Worcester. Here they quickly entered the party that had been welcoming immigrant voters since the days of Thomas Jefferson and James Sullivan, the Democrats. Winning seats as aldermen first, later as delegates to the General Court, they secured themselves from official harassment and gained a share of public patronage. For people who had trouble paying grocers and landlords, and who were frequently subject to seasonal layoffs, political participation was not only an inspiring exercise of liberty, it was also practical. Since the Democrats had been so weakened by the conflicts over slavery in the 1850s and by the war that followed, Irish support proved a blessing. The resurgence of two-party politics became a reality in the 1870s when the Democrats cracked the Republican monopoly in the congressional delegation, largely through Irish-American participation. In the 1880s the Irish began to occupy positions of considerable importance, both symbolic and actual.

The first major city to select an Irish Catholic mayor was Lawrence in 1881. Lawrence in 1880 was roughly the same size, 40,000 people, as Boston had been in the 1820s. Its population was twenty percent Irish-born, and next to Yankees, the Irish were the largest of several ethnic groups among the electorate. John Breen's victory combined support from workingmen from England, Scotland, Germany, and French Canada, as well as some Yankees; but the bulk of his strength came from the Irish. Breen, a native of Tipperary who had built up an undertaker's business among his fellow-countrymen, was both a volunteer fireman and a city councilman before his election. When Breen took office in 1882 he used the patronage at his disposal to bring Irish-Americans into the police, health, and public works departments. Though Breen left office three years later, Irish access to city jobs remained. Irish exclusion in public life was in retreat.

At Boston, the metropolis of Yankee New England, the same pattern appeared in the 1880s, when Patrick Andrew Collins won a congressional seat and Hugh O'Brien won the mayoralty. Collins, a child of the famine migration, was born in 1844 at Ballinafauna in County Cork. His father was a politically active, respectable tenant-farmer; but when he died in 1847, his wife and child were cast adrift in the world. Mrs. Collins chose to migrate to Massachusetts, and it was in Chelsea, just outside Boston, that young Patrick Collins attended public school. When the boy was thirteen, they moved to southern Ohio, and Patrick had a taste of coal-mining; but two years later they came back to Boston, where Patrick Collins became apprentice to an upholsterer.

Collins mastered his trade, but it was politics that excited his imagination. At the age of twenty he joined the Fenian movement for Irish independence, and at twenty-three he won election to Massachusetts's house of representatives. In the same year, 1867, Collins began to study law with a Democratic attorney, while also attending the Harvard law school on a part-time basis. He rose quickly. After three terms in the house he was elected to the state senate, where he successfully sponsored a bill to open state hospitals and prisons to Catholic (as well as Protestant) chaplains. By 1874, when the thirty-year-old Collins was graduated from the law school, he had come remarkably far for the poor son of an Irish tenant.

Now he retired from public office and began to build up a practice. He had married Mary Carey of Boston in 1873, and he soon had family responsibilities. Gradually, as his social and economic position improved, Collins's political orientation shifted. In 1876 he decided to support John Adams's grandson, Charles Francis Adams, who was running for governor as the reform Democrat candidate. At the same time Collins broke with the Fenians, arguing the classic assimilationist position that whatever one's sympathies, Irish politics were foreign, and one must concentrate one's loyalty on America and its affairs. Collins was joining forces with Yankee Democrats in order to bridge the antagonisms that weakened the Democratic party.

In 1882 he was elected to Congress as a reform (Grover Cleveland) Democrat, and Collins served there for three terms. But he was frozen out of the Massachusetts patronage by the new president. Irish Democrats were divided and competing for Yankee alliances, and Cleveland had closer ties with the Brahmin leaders in any case. Ultimately Collins became alienated. Cleveland sought to mollify him in 1893 when he appointed Collins the United States consul-general in London, a prestigious and profitable post. But Collins's involvement in national affairs soon came to an end. He returned to Boston where he ran unsuccessfully for mayor in 1899, before winning successive terms in 1901 and 1903. By this time Collins was a respected elder statesman among Massachusetts Democrats, far from the cutting edge of ethnic politics.

Hugh O'Brien, who never attended college or law school, was almost twenty years older than Collins. O'Brien challenged native stereotypes—as Collins did—by demonstrating that an Irishman could be a prudent, sagacious public official of the highest integrity. His family brought him to Boston in 1832, when he was five years old, and he was educated in the common schools before being apprenticed to the printers of the *Boston Courier*. At the *Courier* O'Brien obtained some elements of a liberal training, since its editor, Joseph T. Buckingham, had broad literary interests, and his paper included book reviews, theatrical commentaries, as well as essays on literature and reform. The young printer also became conversant with "sound principles," since the *Courier* was a Whig organ. Later O'Brien would found his own commercial paper; he did not turn to politics until he was in his late forties and well established.

Because of his early arrival in Boston and his training at the *Courier,* Hugh O'Brien was a much more assimilated, "respectable" gentleman than most of his Irish constituents when he was elected an alderman in 1875. In city politics O'Brien distinguished himself for conscientious hard work, and after several years as an alderman he scored a concrete victory for laboring men by winning enactment of a two-dollar daily minimum wage for city employees. On the strength of this achievement and the support of Patrick Maguire's precinct organization, O'Brien won the mayoralty in 1884. Maguire, who dealt in real estate and published a weekly paper, the *Republic,* had become the leading Irish "boss" in Boston—but his success, like that of Collins and O'Brien, was based on his ability to retain Irish support while accommodating the native Democrats.

The emergence of the pluralism that this Yankee-Irish alliance within the Democratic party represented was symbolized by the selection of the Boston University-trained lawyer Thomas Gargan to deliver the city's Independence Day oration in 1885. Thereafter, for the next generation, the honor was divided equally between Yankees and Irish, who alternated from year to year. As hostile and suspicious as the two groups remained, divided by ethnicity, religion, and class, they had accepted the idea that Boston belonged to both. Ballot-box pragmatism ruled.

Outside the political marketplace, such pluralistic tolerance was far more difficult. But one early testimony to the possibilities was the meteoric career of the editor, poet, and novelist John Boyle O'Reilly. O'Reilly was a romantic man of action, reformer, and literary lion, who arrived in Boston in 1870 at the age of twenty-six. He had spent his youth in Ireland and England as a newspaper apprentice, soldier, and Fenian nationalist. After narrowly escaping the death penalty for subversive activity while in the army, he had been shipped as a convict to Australia. In 1869 he escaped aboard a Nantucket whaler, and in the following year he landed a job as reporter on the *Boston Pilot*. Founded in 1838, and named after the patriotic Dublin journal, the *Pilot* was the oldest and most popular Catholic paper in Boston, supported by laymen as well as churchmen. O'Reilly, whose intellect, magnetic charm, and energy transcended common prejudice, rapidly moved up. In 1876 the recently elevated Archbishop of Boston John J. Williams made him his editor-in-chief and co-partner in operating the *Pilot*. With this forum O'Reilly emerged as a vigorous Irish patriot and the spokesman of a humane, cosmopolitan Catholicism. His poetry moved from romantic, natural themes in the 1870s to reform ideals in the following decade when imperialism, race prejudice, and other forms of oppression—including capitalism—moved him to protest. O'Reilly found friends in literary Boston and Cambridge, and so while Collins, O'Brien, and Gargan were breaking down old political barriers, O'Reilly was enjoying comparable symbolic triumphs. His poetry was selected for the monuments to Wendell Phillips and to the black martyr of the Boston Massacre, Crispus Attucks. In 1889 his verse was part of the rededication ceremony for Plymouth Rock. In O'Reilly, member of several established literary and social clubs, it would seem that cultural acceptance of Irish Catholics was not merely a token, but real and substantial.

Yet appearances are misleading. For one thing O'Reilly was an exceptional personality who combined literary gifts and reform social vision with orthodox Catholicism in a unique way. Moreover, O'Reilly's "sponsors" in Brahmin Massachusetts were chiefly drawn from the older generation of pre-War idealists: Ralph Waldo Emerson, Julia Ward Howe, Thomas Wentworth Higginson, Wendell Phillips, John Greenleaf Whittier. If O'Reilly had lived longer (he died in 1890), perhaps he would have opened the way for other immigrants into the sanctums of literary and aesthetic culture in the commonwealth. But the record of literary, musical, and artistic organizations suggests otherwise. Wealthy Yankees made sure that high culture was their preserve.

Consequently, cultural pluralism emerged in a largely segregated context. "Second-class" associations emerged to satisfy the literary, musical, and artistic interests of aspiring, middle-class Irish-Americans and other newcomers. The simultaneous rise of ethnic philanthropic and social organizations completed the pattern. The late nineteenth century marked the high tide of fraternal clubs and lodges throughout the nation. In Massachusetts such associations flourished within a setting where ethnic self-consciousness and class stratification provided members with a kind of social insulation. Booker T. Washington's classic 1895 Atlanta formula for race relations applied almost equally well to the heterogeneous peoples of Massachusetts: "In all things that are purely social we can be as separate as the fingers, yet one as the hand in all things essential to mutual progress." [2] In their commitment to economic growth and prosperity, the people of Massachusetts were united in a harmony that was only faintly disturbed by socialists and radicals.

In public life the Democratic party was the most prominent agent of inter-group and inter-class coalition in Massachusetts, but the Democrats were a minority party. Between 1860 and 1919 Republicans monopolized Massachusetts's two places in the United States Senate and the vast majority of congressional seats. No Democrat served in Congress from the Bay State until 1876, and a comparable pattern of Republican dominance characterized state politics. The Civil War coalition of farmers and industrialists, of high church, low church, and intermediate Protestants, made Massachusetts a Republican stronghold. Advocating enterprise and industry, protective tariffs and sound currency, in addition to subsidies for transportation and education, Republicans controlled scores of Yankee townships year in

2. Quoted in Leslie H. Fishel, Jr., and Benjamin Quarles, eds., *The Negro American* (Glenview, Ill.: Scott, Foresman, 1967), p. 344.

and year out. Although some party politicians openly exploited anti-Catholic sentiment, Republicans were not so much hostile as they were indifferent to the wishes of immigrant voters. In cities and towns where the French Catholic and later the Italian Catholic voters held a balance of power, by the end of the century Republicans were courting them with rhetoric and petty patronage. More gradually than the Democrats, the Republicans too would function pragmatically, as vehicles for integrating diverse class interests and ethnic groups in a pluralistic society.

Yet the great leaders of the Republican party were old-line, Harvard-educated Yankees George Frisbie Hoar and Henry Cabot Lodge. Between them, Hoar and Lodge illustrated the accommodations that respectable, Yankee Massachusetts was willing to accept in an era of dramatic social change. Their differences over civil rights, immigration restriction, and American imperialism suggested the mixture of conflicting elements that divided Yankees. Unity among Republicans was a matter of repeated compromise, and defections on questions of principle were a recurrent threat.

State Republicans elected George Frisbie Hoar to the Senate in 1877, but Hoar's formative period had occurred before the war. He had been born into a Concord family of Unitarians in 1826. His grandfather Hoar had fought in the battle at Concord Bridge in 1775, and his mother was a daughter of Roger Sherman, the Connecticut delegate who had helped draft both the Declaration of Independence and the Constitution. George was nurtured on Revolutionary idealism before he was sent to Harvard College and the law school in the 1840s. When he left Cambridge, Hoar settled at Worcester, where he soon became active in the Free-Soil party. Like his father, Samuel, and his elder brother Congressman Ebenezer Rockwood Hoar, George opposed slavery and slave expansion. If the Whigs were so bound up with cotton that they were deaf to conscience, then the Hoars were ready to assert their independence. Decades later, Senator Hoar would proudly recall how he had been one of the original founders of the Republican party in Massachusetts at Worcester in 1855. To George Frisbie Hoar, the Republican party would ever after be emblematic of the principles of the

Declaration of Independence—liberty under a free, representative government.

When the war began, George was in his mid-thirties, married, a family man who chose to support the Union war effort at home rather than on the battlefield. Later, in 1868, he was elected to Congress as a radical, and he supported a thorough reconstruction of government and society in the South, including black civil rights. Hoar, who idolized Massachusetts's abolitionist senator, Charles Sumner, whose seat he proudly filled, had firmly established his identity as an old-line Republican of principle by the 1870s.

One of Hoar's principles was to stand by his own party to fight for justice within it rather than bolt when the financial scandals of the Grant administration were revealed and when James G. Blaine, soiled with the corruption of the Crédit Mobilier, won the party's presidential nomination in 1882. Hoar felt a proprietary interest in the party he had helped create and, when he considered the long-term record of the Democrats, he never doubted that the Republican party alone offered the best hope for liberty and progress. Even though Hoar's prewar idealism was already becoming outmoded within his party when he entered the Senate, Hoar clung to his party, preached to it, and, when he lost his battles, stayed to fight again. The year that Hoar came to the Senate as an advocate for the cause of black civil rights, the "compromise of 1877," which traded Republican control of the White House for unchallenged southern white rule in the South, marked the end of the party's egalitarian, reformist era. Hoar, who generally voted with his fellow Republicans on economic policy, was otherwise a maverick sustained by old-fashioned Massachusetts Yankees.

From the standpoint of legislation, Hoar's chief claim to fame is the Sherman Anti-Trust Act of 1890, which he redrafted and guided through shoals of conservative opposition. Though the statute actually did little to impede the progress of monopolies and trusts, Hoar pressed for its adoption because of his commitment, and that of small-town Republicans everywhere, to free, competitive enterprise with opportunities for petty capitalists. In Massachusetts such principles enjoyed overwhelming support across party lines. On other issues, however, Hoar was willing to advocate views that divided his own party.

Hoar's friendly position on black voting rights and his support for woman suffrage were less and less welcome among party contributors and regulars in the 1880s and 1890s. But since these issues were at the periphery of Massachusetts (and national) politics, they did not excite strong antagonisms. Immigration restriction and the development of an overseas American empire, however, were central policy questions, especially in the nineties, and Hoar's views marked a profound division in Massachusetts. Hoar, who had rejected the Know-Nothings in the 1850s, was not about to embrace the American Protective Association, in spite of its growing popularity among Protestant voters. Hoar was equally opposed to the more refined and respectable Immigration Restriction League which, through the device of a literacy test, aimed at keeping out masses of poor immigrants. The mission of America in 1776 had been to serve as the asylum for the oppressed. Hoar, true to family tradition, wanted to keep it that way; but in Massachusetts he spoke for a declining body of opinion, especially among Republicans.

The Spanish-American War and its sequel in the Philippines would further alienate Hoar from party regulars. Unlike some distinguished Boston Brahmins, Hoar supported the American effort in Cuba and stood by President McKinley. But when it came to the conquest of the Philippines and the military suppression of the native independence movement there, Hoar denounced United States policy. In the Senate Hoar worked tirelessly to defeat the peace treaty with Spain that made the nation a colonial power in Asia and the Caribbean. Indeed, had one more Republican or Democrat joined Hoar, the treaty would not have mustered the necessary two-thirds approval. But jingo pressures were intense, and even William Jennings Bryan, the leading Democratic anti-imperialist, yielded. Among Republicans, only Senator Eugene P. Hale of Maine stood by Hoar when the vote was cast. Gloating over the victory, Theodore Roosevelt contemptuously told his friend Henry Cabot Lodge that Hoar's actions could be "pardoned only because he is senile."[3] Roosevelt, Lodge, and indeed most people could not fathom the old man's adherence to the Revolutionary tradition of political independence for all peoples. The right to "life, liberty, and the pursuit of happiness" belonged to the Filipinos, Hoar asserted, and by seizing their liberty, Americans were repealing their own Declaration of Independence. In Massachusetts Hoar's views commanded some respect, especially among the politically heterogeneous members of the Anti-Imperialist League including, among others, the president of the Massachusetts Historical Society, Charles Francis Adams, Jr., and Harvard professor Charles Eliot Norton. But Hoar's outspoken stand represented a strain of individualistic idealism that had become so odd by 1900 that it could be confused with senility. Hoar was an up-to-date, pragmatic, party man, loyal to the collective Republican cause, but he was also loyal to the beliefs of his family and of his own Massachusetts youth. To have embraced imperialism would have been to shed the identity that he had found in Concord, Cambridge, and Worcester.

Hoar's junior Massachusetts colleague in the Senate, Henry Cabot Lodge, was much more comfortable in the political environment of the era. A generation younger than Hoar, having been born in 1850, Lodge's understanding of the old idealism was essentially rhetorical. Lodge spoke the language of principle, but he was worldly and ambitious; and as he matured, he learned that if he clung rigidly to principle, he would be an outsider in a world where power brokers repeatedly laid principle on the shelf. A scrupulous regard for ideals or consistency would have consigned him to the fretful world of drawing-room politics, in which many of his peers dwelled.

In some ways Lodge entered life with every advantage— wealth, social prestige, health, talent, and doting parents. But his very advantages created handicaps in the competitive setting of mass democratic politics. He was definitely not born in a log cabin. The Lodges were relative newcomers, since his

---

3. Quoted in Richard E. Welch, Jr., *George Frisbie Hoar and the Half-Breed Republicans* (Cambridge, Mass.: Harvard University Press, 1971), p. 249n.

grandfather was an Englishman who had immigrated to Massachusetts in the 1790s, after escaping from the black uprising in Santo Domingo. But if the Lodges were relatively recent arrivals, they were successful ones. Henry Cabot Lodge's father, like his grandfather, prospered in trade; he married Anna Cabot, granddaughter of George Cabot, a North Shore merchant who made a fortune during the Revolution and moved to Boston, where he became the patriarch of Massachusetts Federalism. Cabot wealth and Cabot traditions heavily influenced the boy's youth, particularly after his father died, when Henry was twelve years old. His mother believed he resembled the Cabots "in mind & character as well as in looks & manner," and instead of being called Henry, he was called "Cabot." [4] Continually shielded from contact with people outside the family's social circle, Cabot Lodge attended Mr. Dixwell's private preparatory school and toured Europe for a year with his mother and tutor before entering Harvard in 1867. Raised in the Federalist tradition of elitism, and continually reminded of his own social and cultural superiority both before he entered Harvard and while he was there, Henry Cabot Lodge's background suited him splendidly for a life of snobbish complacency. Lodge never wished to escape from his breeding—he was proud of it; but though he became a shrewd and articulate defender of the status quo, he was not personally complacent. Born to hereditary prominence, he felt a compelling drive to make his own mark in the world. After he was graduated from Harvard in 1871, he spent a decade testing possible careers for a man who, already possessing wealth, sought additional recognition and prestige.

Lodge's initial choice was to become a scholar in the field of history. After graduation he had married a distant cousin and spent an extended honeymoon in Europe, where Cabot was an avid admirer of art and architecture. When the couple returned to Boston, Lodge re-entered Harvard, enrolling in the law school and as a graduate student in Henry Adams's course on medieval institutions. Moreover, as one of Adams's favorites, Lodge also accepted a position as assistant editor of the *North*

---

4. Quoted in John A. Garraty, *Henry Cabot Lodge* (New York: Knopf, 1953), p. 5.

American Review. After earning his law degree in 1874, Lodge devoted himself chiefly to historical research and writing, in addition to his editorial duties. His training, which concentrated on the Teutonic origins of Anglo-Saxon political institutions, placed him in the mainstream of the new interest in linking the political and racial heritages of northern Europeans.

Like his mentor, Henry Adams, Lodge was only partly interested in scholarship. Both were deeply fascinated by power and eager to possess it. Adams, believing high office should seek him out because of his own brilliance and his distinguished lineage, sulked because it never did. Lodge, far more flexible and realistic, came to recognize that he would have to labor long, hard, and single-mindedly to grasp political power. But he began among Henry Adams's refined, Harvard-bred coterie of high-principled, conservative reformers. Disgusted by the corruption of the Grant administration and the chicanery associated with Reconstruction in the South, they proposed civil-service examinations so that a meritocracy would control public administration; and they argued that southern Bourbons should be permitted to rule at home in accordance with the interests of their class and race. Ultimately much less fastidious than Adams and his other associates, Lodge started as a Republican reformer whose heroes were the elder Charles Francis Adams and Carl Schurz.

Through the 1870s Lodge dabbled with politics while also emerging as a prolific author of popular American history. Then in 1879 he ran for the Nahant seat in the General Court. Since childhood Lodge had spent summers in Nahant, and he was delighted when he won. Two years later he ran for the state senate and lost, but in spite of this setback he persisted. Henry Adams would never have deigned to run for such a humble office and, once defeated, would have scorned further battles. But Henry Cabot Lodge was more modest; he accepted his bruises and learned about the realities of Massachusetts politics as a participant. Throughout the early 1880s Lodge continued to run and to lose as he now sought a seat in Congress. Ultimately the most profound lesson he drew from his experience was that he must close the gap between himself and the party rank and file and, after being narrowly beaten in 1884 by idealistic defectors who resented his support of James G. Blaine, he became devoted to party loyalty. When Lodge next ran for Congress in 1886, he won—henceforth he would never be defeated.

The years 1883 and 1884 had been crucial for Lodge though he still remained out of office. He had finally broken with his social equals in the Adams circle and become a "professional" Republican. In 1883 he managed the gubernatorial campaign of respectable but lackluster Congressman George D. Robinson against Democratic Governor Benjamin F. Butler. This struggle assumed immense symbolic importance in Massachusetts, since many regarded Governor Butler as a wholly unprincipled "beast."

Butler, a shrewd and brazen opportunist, had begun his career in Lowell as a Democrat who championed Irish Catholic and labor issues in the General Court. During the Civil War he became a Unionist, a political brigadier-general, and then a Republican. Serving as a Radical alongside George Frisbie Hoar in the postwar Congresses, Butler ended up close to General Grant and his cronies. After being defeated for re-election in 1875, Butler championed the inflationary "Greenback" cause before finally returning to the Democratic fold. Butler's willingness to move back and forth among the parties, his relish for patronage politics, and his own cultivation of lower-class and immigrant support convinced many middle- and upper-class people that he was vicious. Snubbed by Harvard and other elite establishments, Butler delighted in twitting his detractors. Indeed, the greatest scandal of Butler's administration was his Thanksgiving proclamation in 1882, a jeremiad pointing to the commonwealth's many sins and calling for repentance and reform. The upright were aghast when they read Butler's harsh criticisms. But Ben Butler had the last laugh, since his proclamation was copied verbatim from the arch-Federalist Governor Christopher Gore's proclamation of 1810. Red-faced and fuming, Republicans were not amused, and the ouster of Butler in 1883 became a holy cause.

But he was popular, and it was an uphill struggle in which Lodge's organizing talents, his energy, and his shrewdness in assiduously presenting "honest" George Robinson to the voters were crucial. When Robinson won by a narrow margin, Lodge's stature in the party soared. He had gone into the political pits to labor not for his own glory, but for the party and Massachusetts. He had succeeded in the grimy, tedious work of meeting people throughout the state, persuading them, speaking at scores of gatherings and arranging dozens more for Robinson. No graduate of Mr. Dixwell's Latin school had ever performed such an achievement. When Lodge went to the Republican convention at Chicago the following year and came back supporting Blaine, some of his Brahmin friends cut him dead. Someone so devoid of principle, so opportunistic, they reasoned, should be beneath their notice. Lodge was hurt, but not so wounded that he altered his course. During the forty years of political activity that followed, Lodge remained a Republican regular, never doubting the wisdom of his judgment. When he subsequently won election to Congress, the wounds he had suffered earlier heightened his sense of satisfaction.

Urbane and wealthy, Cabot and Anna Lodge took naturally to high society in Washington and became part of a truly national elite. At the same time Lodge retained his Massachusetts roots, and his political views were always closely attuned to the Republican majority in the Bay State. By the time Lodge was elevated to the Senate in 1893, he was closely identified with the orthodox positions on industrial tariffs, labor unions, and private capital of his senior colleague Hoar. Yet on other issues Cabot Lodge spoke for a different strain in Massachusetts opinion, and in the Senate he became the pre-eminent leader of the drive to curtail immigration into the United States.

In Massachusetts the movement to restrict immigration was not a distinctively Republican cause. Republicans liked protectionism in the form of tariffs, but they did not want the American labor market protected from low-paid immigrant workers. Indeed immigrant restriction was not a party issue. For different reasons, industrialists and their immigrant employees both favored the traditional policy of welcoming foreigners. But in the 1880s and 1890s especially, Massachusetts natives did become anxious. Now the Irish were being joined by Italians, Germans,

Eastern European Jews, French Canadians, Slavs, Syrians, Portuguese, and Scandinavians. Immigrant birthrates were higher than those of natives, and Roman Catholicism was on the way to becoming the largest denomination in the state. All the trends suggested that in the not-too-distant future Yankees would become a minority in the land of their forefathers. Yankee pride and ethnocentrism grew more self-conscious as a result. Claiming free political institutions, social order, morality, and thrift as their special cultural achievements, Yankees became fearful of continuing, open-ended immigration.

The restriction movement began among a small group of well-educated reformers who viewed the immigrants as a key source of corruption. Because of the immigrants, they maintained, demagogy flourished, and unselfish, meritorious, well-bred people like themselves were displaced from the centers of power by politicians and industrialists who exploited foreigners' ignorance and poverty. Because of the immigrants a vice-ridden proletariat was emerging in the birthplace of liberty. Restrictionists believed that the clannishness of the foreigners exacerbated social divisions, and that their slow pace of assimilation destroyed all hope of restoring the homogeneous, harmonious society that the restrictionists associated with the past, and which they craved. For some elite Yankee Democrats and political independents the Immigration Restriction League, founded at Boston in 1894, offered hope. Public opinion might be awakened and legislation, similar to the recently enacted Chinese exclusion law, could result.

Cabot Lodge was the only prominent Republican in Massachusetts who embraced the league from the outset. His own views, however ethnocentric and snobbish, were also altruistic. Lodge, sharing the prevailing vogue for racial explanations of history and society, wanted Massachusetts and the United States preserved from further dilution by "inferior stocks." Ideally all immigration, except for Englishmen and Scots, would be stopped. But as a realist Lodge understood that such a program could never win public approval, and to propose it would mean political suicide. Already, by 1891, Lodge had stopped making derogatory allusions to the Irish in public—after all, they were voters. Restrictionism under Lodge's guidance would not seem to be directed at any particular national or religious group—it would appear disinterested, high-minded, and couched in the language of the common good. The instrument of the league's indirect approach became the literacy test. Most people believed that literacy was an essential requirement for good citizenship, so by introducing this "non-discriminatory" test the desired result, cutting off the massive new immigration from southern, central, and eastern Europe, could be achieved. Just as Lodge's Bourbon allies in the South were using literacy tests to disfranchise black voters, the league could use the same technique to protect the racial stock of the North.

In advocating restrictionism in this form, Lodge was ahead of other Massachusetts politicians, although he was not alone for long. Workingmen, Yankee and Irish, liked the idea of a protected labor market. Progressives, concerned about political corruption, believed that literacy would help destroy bossism and demagogues. Bigots and xenophobes of every variety found the scheme palatable. By masking racial and ethnic elitism, restrictionism became good politics.

With this proposal Lodge made his mark nationally. In 1896 he reported the results of the "scientific" study his Senate Committee on Immigration had produced. Southern and eastern Europeans were disproportionately poor, diseased, and criminal. Culturally they were "aliens" whose presence in numbers threatened American civilization. American history proved, and here Lodge spoke as an authority, that Anglo-Saxons and northwestern Europeans were the ablest, most achieving peoples. From this platform Lodge launched his literacy-test statute, and it passed both houses of Congress handily. For an America gripped by high unemployment, immigrant restriction was widely attractive. Had it not been for President Grover Cleveland's veto, millions of lives would have been different, and the histories of Massachusetts and the United States altered significantly. Because of the veto, the immigration continued, rising dramatically during the prosperous early years of the new century.

Characteristically, Lodge did not give up. He continued to

lead on this issue both in Massachusetts and in the Senate. The literacy test suffered repeated congressional defeats for a decade after 1897, but finally passed again in 1913 only to be vetoed by the Republican President William Howard Taft. Two years later another version won approval, but this time Woodrow Wilson vetoed. Not until after the First World War, when hypernationalism, the Red Scare, and economic recession sustained a renewed drive for restriction, would it become law. In the thirty-year interval from the time Lodge introduced his literacy bill, hundreds of thousands of Italian and eastern Europeans of various nationalities and faiths had made their way into the Bay State. The ethnic and cultural pluralism Lodge had hoped to stem was to dominate Massachusetts.

Actually, the social vision that had sustained elite restrictionism was already beleaguered by 1900. The neo-Federalist ideal of a homogeneous, hierarchical society united around a single orthodoxy of belief and behavior had always been a reactionary anachronism, even when grafted to "survival-of-the-fittest" social Darwinism. But except for the equally old-fashioned romantic Christian idealism, it had not faced a powerful rival during the post-Civil War era. By the beginning of the new century, however, a new outlook, one that grew out of contemporary experience, had taken shape in Massachusetts and across the country. Pragmatism, the view that the truth of abstract principles could not be established *a priori,* but must be tested by actual practice, was becoming prevalent.

Pragmatism gained adherents in many forms and at many levels. At the highest level the ideas were worked out by Harvard philosophers Charles Peirce, William James, and Josiah Royce; in a formal sense pragmatism was a Massachusetts creation. But at the most common, unself-conscious level pragmatism was the everyday discovery of thousands of people throughout Massachusetts and elsewhere. In simplest terms, pragmatism meant that if an idea worked, it was a good one, regardless. To many self-righteous observers this was the very essence of unprincipled opportunism. All received, "absolute" truths, it appeared, could be laid aside if they did not suit the occasion. Like schoolchildren who discover that they have been speaking "prose" all their lives, politicians discovered that they were pragmatists. From here the step to relativism, where the truth varies according to one's perspective and the circumstances, was a short one. The groundwork was being laid, among common people as well as the most highly educated, for a society in which a wide variety of ideals, even conflicting ones, could peacefully coexist, and in which co-operation and compromise would achieve legitimacy because they were practical.

All these developments occurred in many states and in the nation at large. Yet because of Massachusetts's early experience with industrialization as well as large-scale non-English immigration, it was on the leading edge of the new, pragmatic pluralism. Several generations of Massachusetts people had been actively seeking to reconcile diversity with the ideal of uniformity, and to accommodate old truths with new realities. So it was not entirely coincidental that Oliver Wendell Holmes, the jurist, and his friend the Boston attorney Louis Dembitz Brandeis became central figures in national affairs, bringing legitimacy to pragmatism and relativism in public policy and jurisprudence.

Holmes was born in Boston in 1841. His father, a professor at Harvard Medical School, was a poet and essayist who cut a leading figure in literary circles; and his mother was the daughter of a justice of the Massachusetts Supreme Judicial Court. Young Holmes was raised in a most cultivated setting, and he prepared for Harvard at Mr. Dixwell's school. Holmes endured the pendantry of Harvard in the 1850s, but when the Civil War began, he left—weeks before graduation—to enlist. He was eager to escape from his sedate milieu and to plunge into the world of strenuous action. Earlier in his senior year he had already served as a bodyguard for Wendell Phillips in Boston, and Holmes was committed to abolition and the Union cause. He was romantically attracted to the prospect of valor on behalf of a noble cause, as Samuel Gridley Howe had been decades earlier.

Holmes wanted the war to shape his life, and it did, decisively, though unpredictably. As an officer in the Twentieth Massachusetts regiment, Holmes's war began in tedium far more penetrating than Harvard's, and it was soon joined by horrors more gruesome than the young romantic had ever imagined. From his father, the professor, Holmes had some familiarity with anatomy; but now he saw the bloody fragments scattered on the ground, and he listened to cries of mutilation and death. Before the year was out, he himself was shot through the chest and narrowly escaped death. After several months of recuperation he returned to his regiment; in 1862, at Antietam, he was shot in the neck and briefly left for dead behind Confederate lines. Again Holmes recovered and resumed his duty, and once more he was wounded, taking a ball of grapeshot in the heel. For the third time in twenty months he was a casualty, and by now he had no more enthusiasm for war. He almost wished that his foot had been amputated so he would have been released from the duty of returning to the battlefield. "War, when you are at it," he later declared, "is horrible and dull." [5] When his three-year term was up in 1864, Holmes left to return to Cambridge and Harvard Law School. Though the war continued, neither a sense of idealism nor of duty obliged him to stay; he had had enough.

Holmes was a changed man. His appearance was not much different; he was still the tall, witty, and imaginative young gentleman with bright, piercing blue eyes. But now he was reserved, detached, profoundly skeptical. The stresses of war had stripped away the hopeful shibboleths of liberal antebellum Massachusetts.

"I'm an out and outer of a democrat in theory," Holmes noted while in the army, "but for contact, except at the polls, I loathe the thick-fingered clowns we call the people—especially as the beasts are represented at political centers—vulgar, selfish and base." Repeated experience with the routines of killing fixed him with an aloof identity, and he knew it: "How indifferent one gets to the sight of death—perhaps because one gets

---

5. Memorial Day address, "A Soldier's Faith," 1895. Quoted in George M. Fredrickson, *The Inner Civil War: Northern Intellectuals and the Crisis of the Union* (New York: Harper and Row, 1968), p. 219.

aristocratic and don't value a common life—Then they are apt
to be so dirty it seems natural—'Dust to Dust.' '' [6] Holmes was
a survivor who could no longer commit himself fully to abstractions. Truths were relative, to be tested as his own ideas had
been, in the practical world.

When Holmes completed law school in 1866, he could easily
have become a wealthy establishment lawyer had he so wished.
He boasted a genealogy more distinguished, by Massachusetts
standards, than Cabot Lodge, since he was descended from
seventeenth-century governors Dudley and Bradstreet, the
poetess Ann Bradstreet, and an assortment of Olivers, Lees,
Quincys, and Wendells. His family had, as he put it, for generations "been in the habit of receiving a college education," [7]
and he himself was recognized as both highly disciplined and
brilliant. Moreover, he liked the lawyer's work, the research,
the briefs, the pleadings, the precision and sophistication it demanded. Nevertheless, immersed as he was in the world of affairs, he also edited the *American Law Review* and became an
intellectual in spite of his doubts about ideas and abstractions.

His companions in the early 1870s were the members of the
Metaphysical Club that met in Cambridge. In the evenings
Holmes would join William James, Charles S. Peirce, and
Chauncy Wright, among others, and it was in their discussions
that the principles of pragmatism were first articulated. Later, as
Holmes developed his major treatise, *The Common Law* (1881),
he interpreted legal history as a pragmatic, evolving phenome-
non in which the law, instead of being a set of fixed, absolute
principles, was continuously changing: "The life of the law has
not been logic: it has been experience. The felt necessities of the
time . . . have had a good deal more to do than the syllogism
in determining the rules by which men should be governed." [8]

6. In *Touched with Fire: Civil War Letters and Diary of Oliver Wendell Holmes, Jr.*,
ed. by Mark DeWolfe Howe (Cambridge: Harvard Univ. Press, 1946), pp. 71, 78.

7. Holmes statement, in Harvard Class of 1861 yearbook; quoted in M. D. Howe,
Justice Oliver Wendell Holmes: The Shaping Years, 1841–1870 (Cambridge: Harvard
Univ. Press, 1957), p. 76.

8. Quoted in Mark DeWolfe Howe, *Justice Oliver Wendell Holmes: The Proving
Years, 1870–1882* (Cambridge, Mass.: Harvard University Press, 1963), p. 155.

The consequence of these views was a more flexible, open-minded approach to law than generally prevailed within the legal profession.

A year after *The Common Law* was published, an endowed professorship was created for Holmes at Harvard Law School, and he returned to what he regarded as "the sidelines" of mere theory. Academic law was not his preference, and when the opportunity came to take a seat on the supreme judicial court of the commonwealth, his grandfather Jackson's old bench, Holmes seized it. For the next twenty years Holmes's impact on Massachusetts law and, through it, public policy in other states as well, would mount. Because of his sensitivity to "the felt necessities of the time," including the rights of labor, many of his peers on the bench and at the bar regarded him as a radical. But though he was not a doctrinaire supporter of capitalists, he won their sometimes grudging respect through his genius. One lawyer who often pleaded before Holmes reported that "his questions went so to the root of the case, that it was rather an ordeal to appear before him. In arguing a case you felt that when your sentence was half done he had seen the end of it, and before the argument was a third finished that he had seen the whole course of reasoning and was wondering whether it was sound." [9] In time, Holmes became chief justice in Massachusetts.

Yet when Henry Cabot Lodge proposed to Theodore Roosevelt that Holmes be appointed to the United States Supreme Court in 1902, the idea was controversial. Many lawyers regarded Holmes as too unpredictable, and Senator Hoar, who did not really understand Holmes, believed his mind ran too much "to subtleties and refinements, and no decision of his makes a great landmark in jurisprudence." [10] But Lodge, who never forgot Holmes's kindnesses to him when other Brahmins were turning their backs after he supported Blaine in 1884,

9. James M. Morton, Oct. 9, 1937. Quoted in Felix Frankfurter, "Oliver Wendell Holmes," *Dictionary of American Biography*, Supplement One (New York: Scribners, 1944), 21:422.

10. Quoted in Garraty, *Lodge*, p. 224.

pressed Roosevelt, assuring him that on such key political issues as imperialism Holmes was sound. Once the president was convinced Holmes was not a political renegade, he appointed him to the Court, and Holmes's self-consciously pragmatic jurisprudence, born in Massachusetts, began to be asserted in national rulings.

But one swallow does not make a summer, and Holmes was a lonely, frequently dissenting figure in the Court for years. Only the passage of time and the addition of new judges would change that. In many ways the turning-point came in 1916 when the reforming, Democratic President Woodrow Wilson appointed his advisor, Louis D. Brandeis, to the Court. Though Holmes and Brandeis had important differences in outlook and temperament, there were intellectual bonds between them.

Indeed, it had been the twenty-six-year-old Brandeis who had long ago raised the money to create a professorship specifically for Holmes at Harvard. Brandeis, born in Louisville, Kentucky, in 1856, had come to Harvard Law School in 1875 by way of the Louisville public schools and the *Annen Realschule* in Dresden. Bringing an alien background—his parents were Jewish immigrants from Prague who had settled in Kentucky and founded a grain and produce business a few years before his birth—Louis Brandeis quickly displayed the intellectual and personal aptitude that would place him at the head of his class and at the top of his profession. Soon after he completed law school in 1877, he entered practice in Boston as a partner of his Brahmin classmate Samuel D. Warren, Jr., while he simultaneously clerked for the chief justice of the Massachusetts Supreme Judicial Court. Through these connections Brandeis's legal practice flourished, and within a decade he became a prosperous and prominent member of the Massachusetts bar. Antisemitism, like the more generalized xenophobia that pervaded Yankee circles, was not a serious barrier for Brandeis, whose extraordinary abilities had led influential sponsors to befriend and to employ him. Somewhat in the manner of the exceptional John Boyle O'Reilly, Brandeis was insulated from much hostility by his own brilliance and ascetic charm. To Brandeis even yachting and polo clubs opened their doors.

By the 1890s Brandeis was a wealthy man who had arrived. Now his social conscience awakened, and instead of serving privileged capitalists he turned to advocacy on behalf of common people. In the eyes of many lawyers he emerged as a radical in 1892 when he denounced steel company union-busting at Homestead, Pennsylvania. "Organized capital," he declared, had "hired a private army to shoot at organized labor for resisting an arbitrary cut in wages." [11] Hereafter, as Holmes sought to make law more flexible, Brandeis worked to make it more just and human within the framework of capitalism and competition.

Ultimately, Brandeis rose to national prominence as a conservative defender of individual rights and a foe of monopoly. Brandeis fought railroad and utility monopolies on behalf of individual stockholders and consumers to purify the competitive system. Concerned about the rise of bureaucracy, he also took on the federal government when a lowly official was fired for revealing collusion between the Interior Department and special interests seeking access to Alaskan minerals. Like Holmes, Brandeis was a legal pragmatist. In his most notable case before the Supreme Court, Brandeis defended the Oregon law governing women's working conditions that established the ten-hour day. Brandeis did not argue from abstractions; he argued from experience, confronting the Court with a fact-filled comparative analysis of the impact of excessive hours on health and productivity in the United States and overseas. Here, with regard to the hours of working women, the impact of that long-ago-and-faraway Metaphysical Club of Cambridge pragmatists was apparent in national social policy.

The practical, realistic approach to jurisprudence that Brandeis shared with Holmes gradually came to prevail during the first decades of the twentieth century. Recognition of social realities in courts of law meant that prevailing views of social justice could gain a hearing. Holmes made his greatest direct impact as an advocate of judicial restraint, repeatedly arguing

11. Quoted in Paul A. Freund, "Louis Dembitz Brandeis," *Dictionary of American Biography*, Supplement Two (New York: Scribners, 1958), 22:94.

that legislatures—which were responsive to the Progressives' ideals of social justice in the marketplace—had the right to act whether or not courts agreed with their policies. During this period the Supreme Court was zealously employing the Fourteenth Amendment, which barred states from abridging "the privileges or immunities of citizens," [12] as a bulwark to defend corporate "citizens" from the pressures of labor unions and regulatory legislation. The prevailing ideology on the Court favored a laissez-faire social Darwinism, in which corporations should be allowed to pursue the competitive struggle as they saw fit. Holmes, whose personal outlook was substantially influenced by Darwin's and Spencer's evolutionary views, believed that such beliefs were irrelevant to the issues of legislative power. "The Fourteenth Amendment," he declared in 1905, "does not enact Mr. Herbert Spencer's *Social Statistics.*" [13] Later Holmes commented that legislation was "like buying a ticket to the theatre. If you are sure you want to go to the show and have the money to pay for it, there is an end of the matter. I may think you foolish to want to go, but that has nothing to do with my duty." [14] Holmes did, in fact, think some of the legislation was foolish, and he was skeptical of altruism. By assuming an Olympian posture Holmes enhanced the credibility of his message.

Brandeis, whom President Wilson appointed to the Court in 1916, was heavily criticized during the confirmation proceedings because he had been a partisan of reform. Again and again Brandeis had denounced "industrial absolutism," arguing that it was incompatible with democracy in the long run. [15] It must be transformed by the intervention of labor unions so that industrial democracy might become a reality. Brandeis was the altruistic, socially committed reformer Holmes so doubted, but on the

12. Constitution of the United States.

13. Quoted in Richard Hofstadter, *Social Darwinism in American Thought,* rev. ed. (Boston: Beacon Press, 1955), p. 47.

14. Holmes to Franklin Ford, April 6, 1911, Holmes Letters, Harvard Law School Library, Cambridge, Mass.

15. May 4, 1905, address, "The Opportunity in the Law," in Alpheus Thomas Mason, *Free Government in the Making: Readings in American Political Thought,* second edition (New York: Oxford University Press, 1956), p. 692.

bench they were allies against "judicial sanction" of what Brandeis called the "half-truths" of "survival of the fittest" doctrines.[16]

When they went to the Supreme Court, Holmes and Brandeis left Massachusetts, except to return for summers on the North Shore (for Holmes) and on the Cape (for Brandeis). But the issues that they were now confronting in the national arena were connected fundamentally to the historic dilemmas of individual and corporate rights in Massachusetts. How absolute were the rights of an individual? In what measure could groups prescribe limits on individuals? When people joined in concert to promote their aims, what was their status? In the 1630s the individual consciences of the migrants had been paramount, relative to the English church and state. But in the same decade the corporate good of Massachusetts ruled over the consciences of dissenting individuals like Roger Williams, and groups like the followers of Anne Hutchinson. In 1688 and again in 1775 and 1787 insurgent groups had formed in the name of individual rights to challenge what they saw as usurping state power. Throughout the nineteenth century people had formed voluntary associations that were bent on asserting the rights of their members to free speech and assembly, and on defining the common good even if it meant, as in the case of the Temperance movement, limiting the rights of others. Holmes and Brandeis had been trained in Massachusetts, where conflicts between the individual and the group, between the private and the public good had been repeatedly articulated. Not even conflicts between organized labor and organized capital were new to Massachusetts. Holmes could recall the great Lynn shoemakers' strike of 1860, at the time the largest strike in American history. Brandeis could not forget the strike in Lawrence that closed up Massachusetts's largest mills in 1912. The actors and their interests in the conflicts changed, as did the settings; but whether the arguments were couched in religious or secular terms, whether voiced by Yankees or immigrants, the core political issues fundamental to a republican society remained.

16. Jan. 3, 1915, address, "The Living Law," in Mason, *Free Government*, p. 693.

What was new was the pragmatic willingness to accept social friction. Acknowledging the heterogeneity and competition among Massachusetts citizens and their interests, people learned that tolerance had become a necessity. But it did not come easily to everyone. Memories and traditions, as well as economic and electoral competition, sustained hostilities while they nurtured group consciousness. Haltingly, people adjusted to the multiethnic, urban, industrial character of Massachusetts.

9

The New Industrial
Commonwealth

N twentieth-century Massachusetts, strains between groups and individuals were particularly keen. Every person, it seemed, had several identities, one that was exclusively his own, and others that associated him with an ethnic heritage, an occupation, and a social class. The rights of the majority, acting through the state and public opinion, could infringe on individuals and minorities. Such conflicts occurred repeatedly, from the first decades of the twentieth century onward. In Massachusetts many of the vital issues of contemporary America have been boldly articulated: civil liberties; minority and women's rights; the rights of labor.

Yet Massachusetts was not one continuous, flaming battleground of discord. Parallel to the struggles over corporate and individual rights, Massachusetts was emerging as a substantially pluralistic commonwealth. Electoral politics have channeled ethnic rivalry into routines that excite interest, but not passionate commitment. In time, Massachusetts Yankees, Irish, Italians, and the other ethnic groups have reached accommodations with each other so that in the Bay State, as throughout the United States, boundaries of color and class remain the most formidable sources of hostility and barriers to trust.

Here Massachusetts's electoral history furnishes revealing

symbols of the nature of the emerging pluralism. People have fought vigorously over many questions, but when they have found a candidate who inspires confidence, they have yielded a portion of their ethnic and ideological commitment. Moreover, everyone can identify with some aspect of Massachusetts's past: the idealism of Puritans, Revolutionaries, and reformers; the aristocratic culture of the eighteenth and nineteenth centuries; or the upward struggle of more recent immigrants, the underdogs of the industrial era. People have come into the future bringing their own past and that of the commonwealth. The past is always part of the present, and indeed old names and families have exhibited a rare staying power in politics because people remember, whether in the old industrial cities, the sprawling suburbs, or the countrysides of fields and forests, of rocks, of sand and salt air. If one wishes to escape the past, one must leave Massachusetts, because those who stay cannot forget, and it comes to assimilate newcomers.

In a democracy, conflicts between minorities and majorities are inescapable. In the nineteenth century, Massachusetts was a staging-ground for the minorities of educational reformers, temperance advocates, feminists, and, among others, abolitionists who sought to persuade the majority. In the twentieth century several of the descendants of William Lloyd Garrison and his peers united with a handful of Massachusetts blacks to continue the drive for equal rights. Together they would join in founding the National Association for the Advancement of Colored People, the principal agent of black rights in the new century and ultimately the architect of the national policy of desegregation.

The most remarkable of these people was W. E. Burghardt DuBois, who was born in the Housatonic Valley at Great Barrington in 1869. Raised among his mother's people, who had been in town for generations, DuBois developed a strong, characteristically Massachusetts sense of place:

> The social classes of the town were built partly on landholding farmers and more especially on manufacturers and merchants. . . . The rich people of the town were not very rich nor many in number. The middle class were farmers, merchants and artisans; and beneath these was a small proletariat of Irish and German mill workers.

They lived in slums near the woolen mills and across the river clustering about the Catholic Church. The number of colored people in the town and country was small. They were all, save directly after the [Civil] war, old families, well-known to the old settlers among the whites. The color line was manifest and yet not absolutely drawn. I remember a cousin of mine who brought home a white wife. The chief objection was that he was not able to support her and nobody knew about her family; and knowledge of family history was counted as highly important. Most of the colored people had some white blood from unions several generations past. That they congregated together in their own social life was natural because that was the rule in the town. . . .[1]

Although his family was poor, it was respectable, and DuBois enjoyed Great Barrington, for its surroundings were "a boy's paradise: there were mountains to climb and rivers to wade and swim; lakes to freeze and hills for coasting. There were orchards and caves and wide green fields; and all of it was apparently property of the children." After school he did odd jobs—"splitting kindling, mowing lawns, doing chores."[2] Because his brilliance was recognized in the town school, the principal of the high school encouraged DuBois to prepare for college, and a mill owner's wife purchased the necessary texts in algebra, geometry, Latin, and Greek for him.

When DuBois was graduated in 1884, he delivered a public oration on Wendell Phillips. Though neither he nor his audience knew it, ultimately his own career would carry on Phillips's devotion to human rights and social justice. "My heart was set on Harvard," DuBois later recalled, since "it was the greatest and oldest college and I therefore quite naturally thought it was the one I must attend."[3] But the Great Barrington High School had not prepared him for the entrance exam, nor had he the necessary funds, so he went to work. Soon after, however, white sponsors came forward and offered to send DuBois to the all-black Fisk University in Nashville, Tennessee. Fisk was not

1. W. E. B. DuBois, *Dusk of Dawn: The Autobiography of a Race Concept* (New York: Schocken, 1968), pp. 9–10.

2. DuBois, *Dusk of Dawn*, p. 13.

3. DuBois, *Dusk of Dawn*, p. 20.

Harvard, but he was pleased to go. Going south was an adventure, and for DuBois it would play a crucial role in establishing his sense of himself as a champion of black equality.

For the young black Yankee from the Berkshires, Fisk provided an awakening as to what it meant to be black in America. In the summers DuBois taught school for the children of black sharecroppers in the Tennessee countryside, and as editor of the *Fisk Herald* he began to express "a belligerent attitude toward the color bar." [4] At graduation in 1888 he won a scholarship to enter Harvard, and when he joined the junior class he had already learned to accept the social segregation that prevailed there.

Eagerly, DuBois took advantage of the faculty and library Harvard offered. Philosophy was his first love: "I was repeatedly a guest in the house of William James; he was my friend and guide to clear thinking; I was a member of the Philosophical Club and talked with Royce and Palmer; I sat in an upper room and read Kant's Critique with Santayana." But William James persuaded DuBois to turn toward history and social science because, he told his student, " 'it is hard to earn a living with philosophy.' " [5] Thus DuBois became a protégé of the historian Albert Bushnell Hart and went on, with his study of the suppression of the African slave trade, to become, in 1895, the first black to earn a doctorate at Harvard. DuBois proved that intellectually he had few peers.

For social life DuBois turned to the small, cultivated black community in the vicinity. Some of his most rewarding evenings were spent at the home of Maria Louise Baldwin, the principal of the Agassiz grammar school. Miss Baldwin, who at the age of thirty-three had become the first black principal in Massachusetts in 1889, was a Cambridge native, a graduate of its high school and teaching training school, and a lecturer of note. She was also, in her modest way, a *salonière* for black intellectuals, and her home was the headquarters of the literary Banneker Club and the more wide-ranging Omar Circle. Du-

4. DuBois, *Dusk of Dawn*, pp. 31–32.
5. DuBois, *Dusk of Dawn*, pp. 38, 39.

Bois, who was deeply appreciative and admiring, described her as "always serene, just slightly mocking, refusing to be thundered or domineered into silence and answering always in that low, rich voice—with questionings, with frank admission of uncertainty." For DuBois, who admitted he was then in his "hottest, narrowest, self-centered, confident period," [6] Baldwin made a superb foil. It was in her parlor that DuBois came to know the equally headstrong William Monroe Trotter, his ally years later when they worked on behalf of the NAACP to challenge white supremacy and the Booker T. Washington brand of accommodation. Maria Baldwin's influence not only touched the lives of several thousand students in her forty years at the Agassiz school, she also cultivated the aspirations of passing black Harvard students to whom the college turned a cold shoulder socially.

Trotter, several years younger than DuBois, came from a prominent black family and was a native of Boston who had come to Harvard from the suburban Hyde Park High School in 1891. His father, the son of a Mississippi slave owner and slave mother, had been raised as a free black in Cincinnati. During the Civil War James Monroe Trotter had enlisted in Holmes's friend Nathaniel Hallowell's black regiment, where he rose to the rank of second lieutenant and led the struggle for the principle of equal pay for black soldiers. After the war the senior Trotter settled in Boston, where he became the leading black Democrat. In 1884, one year before Thomas Gargan became the first Irishman to give the Fourth of July address in Boston, Trotter gave the oration in Hyde Park, and three years later President Cleveland named him to succeed Frederick Douglass in the lucrative position of recorder of deeds for the District of Columbia. Notwithstanding political differences, Senator Hoar endorsed Trotter, and he won the post for the two remaining years of Cleveland's administration.

It was no wonder that Monroe Trotter, a junior Phi Beta

---

6. Quoted in Dorothy B. Porter, "Maria Louise Baldwin," *Notable American Women, 1607–1950,* Edward T. James *et al.,* eds., 3 vols. (Cambridge, Mass.: Harvard University Press, 1971), 1:87.

Kappa and a graduate *magna cum laude* of Harvard in 1895, rejected Booker T. Washington's program of manual training for blacks and accommodation to segregation and disfranchisement. Like DuBois, Trotter knew from firsthand experience that intellectual capacity was not a matter of race, and he had grown up competing successfully with whites. Several years after graduation Trotter came to realize that for him the advocacy of equal rights, becoming a "race champion," was more important than respectable prosperity. In 1901, together with George W. Forbes, a black Amherst College graduate, he founded the *Guardian,* a newspaper that quickly became the most militant defender of equal rights in the United States.

Soon Trotter became notorious as a renegade. In 1903 he was jailed for his part in disrupting a speech that Booker T. Washington was giving at the African Methodist Episcopal Zion Church on Columbus Avenue in Boston; and Washington, who did not brook opposition, ever after did his best to denigrate Trotter and destroy his influence. Since Trotter sometimes had a sharp and abusive tongue, and the pages of the *Guardian* were often enlivened with personal invective, Washington had no difficulty in persuading whites. Even the descendants of William Lloyd Garrison, who had known the Trotter family for years, came to regard Monroe Trotter as unreasonable.

Yet he persisted. In 1907 he moved the *Guardian* to the old *Liberator* office, the very building where Garrison had been mobbed, and he adorned his desk with a bust of the abolitionist who would not equivocate or "retreat a single inch," and who insisted that he would be heard. By now Trotter, who had joined DuBois in organizing the Niagara Movement for equal rights, had made himself one of the key spokesmen for the growing minority of blacks who, rejecting "Bookerism," spoke in favor of complete equality of opportunity for blacks—in education, jobs, and politics. Although Trotter was so much the self-righteous individualist that he was temperamentally unsuited to collaboration, he worked for a few years with DuBois; and gradually several key whites, including Oswald Garrison Villard (grandson of Trotter's hero) and Moorfield Storey (former secretary of the abolitionist Senator Charles Sumner), came to respect his principles. By 1910, when the NAACP was formed, Trotter participated as a militant gadfly rather than an insider. He was too irascible for the new organization that would ultimately supplant Booker T. Washington as the quasi-official voice of black Americans to white leaders. DuBois was by now an experienced educator and scholar who had taught for years in Atlanta and who had studied and traveled abroad. He had become more urbane and sophisticated than Trotter; and after his experiences at Fisk and Atlanta, DuBois was ready to compromise lesser points for larger ones. Like his mentor, William James, his idealism merged with his pragmatism.

From here on, his path separated from Trotter's, as DuBois became the chief spokesman of the NAACP and the editor (and frequently author) of its publications. Trotter, though he collaborated with NAACP officials in working successfully in 1911 to defeat a bill in the general court that would have banned interracial marriage in Massachusetts, went his own way. In 1908 he had led in forming the all-black Negro-American Political League which in a few years became a vehicle for his own leadership as the National Equal Rights League, a rival to the largely white NAACP. It was Trotter's independence from the more circumspect NAACP that led to his famous confrontation with President Wilson over the introduction of segregation in the federal bureaucracy.

In 1912 Trotter had led the effort among northern blacks to support Wilson's candidacy in the hope that Wilson would provide greater recognition of equal rights. But soon after taking office the southern members of Wilson's cabinet persuaded the president that segregation should prevail. Trotter, who looked for more, not less, from Wilson, was alarmed. In late 1913 he led a delegation to meet with Wilson, and the president, as Trotter reported in the *Guardian*, "listened attentively to Colored citizens, . . . responded courteously and gave them thirty-five minutes of his time." Yet Wilson did not budge, and a year later Trotter and his colleagues returned. This time Wilson lectured them on the virtues of segregation. It was, he said, "a benefit, and ought to be so regarded by you gentlemen." Trotter, who with his father had been fighting patronizing white supremacists since Lincoln's day, was outraged. Speaking from personal experience he replied to the president: "For fifty years white and colored clerks have been working together in peace and harmony and friendliness, doing so even through two Democratic administrations. Soon after your inauguration began, segregation was drastically introduced." Interrupting, Wilson imperiously declared: "Your manner offends me." But Trotter was undaunted, and for nearly an hour the argument continued. When Trotter later revealed the contents of the interview to reporters, the White House was shocked by this breach of etiquette. But Wilson would not yield, and public opinion, especially in the south, supported his intransigence. Although there were few advocates of official segregation in Massachusetts, and Republicans took pleasure from Wilson's difficulties, informally it was emerging. Trotter himself was denounced by the respected *Boston Evening Transcript* as an "impudent mischief-maker." [7] The white majority in Massachusetts recognized the political rights of the black minority, but the vision of a black man confronting a white official, the president, was offensive.

Several years later, anxieties resulting from minority challenges to majority opinion generated a dramatic confrontation in Massachusetts when the Boston police, of largely Irish background, staged a strike. Coming within the context of ethnic suspicions, widespread labor discontent, and growing concern about political radicals during the "red scare," the strike revealed tensions inherent in the creation of a pluralistic democracy in industrial Massachusetts. Although the conflict was ostensibly Boston's alone, the whole state was involved, and Governor Calvin Coolidge, a modest Northampton lawyer, would parlay his role in the episode into the vice-presidency.

The strike, which had been brewing for weeks, occurred in mid-September 1919. The central issue was whether or not the city would accept a police union affiliated with the American Federation of Labor. When the police went out on strike, an unprecedented step, they were rapidly maneuvered into becoming

---

7. Quoted in Stephen R. Fox, *The Guardian of Boston: William Monroe Trotter* (New York: Atheneum, 1970), pp. 175, 180, 183.

the scapegoats for the mob violence and the destruction of downtown property that resulted. Volunteer policemen, largely recruited from among middle- and upper-class suburban Protestants, together with National Guardsmen from around the state restored order in the weeks that followed, and the strikers were defeated. Calvin Coolidge, the prim symbol of Yankee Americanism, seized the opportunity to vindicate law and order; and indeed Yankee Republicans used the strike to put labor, new immigrants, and the Boston Irish "in their place." The issues that were publicly debated revolved around the rights of labor and the rights of the majority, Governor Coolidge declaring: "There is no right to strike against the public safety by anybody, anywhere, any time." [8] The common good was preeminent—an old, fundamental principle in Massachusetts public life.

Beneath the surface, however, there was an undertow of ethnic division. Long ago the state legislature had reduced Boston's municipal autonomy because of the statewide Yankee Republican suspicion of the dangers of Irish rule. Now, in the aftermath of the First World War, when Irish patriots were protesting the United States's close alliance with Britain, preferring neutrality, some Yankees doubted Irish-American loyalty. Indeed, the prescription of one police strikebreaker was simply to "select a few old-fashioned Yankees—full-blooded Americans to instill a little Americanism" in Boston.[9] Even though the Irish-Americans of Massachusetts had participated heroically under arms in wartime, even though officials of the Catholic Church had firmly supported law and order, staying aloof from the strikers, the old doubts lingered.

Just a few months after the turmoil of the police strike subsided, two robberies occurred south of Boston in Bridgewater and Braintree. Although two men were killed in the Braintree holdup, these incidents were not in themselves remarkable. But

8. Calvin Coolidge telegram to Samuel Gompers, Sept. 14, 1919, quoted in Francis Russell, *A City in Terror—1919—: The Boston Police Strike* (New York: Viking, 1975), p. 191.

9. Quoted in Russell, *A City in Terror*, p. 195.

the effort to solve these crimes, which led to the arrest, trial, and execution of Nicola Sacco and Bartolomeo Vanzetti, became one of the great dramas of Massachusetts history. Just as the trials of Anne Hutchinson and the Salem "witches" had aroused imaginations and readily lent themselves to symbolic interpretations, so did the Sacco and Vanzetti case; but in contrast to them, it developed in the glare of nationwide publicity and became, in the eyes of many, a test of the ability of American democracy to dispense even-handed justice.

Sacco and Vanzetti had come to Massachusetts from Italy in 1908 and had become marginal members of the industrial labor force. By the time of their arrest in 1920, Sacco was settled with a wife and child in South Stoughton, where he was an edger in Kelley's shoe factory; and Vanzetti was living in Plymouth, where he peddled fish, door to door. Both men were in their early thirties, and both were active in a minor way among Italian immigrant anarchists. When they were arrested three weeks after the Braintree robbery, each was carrying a loaded pistol.

Within a few weeks Vanzetti was indicted for the Bridgewater robbery, and after a week-long trial he was convicted on July 1, 1920. A year later, in a trial that lasted six weeks, both Sacco and Vanzetti were convicted of the Braintree crimes. Then for six long years the case remained in litigation, with motions for new trials and finally an appeal to the Massachusetts Supreme Judicial Court. During this period left-liberal activists succeeded in making the case a national, even an international *cause célèbre*. Left-wing and liberal groups believed that the defendants were innocent, and that as Italian anarchists they were victims of ethnic and political prejudice. Their case was used to arouse libertarian sentiments and as a means of challenging the legitimacy of the native white Protestant "establishment."

Finally, when the last appeal was denied, the fate of the two "martyrs" was left to the Republican Governor Alvan Fuller, a bicycle mechanic turned automobile entrepreneur and congressman, whose chief assets at the polls were his great wealth and his companionable nature. Fuller wanted to do right, but as a firm believer in the death penalty he did not mean to err on the side of leniency. Only recently he had denied the request of three Catholic mothers who, backed by a petition of 120,000 people including three ex-governors, had prayed on their knees in his office for their sons' lives. In that instance two of the three convicts were merely accessories to murder, but Fuller, seemingly immune to the pressure of humanitarian appeals, was content that their death sentences be carried out. When Fuller decided to review the Sacco and Vanzetti case and to appoint an advisory committee, headed by President Abbott Lawrence Lowell of Harvard, he wanted to do a thorough job that would appear so fair and meticulous that it would reinforce the legitimacy of Massachusetts government.

From Fuller's standpoint the choice of Lowell to advise him was perfect. By definition a Harvard president could not be corrupt; a man descended from several of the wealthiest, most distinguished Yankee families must be widely respected; and Lowell had long ago proved his civil-libertarian credentials. During the police strike when pressure at Harvard mounted to fire Harold Laski, the temporary lecturer in political science, Lowell, who disagreed with Laski's outspoken support of the strikers, defended him, declaring that if Laski was fired he would resign. What Fuller failed to appreciate was that to outsiders there was no better symbol of smug, self-righteous Yankee establishment than President Lowell. If Lowell's committee found in favor of Sacco and Vanzetti, he was a good choice; if not, the friends of the doomed men would see collusion by the Massachusetts elite.

As it turned out, Lowell's committee, like Governor Fuller, came to the conclusion that Sacco and Vanzetti had been fairly tried and sentenced, so on August 23, 1927, they were executed. That act symbolized Massachusetts's painful, seemingly irreconcilable divisions. W. E. B. DuBois concluded ruefully that "the social community that mobbed Garrison, easily hanged Sacco and Vanzetti." [10] The trial records, as analyzed at the time by the Harvard law professor Felix Frankfurter, showed that a Yankee judge and jury had displayed prejudice,

10. DuBois, *Dusk of Dawn*, p. 40.

that the testimony of immigrant witnesses on behalf of the defendants had been ignored, and led to the conclusion that, if Sacco and Vanzetti had been Yankees, they would never have been indicted, much less convicted. The decision of Lowell, made in good faith, was also a reflection of his own ethnic solidarity. One of Lowell's old Harvard classmates explained to the confounded Frankfurter that he believed Lowell was simply "incapable of seeing that two wops could be right and the Yankee judiciary wrong." [11]

Though they became victims, the fact that the rights of two anticlerical, immigrant anarchists generated profound concern in Massachusetts and the nation was a measure of the emerging liberal pluralism. In the name of the common good, Americans had often ridden roughshod over minorities in the past, sometimes employing the dignity of judicial procedures as in Anne Hutchinson's case, sometimes, as in the Ursuline Convent and Garrison mobs, with direct violence. The Sacco-Vanzetti case, like those of the Scottsboro Boys in Alabama in the 1930s and the Rosenbergs in the early 1950s, was understood as being more than just another prosecution to determine innocence or guilt. In all of them the balance between corporate, majority, and individual rights—procedural and political—was being tested.

The deaths of Nicola Sacco and Bartolomeo Vanzetti signaled the end of the Yankee era in Massachusetts, though few people realized it because of the immediate outcome. Ever since the massive Irish migration had begun three generations back, Yankee hegemony had been challenged. Now, in the second quarter of the twentieth century, it was faltering as the political consequences of the changing population were realized. In 1924, the year that Lodge's immigration restriction went into full force, the Republican presidential candidate, Massachusetts's own Calvin Coolidge, carried the state for the last time. Until then Massachusetts had always been safely Republican (except when Theodore Roosevelt divided the party's vote in 1912); now it became safely Democrat (except for the Eisenhower landslides

11. Quoted in Francis Russell, *Tragedy in Dedham: The Story of the Sacco-Vanzetti Case* (New York: McGraw-Hill, 1971), p. 374.

of 1952 and 1956). Yankees would remain prominent in public life—but only as a competing ethnic group in a pluralistic setting. They could no longer successfully adopt the posture of the special guardians of the commonwealth nor define its objectives in their own terms.

The ethnic and class tensions of Massachusetts in the 1920s, dramatized in the Sacco-Vanzetti case and in the rise of Ku Klux Klan assemblies in central and western counties, were exacerbated by a declining economy. World War I had generated a boom in textiles, shoemaking, shipbuilding, and a wide range of light industries. Even agriculture had enjoyed a modest prosperity. But when the postwar recession came in 1921, the state's economy began to stagnate. The old sources of large-scale employment slid into a long-term decine. Massachusetts, in the vanguard of the industrial revolution in America, also led the way toward industrial depression. Its factories were old; its machinery was old; labor unions were developing, pushing wages higher; and capitalists sought profits elsewhere. Although circumstances had changed radically between the War of 1812 and the First World War, the postwar economic drift, the inability to find quickly new kinds of investment and employment after old ones waned, were similar. When the international depression of the 1930s unfolded, people faced disastrous levels of unemployment—twenty, thirty, even forty percent in some localities. The local and state political response in Massachusetts as throughout the nation was belt-tightening in public services, so still more people were put out of work. State and local government, private capital, no group or individual in Massachusetts, could furnish effective remedies. As never before, people looked to the government at Washington and to the man who came to personify national power, Franklin D. Roosevelt.

This charming, innovative, and ultimately far-sighted leader found palliatives but not genuine remedies for the national economic disaster. Under the stimulus of the New Deal, Massachusetts's economy revived, but it was not until the war economy emerged in 1940 and 1941 that full employment and prosperity returned. The livelihoods of many of its inhabitants were tied directly or indirectly to federal spending, especially in defense. This pattern came to provide Massachusetts with at least a partial means of expanding its economy once again.

When the Second World War ended in 1945, and the shoe and textile industries receded once more in the face of competition from overseas and from the south, defense spending generated by the Cold War and the Korean War in the early 1950s continued to buttress the state's economy. Otis Air Force Base on the Cape, the Hanscom and Westover bases west of Boston, provided substantial direct employment, as did the shipyards at Quincy and Lynn. Even more significant, wartime research in electronics had begun to turn the scientific and technical capabilities of Harvard and the Massachusetts Institute of Technology into immense economic resources. In the 1950s and 1960s, still nourished in part by government research and development funds, eastern Massachusetts enjoyed a small-scale second industrial revolution along Route 128, the superhighway semicircle from Gloucester and Danvers in the northeast, through Lexington and Weston in the west, and southeast through Dedham and Quincy. New high-technology, clean electronic industries burgeoned, and their well-educated, well-paid employees altered the politics of suburban Boston and, in some measure, of the entire state. Coming from diverse social and ethnic backgrounds, sometimes from out of state, these people did not fit the old ethnic categories, nor did they exhibit strong party loyalties.

Electronics was Massachusetts's great new industry, but service activities also grew markedly. Postwar Boston expanded as a center of money management, banking, and insurance. Education, medical, and social services grew rapidly, nourished largely by federal and state appropriations. As a result, a new middle class was emerging, more cosmopolitan and heterogeneous than the predominantly small-town Protestant middle class of preceding generations. Economic and social changes that were national in scope were shaping a context for pluralism to flourish in a state that had been struggling with it for decades. By the beginning of the 1950s a new kind of ethnic politics was emerging that would encourage coalitions across traditional dividing lines in state and congressional elections.

The history of the Kennedy family in Massachusetts public life reveals much of this complex metamorphosis. The first Kennedy, Patrick, came to East Boston in 1848 at the age of twenty-five as part of the great famine exodus. In County Wexford he had been a tenant farmer, but in Boston he found work making barrels, so he became a cooper. After a few years he married a fellow-migrant, Bridget Murphy, and they had three daughters and a son, Patrick Joseph Kennedy, born in 1858, just a few months before his father died. Now a widow, Bridget Kennedy worked heroically to keep her family together, and she succeeded by working in a shop and by taking a job dressing the hair of stylish ladies at the great downtown Jordan Marsh emporium. The baby Patrick was raised by his sisters and, for seven or eight years, attended parochial school before leaving to become a stevedore. It was here, on the East Boston waterfront, in the year that Henry Cabot Lodge graduated from Harvard, that "P. J." Kennedy's real-life Horatio-Alger rise to respectability and power began.

Longshoremen rarely became prosperous, but the brawny, hard-working P. J. Kennedy was a saver of pennies, of dimes, of dollars. After a few years he had saved enough to purchase a run-down saloon in the shadow of Faneuil Hall on Haymarket square. From here he never looked back, gradually expanding his business until he became not only a saloon-keeper in Boston and East Boston but a retail and wholesale liquor dealer. Before he was thirty, Kennedy became a power in East Boston politics, winning election to the state house of representatives in 1886 during O'Brien's mayoralty, and later, in 1892, going to the state senate.

Representative P. J. Kennedy married Mary Hickey in 1887, and the following year Joseph Patrick Kennedy was born. Young Joseph was raised in a privileged, middle-class setting. His prudent and calculating father continued his upward ascent, becoming a prominent fixture in municipal government and a prosperous capitalist with investments in Boston real estate and two small local banks. He carved out his career within the confines of the Boston Irish; but for his son he wished all doors to open. Consequently he cultivated his son's competitive drives and sent him to the elite Boston Latin School where he could prepare for Harvard.

Young Joseph Kennedy was very bright, but not in an academic way, and he only barely made it through the Latin School and into Harvard. But like his father, he did not look back. Harvard presented opportunities for a man on the make to acquire the right social patina, to make useful acquaintances. Given the ambitions of P. J. Kennedy and his son Joe, scholarship was a necessary evil, and many of Joe's highborn Protestant classmates agreed. Judging from his actions after he graduated in 1912, Joe Kennedy aimed to crack the remaining barriers to power and prestige in Massachusetts.

His chosen route was banking, and he quickly landed a job as a state banking examiner—a marvelous opportunity for on-the-job training. From there he quickly moved to acquire the Columbia Trust Company in East Boston, in which his father had long had an interest. At twenty-five he became the youngest bank president in the state and perhaps the nation. But Kennedy was no specialist; as time went on, he sought out opportunities for profit in a wide range of investments including real estate, movie theaters, wartime shipbuilding, and common stocks. Yankee Boston saw him as a pushy, upstart speculator—but no one could deny his shrewd judgment and his talent for getting what he wanted.

In 1914 what he wanted was Rose Fitzgerald, the daughter of John F. ("Honey Fitz") Fitzgerald, Boston's mayor in 1906–1907, and a perennial power in city politics. Rose, who had graduated from Dorchester High School and later studied at the Convent of the Sacred Heart, had been voted Boston's prettiest graduate, a distinction Kennedy appreciated. Rose Fitzgerald was already an accomplished hostess, and Kennedy was confident she would make a splendid wife. Their wedding, which was performed by Cardinal O'Connell, was the highlight of the social season for Irish Boston.

But Kennedy was not content to live in an Irish ghetto, even at its apex. He and Rose settled in Brookline, then mostly Protestant, and as the children came along, enrolled them in private schools where there were few if any Catholics. For a while the family summered at Nantasket, an Irish resort, but they soon tried Cohasset, where old Boston predominated. Here, in a humiliating episode, the Kennedys were barred when they sought admission to the country club. Joe's ultimate response was to create his own resort for his family at Hyannis on the Cape.

Joseph Kennedy wanted a pluralistic Massachusetts, where he could be as good as the "best people" and be an Irish-American Catholic too. But during the teens and twenties that was impossible. Finally he left, moving his family to New York in 1927. By now he was a multimillionaire, having multiplied his fortune in the movie business. Except for spending summers there, the Kennedys became expatriates from Massachusetts. But they would return, and their re-entry into Massachusetts public life after the Second World War revealed how Massachusetts was changing. The agent of their return was John Fitzgerald Kennedy, their eldest surviving son. John had been born at their Brookline home in 1919, he passed summers at Hyannis, he had spent four years at Harvard from 1936 to 1940, but when he came from the Pacific war in 1945, he might as reasonably have sought a congressional seat in New York or Palm Beach as the Eleventh District of Massachusetts. But Jack Kennedy, under his father's tutelage, and with his cousin Joe Kane, an old Boston "pol," for campaign manager, set out to capture the district that James Michael Curley had just vacated in order to resume Boston's mayoralty. The district included, in addition to Cambridge, the North End and East Boston, birthplaces of his grandfathers Fitzgerald and Kennedy. It was an Irish and Italian working-class district with Harvard thrown in. Jack won, and from 1947 until 1953 he served in the House. Yet his own and family ambitions aimed higher.

Opportunity appeared in 1952. Senator Henry Cabot Lodge, grandson of the former senator, was so popular and well entrenched that major Democrats were reluctant to challenge him. Lodge had been in the Senate since 1936 and had regularly defeated Irish Democrats, including James Michael Curley, Joseph Casey, and David I. Walsh, the first Irish Catholic governor and senator in Massachusetts history. To compete with the widely respected Lodge seemed fruitless. But the Kennedys tried. For

Jack it was a contest rich in significance, for Lodge's grandfather had narrowly defeated his own grandfather, Honey Fitz, in the election of 1916. Now the grandsons did battle in a new context.

From the standpoint of issues, little divided the two candidates other than the rhetorical nostrums of their respective parties. Lodge was experienced, honest, personable, and had always been able to attract Irish, Italian, and other ethnic voters to add to his regular Republican support. He was a Brahmin Yankee candidate who had learned to campaign in a plural setting. But in Jack Kennedy he was facing something new in Massachusetts, a fourth-generation Irish immigrant who was so thoroughly "Americanized" that he could surmount ethnic stereotypes. Kennedy's well-financed, well-organized campaign won because he created a favorable impression among all sorts of voters. His ethnicity and family background were assets that he built upon, outdoing Lodge at his own game. Running against the Eisenhower landslide that swept the state and defeated the Democratic governor, Kennedy won by 70,000 votes. "At last," Rose Kennedy exulted, "the Fitzgeralds have evened the score with the Lodges!" [12]

When Kennedy ran again in 1958, the margin of his victory, 875,000 votes, demonstrated the breadth of his appeal. He had transcended ethnic politics in Massachusetts, and he was on his way to surmounting them nationwide. Ethnic politics were not dead, but in a pluralistic setting, they had become far more complicated and more entwined with other issues than ever before.

Joseph Kennedy's ambitions were not confined to his eldest son alone. In 1961, with Jack in the White House and Robert in the Cabinet, he made sure that Jack's seat remained accessible to his youngest child, Edward ("Ted"), who was not yet old enough to enter the Senate. When the new election was held in 1962, it was in many ways a rerun of 1952. After defeating

12. Quoted in Richard J. Whelan, *The Founding Father: The Story of Joseph P. Kennedy and the Family He Raised to Power* (New York: New American Library, 1966), p. 423.

Edward McCormack (nephew of John W. McCormack, Speaker of the House of Representatives) in the primary, Ted Kennedy faced Henry Cabot Lodge's son George. Neither of the two was particularly well qualified for the Senate, except for his wealth and family background, and neither had previously held elective office. That scions of these two families should be again competing for high office testified to the hold that the past still possessed. Kennedy won.

The repetition of the Kennedy-Lodge contest was in some ways misleading, since it suggested that a bi-polar Irish-Catholic–Yankee-Protestant division still dominated the state. In fact, electoral competition was coming to reflect the diversity of Massachusetts inhabitants. In 1957 the Democrat Foster Furcolo became the first Italian-American governor in Massachusetts and the United States; he was then followed by another Italian-American, the Republican John A. Volpe, in a state where Italian-Americans are a distinct minority. Later, in the 1960s, there were Yankee governors from both parties, the Democrat Endicott Peabody and the Republican Francis Sargent. In the following decade the son of Greek immigrants, the Democrat Michael Dukakis, won the governorship. Indeed even though people of Irish background are the most numerous single ethnic group, there has not been an Irish governor since Paul Dever left office in 1953. This over-all diversity became evident at the level of United States senator as well: the Kennedys held the seat John won in 1952 for a generation or more; and the same Massachusetts voters made the Republican Leverett Saltonstall an institution, and after his retirement in 1966 did the same for Republican Edward Brooke, the first black member of the Senate since Reconstruction. Ethnicity remains vitally important, especially within smaller constituencies, but coalition-building across ethnic lines dominates state political organization. As elsewhere in the United States, appeals to the voters focus on personal qualities and even, from time to time, on questions of policy.

Wholly apart from politics, the vitality of the old ethnic consciousness and the ethnic social hierarchy that it sustained have been progressively undermined during recent decades. The Massachusetts economy no longer sustains the old relationships, with Yankee owners and managers ruling immigrant labor, as in the old mill cities. In the last decades of the twentieth century many private employers were national corporations whose managers possessed only the faintest ethnic identities, and labor unions stood between the employer and the employed. Moreover, many people worked for nonprofit enterprises like government and education, so relations between "bosses" and "workers" have been transformed. In addition, large numbers of self-employed professionals and quasi-professionals and small businessmen have emerged, serving all kinds of people. Domestic service, which once reinforced class and ethnic identities all but vanished, and insofar as it survived, relied as in the past on a congeries of impoverished newcomers.

Time also brought a general assimilation toward the national common denominator purveyed in the mass culture. Just as Irish brogues were seldom heard, so the Yankee twang all but disappeared, and Harvard men or women could no longer be identified by accent. Regional and class differences survived, but black dialect was the only really vigorous, distinct ethnic mode of speech, and it was nourished by the single major postwar immigration—in this case from the South. In the generation following the Korean War, Massachusetts became predominantly a heterogeneous, middle-class, suburban state. Under these conditions strong ethnic identities, including hostility to "outsiders," rarely had meaning, and marriages across old ethnic lines became common. Ethnic pluralism survived, but only within the melting pot of mass culture. Social values were changing. Gaining access to the inner sanctum of Yankee society was a vital aspiration for Joseph and Rose Kennedy, but by the 1970s these old longings had become anachronistic. To outsiders, the exclusive Brahmin waltz evenings at the Ritz in Boston became equivalent to the polka nights at the Polish clubs. Such ethnic festivities helped groups preserve the vestiges of their identity across generations and played a minor role in encouraging marriage within the group. But the boundaries of power and prestige, and their sources, had become so inclusive that the old ethnic hierarchy that lingered in the mind was no longer grounded in reality. Wealth, education, personality, and, most of all, performance counted more than ethnicity.

In their acceptance of diverse ethnic identities, the people of Massachusetts found a partial resolution for the chronic tensions between the majority and the minority, between the community and the individual. For at some level of consciousness everyone now thought of himself as part of the majority in some circumstances, and as member of a minority, or even an isolated individual in others. Perhaps it was these realizations that brought Massachusetts people to the forefront in testing new boundaries between individual liberty and community control over issues like school busing, abortion, and gay rights in the last quarter of the twentieth century. The particular conflicts had changed, and so had Massachusetts; it was no longer substantially a world of its own. Yet integrated as it was into the nation, the old questions that had divided its people remained. Did the majority possess the right to overrule the fundamental beliefs of minorities? Where should the boundary lie between individual liberty and community values? Bradford and Winthrop, Adams and Hutchinson, Garrison, Hoar, DuBois, and Holmes had all confronted these issues. By the last decades of the twentieth century, Massachusetts people continued to take a leading role in American debates about the limits of liberty and equality.

Suggestions for Further Reading

One of the joys of pursuing Massachusetts history is discovering the wealth of first-rate scholarship it has stimulated. But any brief list of suggested readings must be arbitrary and can include only a small fraction of the excellent works that exist. Readers are encouraged to pursue their interests from the leads they will find in the footnotes and in bibliographies of the works cited below. These titles, spanning the last two generations of scholarship, are a sampling of the riches that are available.

The Colonial and Revolutionary periods offer the most abundant treasures. The first volume of Charles McLean Andrews's magisterial four-volume *The Colonial Period of American History* (New Haven: Yale University Press, 1934) won a Pulitzer Prize when it was first published, and it remains the most lucid account of the origins and early years of the Plymouth and Massachusetts-Bay settlements. It is gracefully complemented by Samuel Eliot Morison's *Builders of the Bay Colony* (Boston: Houghton Mifflin, 1930, 1958), which presents a dozen biographical portraits of interesting and important people in the seventeenth-century colony. Even more influential among scholars have been Perry Miller's difficult but rewarding studies of Puritan thought: *The New England Mind: The Seventeenth Century* (New York: Macmillan, 1939, and Cambridge, Mass.: Harvard University Press, 1954); and *The New England Mind: From Colony to Province* (Cambridge, Mass.: Harvard University Press, 1953).

Recently there has been a myriad of more narrowly focused, highly analytical studies of a wide range of subjects. Darrett B. Rutman's *Winthrop's Boston* (Chapel Hill, N.C.: University of North Carolina Press, 1965) is a thorough, revealing, well-written examination of urban Boston during its "frontier" decades. The town Rutman illuminates stands in contrast to the cohesive rural community Kenneth A. Lockridge imaginatively and persuasively analyzed in *A New England Town: The First Hundred Years: Dedham, Massachusetts, 1636–1736* (New York: Norton, 1970). Paul Boyer and Stephen Nissenbaum's

237

Salem Possessed: The Social Origins of Witchcraft (Cambridge, Mass.: Harvard University Press, 1974) skillfully traces the pathology of the most infamous episode in Puritan community life. For those interested in getting right back to primary sources, Perry Miller and Thomas H. Johnson's collection, *The Puritans: A Sourcebook of their Writings* (New York: Harper and Row, 1963), furnishes easy access to the prose and poetry of early Massachusetts.

The coming of the Revolution tends to dominate studies of eighteenth-century Massachusetts. Among the most interesting recent works are Robert Gross's *The Minutemen and their World* (New York: Hill and Wang, 1976) and Bernard Bailyn's *The Ordeal of Thomas Hutchinson* (Cambridge, Mass.: Harvard University Press, 1974). Gross's short book, which won the Bancroft prize, looks at the Revolution through the experiences of ordinary farm people, effortlessly merging political and social history. Bailyn's definitive analysis of Hutchinson's career within the context of Massachusetts and the empire, won a National Book Award. It possesses the literary advantages of first-rate biography and the insights of profound erudition. Readers interested in eighteenth-century Boston should consult G. B. Warden's *Boston, 1689–1776* (Boston: Little, Brown, 1970), a clear, reliable narrative, and Esther Forbes's lively, popular *Paul Revere and the World He Lived In* (Boston: Houghton Mifflin, 1942). Robert J. Taylor's *Western Massachusetts in the Revolution* (Providence: Brown University Press, 1954), is a highly informative study that has become a minor classic and helps to offset the eastern bias that creeps into many works. Those who want an eyewitness view of the Revolution as it came to Massachusetts and America will enjoy *Diary and Autobiography of John Adams,* L. H. Butterfield *et al.,* eds. (Cambridge, Mass.: Harvard University Press, 1962) and *Adams Family Correspondence,* L. H. Butterfield *et al.,* eds. (Cambridge, Mass.: Harvard University Press, 1963).

For the early national period two thoughtful and interesting recent monographs on politics are Paul Goodman, *The Democratic-Republicans of Massachusetts* (Cambridge, Mass.: Harvard University Press, 1964); and James M. Banner, Jr., *To the Hartford Convention: The Federalists and the Origins of Party Politics in Massachusetts* (New York: Knopf, 1970). The economic history of the first half of the nineteenth century and beyond is illuminated in Samuel Eliot

Morison's enthusiastic *The Maritime History of Massachusetts, 1783–1860* (Boston: Houghton Mifflin, 1961) and George Sweet Gibb's solid *The Saco-Lowell Shops: Textile Machinery Building in New England, 1813–1949* (Cambridge, Mass.: Harvard University Press, 1950). Oscar and Mary Flug Handlin's *Commonwealth, A Study of the Role of Government in the American Economy: Massachusetts, 1774–1861*(New York: New York University Press, 1947) explores a central theme in Massachusetts's development. Oscar Handlin's searching examination of the arrival of the Irish and their place in Massachusetts, *Boston's Immigrants,* rev. ed. (Cambridge, Mass.: Harvard University Press, 1959) is a classic not only of Massachusetts but of United States history. It is complemented by Stephan Thernstrom's influential monograph, *Poverty and Progress: Social Mobility in a Nineteenth-Century City* [Newburyport] (Cambridge, Mass.: Harvard University Press, 1964), which tests the reality of the Horatio Alger dream.

Massachusetts reformers have been studied chiefly through the medium of individual biography; however, there are some outstanding general works. *The Unitarian Conscience: Harvard Moral Philosophy, 1805–1861* (Cambridge, Mass.: Harvard University Press, 1970), by Daniel Walker Howe, reveals the patterns of thought and belief that conditioned many of the reformers and their constituents. Gerald N. Grob's *The State and the Mentally Ill: A History of Worcester State Hospital in Massachusetts, 1830–1920* (Chapel Hill, N.C.: University of North Carolina Press, 1966), is a penetrating analysis of reformers in action within the framework of current medical thought as well as state politics. Geoffrey Blodgett's study of post-Civil War political reformers illuminates politics and society broadly, considering the monographic focus of *The Gentle Reformers: Massachusetts Democrats in the Cleveland Era* (Cambridge, Mass.: Harvard University Press, 1966). The politics of the late-nineteenth and early-twentieth century are treated in Richard M. Abrams, *Conservatism in a Progressive Era: Massachusetts Politics, 1900–1912* (Cambridge, Mass.: Harvard University Press, 1964) and J. Joseph Huthmacher, *Massachusetts People and Politics, 1919–1933* (Cambridge, Mass.: Harvard University Press, 1959). Two popular studies of dramatic episodes by Francis Russell are both informative and insightful: *A City in Terror—1919—: The Boston Police Strike* (New York: Viking, 1975); and *Tragedy in*

Dedham: The Story of the Sacco-Vanzetti Case (New York: McGraw-Hill, 1971). The indispensable guide to further study of every aspect of Massachusetts history is John D. Haskell, Jr., ed., *Massachusetts: A Bibliography of its History* (Boston: G. K. Hall, 1976). The standard state history remains Albert Bushnell Hart, editor, *Commonwealth History of Massachusetts, Colony, Province, and State* (New York: States History Company, 1927–1930), in five volumes.

Index